Praise for POE

"Di Cintio's Iran yi[illegible] country's most beguiling images: pomegranate groves, poets' mausoleums, ripening dates, poetry over dinner and village wrestling tournaments." —*The Globe and Mail*

"A charming retreat. . . . *Poets & Pahlevans* is so graceful and sympathetic as to make anyone fall in love with [Iran]. . . . The result is finely balanced, taking into account both the romance and wretchedness of modern Iran. . . . Di Cintio has a poet's eye for imagery and his descriptions are marvellous, whether of fallen sprays of scarlet blossoms, the play of light on mosaics or the twisting backstreets of venerable cities." —*Calgary Herald*

"Like Michael Moore . . . in the documentary *Roger and Me*, Di Cintio is on a quest and he doggedly follows up on every lead. . . . From the well-known tourist destinations of Esfahan, Shiraz and Bam . . . to the most obscure Kurdish village, the glimpses of the lives of ordinary Iranians are memorable."
—*Winnipeg Free Press*

Praise for HARMATTAN

"Marcello Di Cintio is a fine, fine talent to be savoured."
—Wayson Choy

"An honest writer, rendering not only the marvels of what he sees and feels, but the entire odyssey, his vulnerabilities, flaws and low points . . . Di Cintio's travelogue stands apart from another's by inviting the reader into his thoughts." —*Calgary Herald*

"This book isn't just a good travelogue, it's a great story; you don't have to be a traveller to appreciate it." —*See* (Edmonton)

"Like the Harmattan wind itself, Di Cintio's story blows into the reader and swirls images around, leaving a dusty layer of grit to mull over." —*Georgia Straight* poets &

MARCELLO DI CINTIO

PAHLEVANS

a JOURNEY into the HEART of IRAN

vintage canada

VINTAGE CANADA EDITION, 2007

Published in Canada by Vintage Canada, a division of Random House of Canada Limited, Toronto, in 2007. Originally published in hardcover in Canada by Alfred A. Knopf Canada, a division of Random House of Canada Limited, Toronto, in 2006. Distributed by Random House of Canada Limited, Toronto.

www.randomhouse.ca

Pages 293 to 294 constitute a continuation of the copyright page.

Library and Archives Canada Cataloguing in Publication

Di Cintio, Marcello, 1973–
Poets & pahlevans : a journey into the heart of Iran /
Marcello Di Cintio.

ISBN 978-0-676-97733-2

1. Di Cintio, Marcello, 1973– —Travel—Iran. 2. Iran—Description and travel. 3. Wrestling—Iran. I. Title. II. Title: Poets and pahlevans.

DS259.2.D52 2007 915.5045'44 C2007-900757-0

Text design: Kelly Hill

Printed and bound in Canada

2 4 6 8 9 7 5 3 1

For Moonira, with love

IRAN

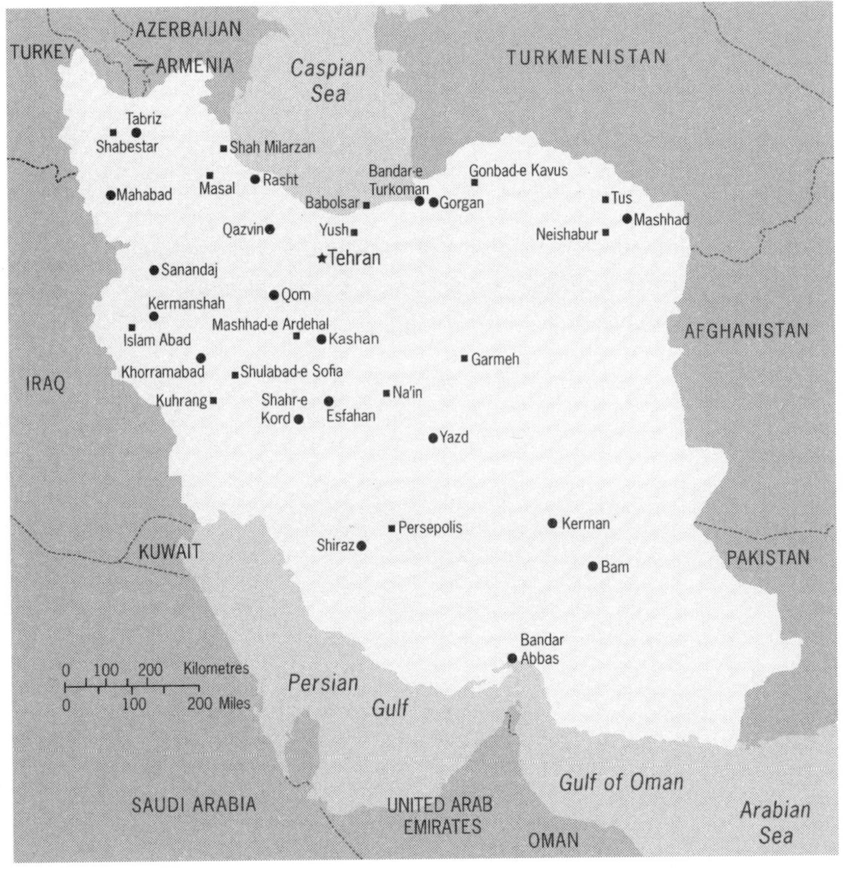

AZERBAIJAN
TURKEY
ARMENIA
Caspian Sea
TURKMENISTAN
Tabriz
Shabestar
Shah Milarzan
Bandar-e Turkoman
Gonbad-e Kavus
Rasht
Masal
Mahabad
Babolsar
Gorgan
Tus
Mashhad
Neishabur
Qazvin
Yush
Tehran
Sanandaj
Qom
Kermanshah
Mashhad-e Ardehal
Islam Abad
Kashan
AFGHANISTAN
Garmeh
Khorramabad
Shulabad-e Sofia
IRAQ
Na'in
Kuhrang
Shahr-e Kord
Esfahan
Yazd
Persepolis
Kerman
Shiraz
KUWAIT
Bam
PAKISTAN
Bandar Abbas
0 100 200 Kilometres
0 100 200 Miles
Persian Gulf
Gulf of Oman
SAUDI ARABIA
UNITED ARAB EMIRATES
OMAN
Arabian Sea

What you most want,
what you travel around wishing to find,
lose yourself as lovers lose themselves,
and you'll be that.

FARID AL-DIN ATTAR NEISHABURI

Know then that the art of wrestling is accepted and praised by Kings and Sultans, and that of those who practise it, most are pure and righteous.

WAEZ-E KASHEFI

1

Into Iran

And now they meet – now rise, and now descend,
And strong and fierce their sinewy arms extend;
Wrestling with all their strength they grasp and strain,
And blood and sweat flow copious on the plain;
Like raging elephants they furious close;
Commutual wounds are given and wrenching blows.
Sohrab now claps his hands, and forward springs
Impatiently, and round the Champion clings;
Seizes his girdle belt, with power to tear
The very earth asunder . . .

An old man recites poetry into a microphone. The measured verses float over the assembled crowd through a static-garbled loudspeaker. When the poem ends he calls two wrestlers to the centre of the circle. Both are barefoot, and both brush the ground with their fingertips before touching their lips and forehead. This is an invocation to Allah, something I don't quite understand. Village men sit on the perimeter in their white turbans and old fedoras, smoke cigarettes and spit out black sunflower seeds. They shout and cheer their muscled heroes.

The wrestlers shake hands and kiss each other on both cheeks, then lock their arms around each other in a warriors' embrace. Their bodies, now merged, are tense and already sweating. I can see their faces: both are nervous but resolute. Their stillness is momentary. When a referee taps them on their shoulders the men clash.

The poetry, epic tales of ancient wars and legendary heroes, was meant to inspire the wrestlers in their battle, but now the crowd's roar replaces the old verses in their scarred ears. They push each other back and forth in the circle, maintaining their grip around each other's waist. Their knuckles blanch. The dust mingles with their sweat and slicks their legs with salty mud. The mob wave their arms and holler instructions in the village dialect. Young boys bounce on their grandfathers' laps.

Then one wrestler thrusts his body forward. His grip turns to stone and he lifts his opponent from his feet. The noise of the crowd swells. The man hurls his rival to the ground and crashes down on top of him. They are invisible in the cloud of dust until the referee helps them stand. Both are filthy and exhausted, but only one man is a winner. The referee raises his arm and the two wrestlers shake hands and kiss again. The victor strides into the throng of his fans and is immersed in their cheers. The loser leaves alone.

When I pressed the button at the Iranian consulate in Istanbul I had no reason to be confident. I wasn't granted a visa from the embassy in Ottawa and the verdict on my visa in Istanbul had already been delayed twice. I did not know why. Admitting I was a writer was, in retrospect, a strategic error; Iran is famously wary of foreign "journalists." Also, Toronto was in the middle of its SARS crisis. Canadians were being turned away at borders around the world. The man at the embassy who accepted my visa application wasn't overly diligent on this point. "Do you have SARS?" he asked. I said no and that was that. I worried, though, that his superiors might be less cavalier.

I waited for nearly two weeks, wandering through the fabulous mosques that crown each of Istanbul's hills and point the way to heaven with their slender minarets. Five times a day the call to prayer boomed out over the city and gave a moment's respite from the Turkish pop music blaring from every storefront and taxicab. Fashionable Istanbulus smoked water pipes and drank tea in popular garden cafés. The bazaars were filled with briny olives, Turkish silks, Ottoman antiques and cheesy belly-dance costumes. It had been three years since my last visit to the Middle East and it was a pleasure to be back among the pistachio vendors, tea houses and honey-soaked pastries.

But for all Istanbul's charms, my mind was a thousand kilometres east. I'd spent the last two years infatuated with Iran. I had read Persian history and become obsessed with Iran's politics, but it was the Persian love for poetry that first drew me to the place. I learned that all Iranians, even small children, could recite poetry from memory. Poets who have been dead for centuries are revered. Their verses resonate over time and colour everyday language. I wanted to investigate this devotion and be in a place where *bazaaris* and taxi drivers spoke in measured verse. Istanbul was a poor consolation. I wanted to be in Iran.

While the consulate deliberated on my visa application, I bought my ticket for the Trans-Asya Express to Tehran, and did all the things I knew I would not be able to do once I crossed the border. I watched American action films in modern cinemas. I went to European-styled coffee shops to sip espresso, and drank pints of Efes lager in noisy bars. I read a copy of Salman Rushdie's *Fury* I found in a used bookstore.

I returned to the consulate. When the visa official opened the door he was not smiling. Neither was I. "Mr. Marcello?"

he asked. I nodded. Then he tapped my passport against my chest and opened it to a fresh visa sticker. "You have one month. Have good times in Iran."

The Haydarapasa train station stands on the banks of the Bosphorus Strait on the very edge of the continent. Asia begins here, and from Haydarapasa there is only east. I went to the station early, and was the first passenger on the train. The car was dark, but enough light filtered in through the window for me to find my cabin and stow my rucksack beneath a seat.

Another man entered the cabin. He was in his fifties, balding and with a thick white moustache. He smiled and greeted me, but beyond his *salaam* I didn't know what he said.

"I'm sorry, but I don't understand."

"You are a foreigner," he said in English. I was relieved. "Tourist?"

"Yes," I said, though I hate that designation.

"I am Reza," he said. "What is your country?"

"Canada."

He repeated "Canada" back to me, pausing almost reverently after each syllable. "Ca. Na. Da. Canada is good?"

"Yes, Canada *khub*."

"You can speak some Farsi?"

"A little," I said, embarrassed because I should have been able to speak much more. I had spent the previous months studying Farsi with a private tutor. I had met my teacher, Khadije, through a woman at a Persian restaurant. "I teach children mostly," she said on the phone. "But I can teach you, too, if you like." We convened in a vacant room at the university for our first lesson. She was a pious Muslim and wore an all-encompassing black chador. There was another woman there, a friend of Khadije's who also wore a chador. I thought she might share teaching duties with Khadije, but instead she sat at the back of the room through the lesson and rarely spoke. It occurred to me later that she was our chaperone.

I got to know Khadije as the weekly lessons progressed. After about a month the chaperone stopped coming. Neither Khadije nor I spoke of this, but I had earned her trust. I was, however, a poor student. The gargled Farsi consonants tended to stick in the back of my throat. Khadije was patient. "Once you get to Iran it will all come very fast," she promised. Khadije would have been disappointed that my Farsi froze the moment I faced my first "real" Iranian.

"I will teach you Farsi," Reza announced. "By the time we reach Tehran you will be fluent." Then he pointed at my right ear. "You are a *koshti giri*. A wrestler."

I touched my ear. Back home, nobody commented on my cauliflower ears. I never knew if people didn't notice or simply felt it was rude to say anything. I scarred both ears during my days on the varsity wrestling team, but my right was the worst. It is a common injury for wrestlers. A solid bash on the ear can cause a blood clot between the layers of cartilage. If the clot is not drained in time the cartilage dies, shrivels and hardens. The cartilage on my right ear was so thick I had to press the headphones against my head to follow the in-flight movie. Cauliflower ears were about all I earned on the mat; a shoebox at home contained a sparse collection of medals.

Wrestling also brought me to Iran. I'd read stories of the old wrestling champions of Persia, the *pahlevans.* Modelled on the mythical warriors in Persian poetry, they embodied a masculine ideal. They were modest and dignified, with strength of character as well as flesh. They were perfect men, and their art is still practised in Iran. Far from the modern gymnasiums barefoot men still grapple in the dust and sand. Athletes wear sacred costumes, and music, prayers and poetry still stir them into battle.

After university, I traded my wrestling career for writing. The two pursuits felt contradictory. Each required all my energy and I didn't think I could ever do both. So instead of struggling on the mat I struggled at my desk. By the time I turned thirty my wrestler's body was gone. The tales of the pahlevans, though, made my soft muscles twitch. These were men who lived poetry and athleticism at once. I envied them and wanted to witness this marriage of muscle and verse. But more than that, I wanted it for myself.

Four months before the voyage, I decided that if I was to comprehend Persian wrestling, I had to feel like a wrestler again. I returned to the mats. It had been seven years since I wrestled and I recognized few of the men in the room. They glanced up at me without smiles and continued lacing up their boots. Two men passed wet mops back and forth across the mat, filling the room with the stench of disinfectant. My old coach spotted me and came to shake my hand.

"I want to start wrestling again," I said.

He raised an eyebrow. "You in shape?"

"Not really."

He sighed. "All right. Just don't overdo it."

I was exhausted by the time the warm-up was finished. My body was weak and slow, and the cartwheels and somersaults left me dizzy. Still, I was excited. I drilled manoeuvres with a wrestler ten years my junior until the coach divided everyone into groups for live wrestling. He looked at me. "Maybe you should sit this out," he said.

"I'll be fine."

My partners and I found a spot of mat and waited for the whistle. My first rival jumped on my legs, lifted me up and brought me to the ground with embarrassing efficiency. I stood up and he did it again. For half an hour my partners tossed, tripped and twisted me to the ground. I was a fool to think that I could keep up with younger, fitter men after seven dormant years. One wrestler rewarded my arrogance near the end of practice with a tight gut wrench that cracked one of my ribs. I moaned with pain and the coach shrugged.

In the shower the next morning my fingers found all the other tiny injuries inflicted the previous night. Fingertip-shaped bruises dotted my upper arms. I had welts on my calves that made my legs look like purple marble. Under the hot water, abrasions burned on my forehead and behind my ears. My girlfriend, Moonira, was shocked, but my battered body pleased me in a way I hadn't felt in years. I had missed these pains. The marks on my skin mapped a return to a place I'd abandoned. I traced my bruises the same way I traced my maps of the Middle East. I was going somewhere.

My twice-weekly training did not result in the level of fitness I had enjoyed when I was a full-time athlete. I spent much of my mat time being pummelled by the more skilled members of the team. Still, I felt strong again. After a few weeks I lost some weight and my arms began to tighten. By the time I left for Istanbul I was starting to score the occasional takedown. I revelled in each small victory and laughed out loud when my body remembered obscure throws, surprising me as much as my practice partners.

I reached into my rucksack to show Reza my Farsi phrase book and I felt a brief flash of pain in my side. I winced at my cracked rib, but Reza didn't notice. "You are lucky to be sitting with me," he said. "I will also teach you about Iran. You know, I used to be a tour guide. Ten or fifteen years ago. I took foreigners around Iran. Showed them all the beautiful places. Do you know about Shiraz? About Persepolis? It is very beautiful. Tourists love it."

"Yes, I read about Shiraz."

"Many tourists used to come to Iran. Many people from the West. Things are different now. Now nobody comes. Now you will have the place to yourself."

"Now" was what followed exploded planes and fallen towers. It was the summer of 2003. Well-meaning people said I must be brave to go to Iran. They reminded me of the wars in Afghanistan and Iraq. "It is too close," they said, as if stray bullets could fly across borders. The dust of those towers clouded Western eyes. For too many people, the entire Middle East was a fountain of hate.

Two men entered the compartment laden with boxes and suitcases. They whispered greetings to Reza and me, and did their best to stow their baggage beneath the seats. Reza pointed at me with his chin and said something that ended in the word *Canada*. The men looked at me, then back to the old man. "Farsi?" The old man shook his head.

We slept early that night. Reza's snores were extraordinary. In the morning I shared breakfast with the men in the cabin: bread, chocolate spread and a delicious preserve made of honey and nuts. They poured me a Nescafé. When I told them I drank my coffee black they made faces and dumped handfuls of sugar cubes into their cups. Afterwards we sucked on tiny bitter limes.

The two young men, Habib and Davood, were shoe salesmen from Tehran. Their bags were filled with children's shoes and shoemaking materials, as well as some phony designer T-shirts and ball caps. Habib was interested in my chunky hiking sandals. He asked to borrow one and while he sketched its design onto a piece of paper, I asked them about traditional wrestling in Iran. "I have not seen it," Davood said. "This sort of wrestling is not found in the city. Only in the villages."

The train continued its way eastward across Turkey, stopping regularly to pick up passengers. A large group of women came aboard at one station. They wore makeup and stylish form-fitting clothes. Their heads were uncovered and one woman had dark roots showing under her blonde dye-job.

Davood nodded towards them. "You see those women?" he said. "They are Iranian. Watch them. When they reach the border they will put on their hejab."

The sky was dark with clouds when we reached the western shores of Lake Van. The train tracks ended at the lake. Workmen unattached the cargo cars from the train and loaded it onto a ferry. We would travel across the lake by boat—passengers on the upper deck, the train cars in the hold—then meet up with the Iranian train at the other side of the lake. For all my love of trains I wished I had opted for the quicker bus.

The weary passengers trudged off the train and onto the ferry. For two days we had been sleeping in our clothes. Every man's face was rough with stubble. Even the stylish women who boarded the train that afternoon were already uncombed and dishevelled. It was as if sitting inside the cabins increased everyone's personal entropy. We watched the cargo cars being loaded onto the ferry without saying much to each other.

The mood lightened once we boarded the ferry, but there was nothing beautiful about Lake Van that day. The elephant-skin water was obscured by fog, and the wind made it too cold for sitting on the deck. The passengers crowded the lounge area and sat on cracked plastic chairs. Raised edges on the tables prevented tea glasses from tumbling to the floor. My cabinmates and I shared bread and canned chicken. Others bought potato chips and tea from the *bufe* on board. I found a private table to read, but once word got around that a foreigner was on board everyone with even a smattering of English took a turn greeting me. One man showed me the phone number of a friend who lived in Canada and asked me if I could tell which city he lived in by the area code. Another man, a "music teacher and a Christian," with startlingly blue eyes, wanted to talk about Jesus. I switched the subject to wrestling and he called a friend over. "This is Kamal," he said, placing his hand on his friend's shoulder. "He is from Babolsar near the Caspian Sea. He has friends who wrestle there."

I asked Kamal about wrestling. There were competitions on the Caspian Sea coast at the beginning of summer. He wrote down his address in Farsi for me, two lines of squiggles that I couldn't read. "Call me if you come to Babolsar. I have a friend who speaks English." I thanked him and he walked away. The Christian left me his phone number in Tehran and told me to call him if I ever needed anything.

At the other side of the lake, the Van train station was busy. Westbound passengers waited for the cargo cars to shunt off the ferry before they could board. Those of us going into Iran waited for the Iranian train to arrive. It was late and nobody knew when we could expect it. We crammed into the tiny station house to avoid the wind. Children, oblivious to the delay, played amid the tables and chairs. The rest smoked cigarettes, drank tea and spat the husks of melon seeds onto the floor. A television in the corner showed a Turkish newscast, images of Americans in Iraq.

The Iranian train finally arrived, and I again shared a cabin with Davood, Habib and Reza. The cabin was laid with ornate Persian rugs and there was a box for every passenger containing a complimentary towel, a toothbrush and tube of toothpaste, a small bag of pistachios, a packet of tea, polyester sheets for the beds and a can of tuna. Reza was giddy. "This train is much better than the Turkish train," he said. "And you can keep your sheets." My cabinmates and I taught each other the Farsi and English names for all the items in our boxes. Habib had trouble with the *th* in *toothpaste* and kept lisping *toospaste* long after we laid our free sheets over our beds and turned out the light.

In the morning we reached Kapikoy, the last stop before Iran. All three of my cabinmates rushed into the station. Each returned with two large cans of Efes Strong, a Turkish beer.

I'd been craving a beer for two days but decided against drinking in the cabin for fear of causing offence.

"I thought you were Muslims," I said when they returned.

"Yes, but we drink sometimes."

Habib drained half a can in one long swig. Then he belched and held his stomach. "Why are you drinking so quickly?" I asked.

"Soon we will reach the border. Beer is illegal in Iran."

"We have been in Turkey for two days. You could have bought beer any time, even on the train," I said. "Why did you wait?"

"Because we are almost there."

Habib pointed out the window. Women were busy putting long coats over their clothes and headscarves over their hair. The Islamic Republic of Iran was within sight. This was the last stop for secularism, and last call for alcohol.

The train trudged over the border and made a brief stop in Tabriz before continuing on to the capital. Davood and Habib turned serious as we approached Tehran. They started to rifle through their baggage, open plastic packets of T-shirts and shuffle items from one bag to another. Davood was sweating, and Habib's tone of voice hardened. Reza watched them, grinned and shook his head. When Davood and Habib charged out of the cabin, I asked him what the matter was.

"These men are smuggling shoes and clothes into Iran. They are foolish. They will have to pay a big bribe."

Sure enough, when the men returned Habib pulled an American hundred-dollar bill from his pocket. He waved it at me and said something to the old man.

"He wants to know if you can make change for him. Do you have two fifty-dollar bills?"

I made change for Habib and he rushed out of the cabin once again, presumably to grease the palm of the onboard customs official. In the meantime, Davood frantically loaded a red suitcase with contraband clothing. He spoke to me in jittery English. "Marcello. This suitcase you. No me. Okay? This clothes, this shirts, this hats you. You carry. Okay? No me. You carry."

He wanted me to bring the suitcase through customs for him to avoid a hefty customs charge. "Why not?" I shrugged. I knew there was nothing but clothes in the suitcase, and I trusted Davood.

In Tehran, the customs officer never questioned why I would have both a rucksack and a bulky suitcase. He glanced over my things and waved me through. I waited for my friends with Davood's wife and brothers. Davood and Habib, in spite of their bribes, were shaken down by the officials. After nearly two hours they emerged, frazzled and sweaty, but with all of their baggage.

"Okay?" I asked Davood.

"Okay," he said. To thank me for being his accomplice, he and his brothers drove me through the darkened Tehran streets and found me a hotel.

2

TEHRAN

I woke late the next morning, too late for the hotel's offering of complimentary tea and eggs. The hotel was more expensive than I could afford, so I went in search of cheaper accommodation.

Tehran greeted me with traffic. Iranian-built Paykan sedans clogged the streets and narrowly missed collision. Buses travelled on lanes that ran against the flow of traffic. Motorists ignored stoplights and treated pedestrians with contempt. I learned quickly that crossing the street required a precise amount of bravery: too little and I waited on the curb for an age, too much and I risked death. The sidewalks were no better. Motorcyclists, frustrated by the gridlock on the road, bumped over curbs and sped along the walkways.

I marvelled at the locals who waded into the streets with a fearlessness I could only attribute to faith. Only those convinced of paradise could walk with such assurance.

I found a cheap hotel on a street lined with lighting fixture shops, deposited my bag in a windowless room and went in search of lunch, though the thick summer pollution nearly killed my appetite. After a few breaths I felt the smog cling to the back of my throat like an oily rag. I looked up at the drab cement buildings and cracked sidewalks and decided that Tehran did not look like Iran, or at least what I thought Iran would be. I expected domed buildings, mosaics, fruit stalls and men in robes. Aside from the women in headscarves and the curvy arabesque neon, Tehran seemed a grimy, generic metropolis.

I saw the slogans on Taleqani Street. Down with the USA. When the US Praises Us We Should Mourn. We Will Make America Face Severe Defeat. Amid the painted slogans were the murals. An American flag with stripes twisting into barbed wire. A skull-faced Statue of Liberty. A handgun, starred and striped. All along the wall of the former American embassy, renamed the "US Den of Espionage," were artistic expressions of political hatred.

In the winter of 1979, Iranian students slipped inside a basement embassy window and, with Ayatollah Khomeini's blessing, took fifty-two Americans hostage. For 444 days the world watched bound and blindfolded Americans displayed as trophies of the Islamic Revolution that had unseated the Shah a few months earlier. Fierce women in black chadors chanted "Death to America" for television cameras. Street vendors sold American flags to be burned. A rescue attempt ended in the deaths of eight American soldiers when the aircraft collided in a sandstorm over Saudi Arabia, proving to some that God was on the side of the revolution. The attempted rescue was portrayed in one of the murals as two charred helicopters lying twisted in the Arabian Desert. For many Westerners, especially Americans, the word *Iran* still conjures images of rage and burning flags.

I was eight years old at the height of the crisis and didn't see those images. I did, however, follow pro wrestling. I do not remember the hostages, but I remember the Iron Sheik. Born Khosrow Vaziri, the Iron Sheik was a wrestler from Tehran and, allegedly, a former bodyguard for the Shah. He falsely claimed to be the 1968 Olympic wrestling champion. His fame came from his pro wrestling career, which began around the same time as the hostage crisis. While adults watched American flags burn on the news, I watched the Sheik insult America and dispatch opponent after opponent with his dreaded "camel clutch." He wore a turban and curved toe boots, waved a mock Iranian flag emblazoned with Khomeini's face, and often led a live camel to the ring. His evil was a meter of the public perception of Iran. He was another of America's moustached enemies.

I thought of the Iron Sheik as I walked past the Den of Espionage. The building does not feature on any tourist brochure, but it is one of the capital's most popular attractions, especially for curious Westerners. As I stared at the murals I was surprised at how little they affected me. I could not hear the shouted rage of 1979. To me this was just an open-air museum of political kitsch. The Iranian military occupied the building and armed sentries on watchtowers made a show of discouraging my camera. I understood their caution, but the slogans were in English. Weren't they intended for me?

I continued north from the Den of Espionage, and followed a pollution-choked highway for about a kilometre to the Shiridi Sports Centre where the headquarters of the national wrestling federation was located. I hoped to find some information about traditional wrestling events across Iran. I made a few inquiries in my halting Farsi and was quickly ushered into a room where I was served tea and told to wait. Eventually four middle-aged men came in. Each had thick cauliflower ears and broad shoulders beneath his business suit. The former titans shook my hand then eased their bulk into swivelling office chairs. One of the men could speak some English and was able to translate for me. I introduced myself and told them about my travel plans.

They told me that the traditional wrestling styles were still widely practised, and were very important historically. The sport of judo, for example, was derived from the *bachoukheh* style of wrestling popular in Khorasan Province in eastern Iran, they said. Unfortunately, none of the men could give me dates or venues for any competitions. "They happen in small villages. Sometimes at weddings or after the rice harvest. It is difficult to get a schedule for such things," a man said. They gave me the address of a sports centre, or *varzeshga*, in Mashhad, where I could see some bachoukheh wrestling, and the phone number of a man in Babolsar who would help me seek out some wrestling there. They also told me to visit the *zurkhanes*, traditional wrestling halls, which are found throughout Iran. Then they drained their tea glasses and wished me luck. This was the best they could do.

I visited the Golestan Palace the next morning. After wandering through the sumptuous halls of Iran's former kings, I took a moment's pause amid the flowers and manicured lawns in front of the palace. Two white swans swam in the central fountain. A thin man with thick glasses approached and sat next to me. "Excuse me, do you speak English?" He opened up a leather satchel and pulled out a copy of the *Guardian* newspaper. It was yellowed and old. "If you have the time, will you translate some words for me?" There were a few circled words in the text of the newspaper. He recorded the vocabulary in a notebook. Afterwards he folded up the paper and announced, "Now we will have a conversation."

I wondered how long he had waited for a foreigner to pass so he could practise his English. We worked our way through the usual chat about my name, job, country and family. Then the discussion turned to politics. He wanted to know what I thought about the Israeli-Palestinian conflict, about the American invasion of Iraq and about September 11.

I paused. People had warned me against having open discussions about politics in Iran. A friend who ran an Iranian supermarket back home said, "You never know who might be listening." I answered the man's questions with deliberate ambiguity, and was relieved that he wanted to talk about the United States rather than his own government.

"Everybody hates America. And everyone hates George Bush," he said. Defensively, he lifted up his palms. "Please understand me. I love Americans. They are good people. I want them to come to Iran. But their government is very bad. George Bush is very bad. They hate Muslims. What do you think?" I told him I didn't agree with American policies either. "Canada should protest the American government," he said.

"Sometimes we do," I said. Before I left home, thousands of Canadians protested in the streets against America's war in Iraq. The prime minister opted out of joining the American-led invasion. This was one of the most popular government decisions in recent memory. I told this to the man and he was happy.

"George Bush is a terrorist," he said.

When I returned to my hotel, I picked up my room key from the manager at the front desk. Before I went upstairs he placed his hand on his chest and said, "George Bush."

"I don't understand," I said.

He lifted a pen from the desk and drew a heart on a scrap of paper. He pointed to it and said, again, "George Bush."

"You like George Bush?"

"Yes. Yes. I love him. Everyone in Iran love him."

I said nothing. The man pointed to a photo of Khomeini on the wall behind him. "I hate him," he whispered. Then he looked at me hard and said, "Iran terrorists."

That night I dined with Said Ershadi. His niece was a friend of mine in Calgary and as soon as I called him from my hotel he invited me to his home for dinner. Ershadi was in his fifties and lived in a northern suburb, an upscale neighbourhood far from my hotel. The taxi ride took over an hour, and cost more than my hotel room.

Both Said and his wife met me at the front door. Said invited me to sit in the salon with him while his wife quietly tended to dinner in the kitchen. Due to the presence of an unrelated male in her house, she wore her headscarf.

Said clicked on a Gypsy Kings CD and joined me on the sofa. He was a poet and a translator who spoke four languages. We discussed Persian poetry and he gave me copies of poems written by contemporary Iranian writers. He read each poem aloud, using a magnifying glass to compensate for his poor vision. "Nowadays most people write watery poetry," he said, "but these are very good." I asked Said the status of poetry nowadays.

"Today, people think that poetry is old-fashioned. If you give a man a poem he does not know whether to boil it or fry it."

"Why not?"

"There was a time when there was room in men's minds for poetry. Now men have to remember where are all the potholes in the road so they do not smash their car. They have no space left for poetry." I was happy for his hospitality, but I was disappointed by what he told me.

The doorbell rang. It was one of Said's English students, Mitra, and her five-year-old daughter. They were invited to join us for dinner. Said instructed Mitra to greet me in English. "Hello. How are you? Welcome." Speaking English to a stranger made her blush, but she immediately removed her headscarf and hung it on a peg beside the door. Beneath her overcoat she wore a form-fitting red shirt and black trousers. She smiled and fled into the kitchen to help Said's wife with dinner.

"She dresses very Western," I said to Said.

"Yes. She is modern. Young women are not interested in hejab."

While I spoke with Said, Mitra's daughter crept up beside us to listen to our English. Once, as I was looking away, she placed a tiny white flower gingerly on my knee. When I noticed it I turned to thank her. Giggling, she ran to hide behind her mother's legs.

The next day, I noticed an odd sculpture on the sidewalk near my hotel. Fresh tomatoes, onions and kebab skewers were balanced together on a squat stool. Next to this, a narrow stairwell led below street level. I followed it down into an Iranian tea house.

Before leaving for Iran, I had read about traditional Iranian tea houses with coloured lamps and soft cushions on couches laid with rugs. This room was thick with tobacco and lit with anaemic fluorescent tubes. An air conditioner rattled at the foot of the stairwell. Ten sad-eyed men sat at dented metal tables, hunched over tiny glasses of tea and sucking on *qalyun*s, the bulky Persian water pipes. When I entered the room every conversation stopped, and every face turned to look at me.

I ordered tea and a qalyun with apple-flavoured tobacco. The scene was somewhat familiar. During a trip to Cairo a few years before, I had discovered the joys of the qalyun, and the beautiful blue pipe that sat in my living room back in Canada was one of my favourite souvenirs. When the owner delivered my qalyun I took a long, bubbling pull on the hose and thought of the first Persian poem I ever learned:

> The Water Pipe takes pleasure at thy lips
> And in thy mouth its reed turned to sugar cane;
> 'Tis not tobacco smoke which wreathes thy head
> But clouds which turn about the moon and turn again.

Then the owner brought my tea. I took two roughly hewn chunks of sugar from a pink plastic bowl and dropped them into my scalding tea. I looked for a spoon but I had not been given one. I looked around. None of the other men had spoons either.

The owner had been watching me. He came to my table and asked if I spoke Farsi.

"A little."

"Where are you from?"

"Canada."

"You do not have tea in Canada? Ha! Wait." He shouted for one of his minions in the back of the room to bring him a glass of tea. "Look." He poured the hot tea into the saucer. Then he lifted a lump of sugar from the sugarbowl, dipped it in the tea and placed it between his front teeth. He raised the saucer to his lips and sucked the tea into his mouth over the sugar. "No spoon," he said, with the half-melted sugar lump still in his teeth. He stood up. "Come." He picked up my qalyun and led me to the table he shared with his friends. He introduced me to everyone. "Foreigners never come here," he said.

A man stomped down the stairs and broke up our conversation. He was in his fifties and balding with white tufts of hair over his ears. Everyone knew him and shouted out their *salaams*. He scowled as he greeted the room, even though his eyes smiled. With his undershirt visible beneath his threadbare white shirt the man looked like a thin Marlon Brando.

He took the seat across the table from me. The other men introduced us and told him I was from Canada. His eyes widened. "Canada!" he growled. "I speak English very good." He had the low rumbling voicc of a lion. "I live England four years. Then Germany. Now Iran. *Perssssia*." To illustrate his proficiency in English he started conjugating verbs. "Yesterday I came. Today I come. Tomorrow I *will* come. . . ."

When I tried to speak to him in Farsi he shouted at me. "You are from Canada! You speak Farsi! I speak English! No Farsi! No Farsi!" His tirade continued and his mock rage increased until the tea house trembled with his baritone roar and everyone's laughter. Only at the end of his rant did the man allow a smile to crack his face and a chuckle to quake his shoulders.

A bespectacled man peeked up from behind his newspaper. He pointed at Brando and said, "This man thinks he can speak English better than Tony Blair." Brando started to rage all over again. I thought he might holler for Stella.

I spent two hours with the men, and lost track of how much tea I drank. I replaced the Tehrani smog in my lungs with the cool, sweet tobacco smoke. I told them about my travel plans, and my intention to visit as much of Iran as I could manage. Upon hearing about my interest in wrestling, the owner called his son over from the back of the room. "My son is a wrestler. This weekend he will become the champion of Tehran." The boy, with a face marked with mat burns and ears swollen and red, blushed at his father's pride.

When I finally stood to leave, I shook all the men's hands. Brando growled, "If you need something, you come talk to me. I am here every day."

Later I visited Davood at his shoe store. He seemed pleased to see me. I photographed him as he stood beside a display of the children's shoes I had helped smuggle in from Istanbul. "When will you leave Tehran?" he asked.

"Tomorrow, I hope."

He was disappointed. He wanted to invite me to his home for dinner, but he already had plans that evening with his wife's family. "My friends can take you out," he said. "One of them has a car and speaks English." He called his friends on his cellphone and arranged for them to meet me at my hotel that evening. Ali and Mohammed were happy to take me on a nighttime tour of Tehran. Jennifer Lopez droned from Ali's futuristic car stereo.

"I read that female singers are illegal in Iran?" I asked.

"Yes. Everything is illegal in Iran," Ali complained. "We get music from the Internet."

We drove up and down the Tehran expressways, and cruised along Africa Street, a trendy promenade in northern Tehran. Stylish young Tehranis walked in packs along the sidewalks. They window-shopped, ducked in and out of pizzerias, and gabbed on their cellphones. Aside from the headscarves and long overcoats worn by all the women, this could have been any hip neighbourhood in the world.

Ayatollah Khomeini scowled down from giant murals on the sides of buildings. His countenance was a constant reminder that Iranians had him to thank for the lives they led. Ali pointed up at one of the murals. "Do you know who that is?" he asked. I nodded. "We are tired of seeing his picture. And tomorrow is the holiday of his death."

The anniversary of Ayatollah Khomeini's death in 1989 was a national holiday that bore the full-mouthed title: the "Heart-Rending Departure of the Great Leader of the Islamic Republic of Iran." Khomeini's funeral was an unprecedented orgy of mob grief. Over a million mourners crowded the burial site. Men flagellated themselves to express their grief and the crowd of mourners surged out of control. They swarmed the coffin to glimpse the dead Ayatollah and to grab a shred of his burial shroud as a souvenir. During the melee, the coffin tipped over and Khomeini's corpse slumped out onto the square. Ten thousand people were injured that day. The funeral was rescheduled and Khomeini was laid below the ground in a steel casket to protect against morbid souvenir-hunters.

As we drove along the highway, I noticed that Khomeini's face was not the only image gracing the sides of buildings.

Other murals portrayed *shaahedeh*, martyrs of Iran's eight-year war with Iraq. Some were simple likenesses, young faces with thin beards and heavy eyes. Others were more graphic. Crumpled bodies. Pools of vivid blood. Sometimes paintings of flowers and flowing Persian poetry festooned the scenes of bloodshed.

The car turned a corner and passed a group of women standing on the side of the street. Mohammed pointed to them. "Those are prostitutes," he announced.

"Really? How can you tell?"

"It is very obvious."

I glanced back at them through the side mirror. They wore loose-fitting overcoats and headscarves just like most of the other women I'd seen in Tehran. I wanted to ask what identified the women as prostitutes and who their customers were but I didn't want my hosts to misinterpret my curiosity.

They brought me to Bam Tehran, a hillside park overlooking the city. Tehrani families were enjoying some clean air outside of the city centre. From the park, the lights of Tehran were made soft through their filter of smog. We paused to listen to a trio of young girls singing Persian pop songs, and my friends snickered at the couples discreetly courting among the trees. The park was much like parks back home. There were stalls selling snacks, plastic toys and disposable cameras. Mothers pushed strollers while fathers held camcorders. The place seemed busy, but Ali said it was a slow night.

We drove to a restaurant near the park and shared plates of rice, salad and lamb *shishlik* kebabs. Ali and Mohammed let me taste their *dugh*, a drink made of sour milk, salt and garlic. I opted for a Parsi Cola. We finished our meals and Ali paid for it all. I protested, but he insisted I was a guest.

Back at my hotel, I packed for the next day's journey. Tehran's steel and smog had left me cold and I was anxious to continue my travels in Iran. Still, I felt a tinge of regret on my leaving. Everyone I met—whether it was Marlon Brando and his friends, bulky old wrestlers or the young girl with her white flower—had received me with generosity and warmth. On my arrival, Tehran had seemed a poor introduction to Iran, but the Iranian capital was wholly redeemed by the Persians.

3

THE PAHLEVANS OF QAZVIN

I found ancient poetry inked in blue tattoos, etched on the worn muscles of an old wrestler. I held my breath, and my own unadorned chest swelled in the pahlevan's presence. I was in Iran to find the emotional link between poetry and wrestling. In Qazvin I witnessed the concept made flesh.

Due to holiday traffic, it took more than three hours to travel the hundred kilometres from Tehran west to Qazvin. It was the beginning of a rare four-day holiday. That year, Heart-Rending Departure Day fell on a Wednesday and was followed by the Anniversary of the Arrest of Ayatollah Khomeini, another national holiday. Then came the regular Friday holy day. I had considered joining the throngs of mourners who made yearly pilgrimages to Khomeini's shrine south of Tehran, but an official at the Canadian embassy cautioned against it. Although he couldn't recall any problems with foreigners in the past, he was unsure how welcome a Western observer would feel among thousands of bereaved Iranians. He also told me that most vacationing Tehranis would head towards the beaches of the Caspian Sea and that the roads north would be jammed. I went west, but even that highway was clogged.

When I arrived in Qazvin I dropped my rucksack at the Hotel Iran. A dubbed version of *Annie Hall* played on the lobby television and I resisted the temptation to stay and watch Woody Allen speak Farsi. Instead I wandered towards the town centre. Qazvin seemed a ghost town. There were only beggar women on the streets. They hid under their chadors and sat motionless on the sidewalk in front of the mosques, extending hands from beneath black fabric.

Most of the shops were closed but I happened on an open tea house and went inside. The place was not unlike Brando's tea house in Tehran. It was another dusty gathering place for men. The inside was dark and cluttered with teapots, ashtrays and crates of empty Parsi Cola bottles. Water pipes filled the shelves. I took a seat at a table beneath a photo of Khomeini and nodded a greeting to the rough-shaven men. Two men wore wrinkled suits and fedoras like old jazz musicians. They spoke in whispers so as not to disturb a scratchy radio broadcast of the ceremony at the Holy Shrine of Imam Khomeini. A cross-eyed man brought me tea, then returned to the sink to wash dishes. I finished my tea and watched as the leaves collected in the bottom of my glass like stubble.

I beckoned the shop owner and ordered another tea and a qalyun. He struggled to understand my Farsi, and paused a moment to try to place my accent. I puffed a cloud of sweet smoke to the ceiling as a dirge drifted from the radio. A man next to me fingered his prayer beads. Another slurped lamb stew from a metal bowl. The mood in the room was heavy and sad.

The tea-house owner walked towards two men sitting at the back of the room. He murmured something to them and they glanced up at me. The men smiled and waved me over, pointing up at a clattering air conditioner as if to say it was cooler back there. The cross-eyed man grabbed my qalyun to bring it to the back of the room. I met the shop owner, Afshin, and his two friends, a middle-aged man named Ali and Babak, a man my age who said he was studying English in university.

Babak asked me what I was doing in Iran. I told him about my interest in old Persian wrestling and asked if they had heard of a style called *baghal-be baghal.* I had read that in the past it had been popular in the area around Qazvin. The men frowned. No one had heard of it. Babak said that later he would take me to a zurkhane. "There we can find somebody who knows about this sort of wrestling, but let us finish our tea."

Afshin brought me another cup of tea, this time with a spoon. I pushed the spoon aside, dipped a sugar lump in my tea then held it in my teeth. The men laughed. "Do you understand why we drink tea like this?" asked Babak. "Some years ago the Iranian mullahs argued with the sugar sellers from Russia. The mullahs said that the sugar sellers cheated them and they wanted their money back. The sellers said they did not owe the mullahs anything. So, at the mosque on Friday, the mullahs said that sugar was *haram.* It was 'dirty' like pig meat and whisky, and good Muslims should not use it.

"The sugar sellers were now in trouble because nobody is buying their sugar, so they gave the money back to the mullahs. The next Friday, the mullahs went to the mosque and said, 'Sugar is still haram, but you clean the sugar by dipping it into your tea.' Then the people could put sugar in their tea and be good Muslims."

Babak and I stood to leave after we finished our tea. Afshin would not allow me to pay. I shook his hand and followed Babak down Shaahedeh Street towards the zurkhane. The tiles over the doorway were painted with wrestlers. One scene depicted one man tossing his opponent in some kind of throw. There was also a moustached man swinging a pair of bulky clubs. White calligraphy and patterns of flowers and vines swirled between the bare-chested strongmen.

Babak spoke to a young man selling T-shirts and underwear from a stall nearby. He found a key and opened the zurkhane door for us. We stepped inside a room that smelled of old sweat. The place was a cross between a gymnasium and a religious shrine. Photos and paintings of wrestlers covered the walls. Most were faded and discoloured. In one photo, two men stood next to each other with their arms locked and chests bulging. In another, a wrestler posed next to a pair of heavy clubs and frowned through a moustache. There were also paintings of Imam Ali, the first Shiite Imam and son-in-law of the Prophet Mohammed, clutching his sword. Another portrayed the clean-shaven prophet himself with his head cocked to one side and his robe slipping off his shoulder. It seemed oddly feminine. I was surprised to see this image of the Prophet, but would see the same posters all around the country, hanging in teahouses and for sale in the bazaars. The Shiites of Iran do not have the same prohibition against portrayals of the Prophet as do Muslims elsewhere.

An old man sat in the corner of the room. He rose slowly to greet us, supporting himself on a carved wooden cane. His face was covered with stubble and his lips were sucked in beneath his thick moustache. Large round ears pushed through his messy hair. He seemed clownish and awkward, but Babak approached him with reverence.

"This is Karim Qazvini," Babak told me. "He is weak because he was in a car accident, but he is a master wrestler. A *pahlevan*. You see his picture on the wall?" Babak gestured towards a painted portrait of a well-muscled man wearing a red, white and green–striped sash with a gold medallion of Imam Ali. The man in the painting was young and strong and frowned out of the picture, but there was no doubt this was once Qazvini. He and the old man before me had the same tea-saucer ears.

Qazvini gave me a tour of the zurkhane. He leaned on Babak as he walked. A small set of free weights sat in one corner, but most of the exercise equipment in the zurkhane resembled archaic implements of war. There was a stack of the weighted clubs I'd seen depicted in the tilework outside (Qazvini called these *mils*), several large wooden shields and two steel "bows" weighted with metal rings. In the middle of the zurkhane was the *gohd*, a metre-deep octagonal pit where the athletes practised their sport.

The T-shirt boy followed us into the zurkhane and Qazvini sent him to fetch us tea. "We used to bring sick men and women into the zurkhane," Qazvini said. "We laid them in the corner and collected the sweat of the Master Pahlevan as he performed his exercises. Then we gave the sweat to the sick person to drink. The sweat was like medicine. The person would be healed."

"When did they stop doing this?" I asked.

"Sixty years ago. Nobody believes any more. Almost all the old pahlevans are dead, and young people are more interested in opium these days."

"Why are you here all alone?" I asked him.

"The men gather here almost every evening to do the exercises, but sometimes I come during the day. I come to relax. And to pray. For me it is a holy place." He took a sip of tea and whispered something to Babak.

Babak turned to me. "There is no ritual tonight because of the holiday, but the wrestlers will be here tomorrow morning. You are invited to attend. You will be the guest of Pahlevan Qazvini."

Babak met me at the hotel the next morning and we arrived at the zurkhane early. Qazvini was already there and invited us to sit next to him. One man, the *morshed*, climbed into a small booth above the gohd and began to play a drum embossed with the image of Imam Ali on its skin. The morshed wore no shirt and his long stringy hair waved back and forth as he played. Soon his chest began to shine with sweat.

Men arrived one by one and removed their shoes at the door. The morshed never stopped his drumming, and welcomed each man into the zurkhane with a snappy flourish of drumbeats and a blessing shouted into the microphone. The men shouted back a response. Babak told me it was a prayer for Imam Ali, Imam Hossein and the Prophet. Occasionally, the morshed greeted a man by clanging a bell. This signified that a Master Pahlevan had entered and should be honoured. Before doing anything else, each man went to the back of the room to greet Qazvini. He was the most revered man in the room.

Two teenaged boys served tea, then each man was offered a length of blood-red cloth. Those who wished to participate in the exercises wrapped the cloth over their trousers, around their waist and between their legs.

Qazvini began the exercises. He shuffled into a corner of the room, lay on his back, lifted his legs and crossed his ankles in the air. Another man handed him two heavy wooden shields. Qazvini gripped the shields and rotated them over his chest while rolling back and forth on his back. He sang while he laboured, and his voice, frail the day before, filled the zurkhane. "He is singing poetry," Babak told me. "He is asking for help from Imam Ali." Qazvini turned the shields for nearly ten minutes. The man was too weak to walk unaided, but inspired by the sound of drums, the respect of men and the sound of prayer, the old warrior was strong again.

After Qazvini was finished the other men removed their shirts and stepped down into the gohd. "It is like stepping into a grave," Babak said. "It reminds the men that they are mortal and should act humble." The men touched the floor with their lips and their foreheads. Each man chose a pair of mils from the edge of the gohd, kissed them and rotated them behind his back. The drumming of the morshed set the pace of the exercise and soon a dozen men were swinging heavy clubs in unison. Men began to sweat, stink and shine.

When the exercise was done, the men returned the clubs and each chose a short wooden plank from a pile. They formed a circle around the perimeter of the gohd. One man walked around the gohd greeting each man and asked permission to lead the ritual. After this brief formality he stepped into the centre and led the men in a series of push-up exercises using the plank. The drumming continued and the morshed began to sing:

> Oh Friend, show me your face.
> From behind the curtain show me your face.
> Solve one hundred of our problems, Friend.

A series of ritualized stretching exercises followed the push-ups. Then the men jogged in place and swung their mils a second time. Afterwards, the pahlevans took turns spinning in the gohd. With arms held aloft the men spun themselves into blurs. The novices ended up losing their balance and falling against their comrades, but the skilled men whirled in the centre of the gohd at fantastic speed.

The whirling required skill and precision. It was not a dance or the sort of dervish whirls that bring Sufis closer to God. It was martial. The spinning was an expression of strength and power. Like the clubs and shields, the men transformed themselves into muscled implements of war.

Afterwards, the morshed invited the assembled to pray for the son of one of the men who had fallen ill. The men turned to face Mecca, closed their eyes and murmured their invocation. Then the morshed officially welcomed me to the zurkhane. He told the gathering that I was a wrestler from

Canada who wanted to learn about baghal-be baghal. The men turned to me and greeted me in unison. I didn't know the proper response so placed my hand over my heart and bowed my head to the group. The men bowed back.

The ritual was over. The pahlevans crawled out of the gohd to look for their clothes. An old man in a yellow golf shirt approached me. He hadn't participated in the ritual that day but he was a Master Pahlevan like Qazvini. His name was Ali Vakili. "Many years ago I was a baghal-be baghal wrestler," he said. "If you like you can come to my home and I can show you some pictures." We arranged to visit his home the next day.

I received another invitation outside the zurkhane. Two men in their twenties, the only young men in the zurkhane that day, approached and offered me dinner in their homes. Babak placed his hand on my shoulder. "Marcello, do you know what is *ta'arof*?"

I smiled. An Iranian friend in Canada warned me about ta'arof, the uniquely Persian phenomenon of ritualized insincerity. She told me that I should refuse any invitation or offer of generosity at least three times before I accepted it. Nearly every shopkeeper and taxi driver refused to charge me at first, each saying *befarmyyid*, "You are welcome," a couple of times before eventually accepting my money. Ta'arof is the foundation of Persian etiquette and as important as the initial "Salaam." For the invited person to accept these offers of hospitality without first refusing three times would be as rude as the host's not offering at all.

"No, thank you," I said to the two men.

"It is no trouble. You are welcome."

"Thank you, but no."

"*Khoda hafez.*" They shook my hand and walked away.

I turned to Babak. "Was Pahlevan Vakili's invitation also ta'arof?"

"No. He wanted you to come to his house."

"How do you know? I didn't refuse him."

"Sometimes you can just know. I am Iranian. I know the difference. But until you learn, you should say no to everything."

Babak and I walked from the zurkhane to Azadi Square. The fountains were on and Iranian families sprawled out on the grass enjoying picnics, oblivious to the traffic screaming by. I thanked Babak for his help and said goodbye, but he had other ideas.

"Do you want to drink with me tonight?"

"Drink what?"

"*Araq*. Iranian whisky."

"Alcohol?"

"Yes."

"It is illegal here, isn't it?"

"Yes, everything is illegal in Iran. But I have a friend who makes it. I drink it very often. Many people do. He called me yesterday and told me he has some. Tonight I will go drink. Would you like to come?"

"Yes, please."

I met Babak later that night at my hotel, but I was wary about drinking in my room. I didn't want my hotel manager to get suspicious and call the police. "We will go to my friend's house," Babak said. "Don't worry." He was immensely excited. We took a taxi to a flower shop a few kilometres out of the town centre. Babak's distiller friend was the owner. So far my experience with Iran's criminal underworld consisted of florist/bootleggers and children's shoe salesmen/smugglers.

Babak's friend helped a woman with a giant bouquet of fake lilies. Then he brought us behind the counter and handed Babak a plastic bag filled with clear liquid. The florist turned to me and joked, "This is Bordeaux. Our finest wine."

I laughed and Babak said, "You see, my friend is very funny."

"What is it made of?" I asked.

"Raisins. It does not taste good but it has strength."

We took a shared taxi back into the city centre. There were three other passengers in the car, plus the driver, and Babak was nervous. "We should have hired a taxi ourselves," he whispered to me, in English. Then he discreetly sniffed. "Marcello, I think the bag is leaking. This is very bad. Can you smell the alcohol?"

I couldn't smell anything. "I think we are okay," I said.

Babak relaxed a little when we left the taxi. As we walked towards Babak's friend's house, Babak asked, abruptly, "Will you have sexual relations while you are in Iran?"

I told him that I had a girlfriend back home. "I will be a good boy," I said.

He told me that he didn't have a girlfriend in Qazvin but there were three women in Esfahan whom he slept with whenever he visited.

"Are they prostitutes?"

"No. They are women who like to have sex. I meet them on the street. Or in shared taxicabs. You can see them."

"How do you know a woman wants to have sex?"

"Their clothing. They have bad *hejab.* Sometimes they have too much makeup. Sometimes they wear their hejab too far back on their heads. It is easy to tell, and if you want sex you just ask. Then they say yes or no, and tell you if they want money." He turned to me. "I wish I had my own house. Then you could fuck some Iranian slut."

I changed the subject and asked Babak if poetry was important to him. "Poetry is only for old men and lovers," he scoffed.

We reached the house and rang the bell at the front gate. A tall, chubby man with thick glasses opened the door. "This is my friend Azad," Babak said. "He is my best friend. You stay here and I will go get food. We must eat before we drink or our stomach will have pains." While Babak fetched snacks

Azad showed me photos from his thinner, athletic days as a local karate champion.

Babak returned with some bread and sliced meat, a tub of yogurt and a bag of potato chips. After we ate a few sandwiches, Babak transferred the araq into an empty soda bottle and poured us each a glass. It smelled like kerosene. We clinked glasses and shot it back. The araq seared a path down my throat and left only a vague raisin aftertaste. Azad and Babak chased their drink down with a yogurt-dipped chip. "You must eat the yogurt to take away the taste," Babak instructed, then promptly refilled our glasses.

The conversation moved swiftly to politics. Both Babak and Azad railed against the Iranian government, and as we started buzzing from the drink, they became more spirited. "The mother-fucking mullahs!" Babak shouted. Each time he mentioned the government he twirled his index finger over his head. It was a derogatory reference to the men in turbans who rule Iran. "Iranians love George Bush. And we love Clinton, too. We hope that Bush comes and takes away our government like he did in Afghanistan and Iraq."

"Are you serious?" I asked. At the time, the United States was in the middle of an air campaign over Baghdad. Newspapers carried photos of burned buildings and reported on the wayward bombs that crashed into Iraqi bazaars. "People are dying because of the American attacks. Innocent people. You want this in Iran?"

"That is the price you must pay for freedom."

"What if a bomb landed on your family?" I asked. "On your mother?" I wouldn't have said this if I wasn't drunk, and I immediately regretted it. Babak didn't answer. Instead he stood up and said, "I am going to the water circulation."

"The what?"

"The water circulation. The WC." Then he disappeared down the hall.

Babak was gone for almost twenty minutes. When he returned his belt was undone and he was holding his stomach. "Sorry I took so long. I was making a statue of Khomeini in the toilet." Azad and I grimaced.

"I hate Iran," Babak slurred as he sat back down. "And I hate Islam. The Quran is not our book. It is the book of the Arabs. We are Persians." He paused and shot back the last of the araq, chased it with a chip, and said, "Marcello, I would do anything to leave this place."

Babak's rage against Islam made me uneasy. He sensed my discomfort and the conversation moved on to more benign topics. Music. Food. The misanthropic roadways in Tehran. Babak told me that Iranian traffic spawned an entire sexist slang based on automobiles. "A woman who is a virgin, we say 'zero kilometre.' If she is not a virgin, she is an 'overturned car.' If she is pregnant, she has 'been in an accident.' Her ass is 'hubcaps' and her tits," Babak held out his hands in front of his chest, "'headlights.'" We laughed like teenagers in a locker room.

"How long will you be in Iran?" Babak asked.

"I don't know. As long as I can. I don't know if I will be able to extend my visa for more than two months, though."

"You want to go everywhere, but will you do everything?"

"What do you mean?"

"Is there anything that you would not do while you are in Iran?" Babak asked.

"Like I said before, I have a girlfriend in Canada so I won't overturn any cars."

Babak grinned. "But would you ever lie?"

"To her?"

"To anybody."

"Tomorrow, if the police find me and ask me if I was drinking with these men," I pointed at them both, "I will say, 'No. I do not know them.'"

They both laughed. "And we would say the same!"

We finished the araq and gathered up the trash. Each of us stumbled a bit when we rose to leave. "We will walk you back to your hotel," Babak said. Azad lifted a bottle of cologne from a shelf and sprayed my chest. It smelled sickly of flowers. Outside the air was cool and the streets deserted aside from a lone cigarette seller at the nearby roundabout. Azad bought two cigarettes and he and Babak smoked as we walked up the street.

Azad broke the quiet and started to sing into the darkness. "He is singing poetry," Babak said. "It is a poem about wine from Omar Khayyám." He translated it for me:

> And David's lips are locked; but in divine
> High-piping Pahlevi with "Wine! Wine! Wine!
> Red Wine!"—the Nightingale cries to the Rose
> That sallow cheek of hers to incarnadine.

Then Babak began to recite poetry, too:

> Pour the red wine with control like rose water into the bowl,
> While fragrant breeze will roll and sweet incense refine
> With a harp on display we ask the players to play,
> While clapping we sing and say and dancing, our heads
>   decline.

All the way back to the Hotel Iran my friends took turns releasing poetry from their memories into the night. Babak had proven himself wrong. Poetry was not just for old men and lovers. The araq loosened the poetry from their minds and it slipped off their tongues. I smiled the entire way back to my hotel but felt a pang of jealousy. I had no poetry of my own to offer.

Babak and I rang Pahlevan Vakili's door the next afternoon. He led us to his living room, where his grandson brought us tea. The décor reminded me of my grandmother's house. Silk flowers filled brass vases and the coffee table was covered by an embroidered cloth.

Vakili said that in baghal-be baghal wrestling, which means "side to side" in Farsi, athletes fought outside, usually at wedding ceremonies, but the style was no longer practised. "It was very rough," he said. "We would hit each other sometimes." He rolled up his sleeve and showed me a flap of loose skin that hung under his arm. "I used to be a champion, but I injured my arm in a baghal-be baghal match. My opponent fell on my arm and the muscle ripped. If I had stopped wrestling the injury would have healed but when I was young I was stubborn. I did not stop. Now my arm looks like this." He tapped the flap of flesh and it swung under his arm.

"Sometimes I still go into the gohd at the zurkhane, but I use very small mils. I used to use those." He pointed to a pair of massive mils sitting next to his fireplace. "Try to pick them up." I could barely lift one off the carpet with both hands. Vakili opened a yellowed photo album and showed us pictures of himself juggling the immense clubs at a competition in Tehran. Another photo showed Vakili wearing a medal awarded to him by Reza Shah. Vakili sent his grandson to bring me his pair of weathered wrestling trousers. They were made of leather and denim and were covered with swirling coloured embroidery. "These are over one hundred years old," he said. "They are part of my youth. I could never part with them."

"How old are you now?" I asked.

"Eighty years."

I told him he didn't look older than sixty. He nodded. "I know. I have been in the zurkhane since I could grow a beard. And I have refused cigarettes a thousand times."

His grandson left the room and returned with a tray of biscuits, baby cucumbers and some slightly rotting strawberries. Vakili invited me to eat, and I asked him about the ideals of the pahlevan.

"To be a pahlevan, you must show your skills in the zurkhane. Years ago, we used to wrestle in the gohd. The wrestling was called *koshti pahlevani* but wrestling was not the most important thing. To be a pahlevan, you had to have a pure heart, pure words and pure actions. The pahlevans used to make food for the poor and help old women. They were honest and respectful. They were good men. Like Mohammed and Imam Ali. That is why the morshed rings the bell when the Master Pahlevans go into the zurkhane."

Vakili told me that now men will pay the morshed to honour them. Money and greed have cheapened the tradition. Men purchase respect rather than earn it with moral deeds. "Some good actions have ended in our society," he said. "Most people do not know how to wrestle koshti pahlevani any more. So the zurkhane is for exercising, and to be with your brothers. In the zurkhane we can keep your body strong and think about Allah."

"Is this why the morshed sings poetry about Islam?" I asked.

"Yes, but it was not always this way. Before the Revolution we used to sing *Shahnomeh*."

Vakili savoured the word on his tongue. *Shahnomeh*, or "Book of Kings," was the masterwork of the eleventh-century poet Ferdosi. The epic poem recalls a thousand years of Persian history, from early creation myths to the Arab invasions of the eleventh century, and was filled with stories of valour and tragedy. The book's central hero, a Hercules-like warrior named Rostam, was the archetypal pahlevan. The most famous episode in the book comes when Rostam slays his rival Sohrab in battle, discovering later that Sohrab was his only son. I found paintings of Rostam, clad in battle armour and crying over the body of his slain son, on the walls of tea houses and restaurants all around Iran.

Vakili closed his eyes and began to recite verses from memory. I couldn't understand his Farsi, but the words came in beautiful measured lines. His head nodded slightly with the rhythm of each verse. When he was finished he said, "Since the Revolution we sing songs for Imam Ali. But *Shahnomeh* is better for the zurkhane. It is strong poetry. And powerful. I am a religious man, a good Muslim, but religious poetry is too weak for wrestling. When you are in the zurkhane and hear the poetry you are inspired. You think you are Rostam and it makes you strong."

He sat forward in his chair and pointed to his chest. "I have *Shahnomeh* right here." I thought he meant he held the poetry in his heart, but then he unbuttoned his shirt. His flesh was decorated with rough blue tattoos. Two Persian lions battled an eagle in the centre of his chest. On his arms, mythic warriors, drawn from ancient verses, brandished swords and frowned from beneath their iron helmets. A winged maiden flew along his wrist. They were characters from *Shahnomeh.* He touched each tattoo, his fingers light with reverence. "Here is Sohrab, and this is Rostam. And here is Manijeh, Afrasiyab's daughter and wife of Bijan." He said these names as if I should know them all.

"The tattoos represent strength." Vakili took a sip of tea. "In my time there were pahlevans who had the strength of forty or fifty men. Today the young are weak with drugs. The government wants to keep them weak so they can control them. If the zurkhane and koshti pahlevani became popular again we could change this country. It could be as it once was."

I rose to leave and Vakili shook my hand. He had the grip of a bear and my knuckles popped. He looked at me sternly and said, "Be sure to tell the whole story. Tell people in Canada that there are still good men in Iran."

4

In the Holy City

Mashhad is a place of pilgrimage. It is Iran's holiest city and the burial site of Imam Reza, the much-adored eighth Imam of Shia Islam. His shrine complex is a collection of some of the most beautiful religious buildings in the world. Mashhad owes its prominence, if not its very existence, to Imam Reza. The city emerged around his tomb and all roads emanate from the golden dome of the *haram* like rays from the sun. Millions of pilgrims visit the shrine each year.

But there were other pilgrimages to be made around the holy city. The figures on Pahlevan Vakili's arms and chest inspired my fourteen-hour bus trip from Qazvin to Mashhad. I sought out the source of the poetry that danced on his flesh. I arrived at five in the morning, then found a bus headed east along the old Quchan road towards Tus. The highway was dusty and unsightly, lined with auto parts shops and crumbling mud-brick buildings, but the road ended at a lush garden and the shrine of the poet Ferdosi.

Ferdosi's tomb, an imposing block of stark white stone, marks the exact spot of the poet's death. Verses from his poetry are etched into the marble, including the phrase "Let not this body live if there is no Iran." The monument was muscular and dramatic, and seemed more suited for a warrior than a writer, but it befitted the poet's masterwork. Ferdosi's sprawling *Shahnomeh*, an epic poem of thirty thousand couplets, clangs with the noise of swords and combat. Its rhythms echo the drums of war.

Ferdosi's life story is dear to the Persians. Born Abdul Qasim Mansur in AD 935, Ferdosi was commissioned to write *Shahnomeh* by the Turkish Sultan, Mahmud. The Sultan promised Ferdosi a gold coin for every couplet of the poem. The poet accepted the commission in the hope of earning enough money for his only daughter's dowry. Ferdosi spent over thirty years writing *Shahnomeh* before presenting the finished work to Mahmud. The Sultan, astonished by the size of the manuscript and angry the book covered a millennium of history without mentioning the Turks, reneged on his contract with Ferdosi and offered him silver rather than gold.

Ferdosi was bathing in the *hamam* when the payment arrived. Mahmud's courier approached the poet across the steam-slick stones and presented Ferdosi with the silver. "I did not labour for thirty years to be paid with trinkets!" Ferdosi spat beneath the hamam's glass-studded dome. Then he gave a third of the silver to the courier, a third to the bathhouse keeper and a third to a tea-seller. When the sultan heard of this insult he sentenced Ferdosi to death. Only the poet's pleas for mercy, and a hastily composed elegy honouring Mahmud, saved Ferdosi from being trampled to death by elephants.

Years later the Sultan decided to pay Ferdosi the commission he promised; he could not deny that *Shahnomeh* was a masterpiece. He sent Ferdosi bales of indigo worth sixty thousand gold coins, but it was too late. Legend holds that the Sultan's camels arrived at the city gate just as Ferdosi's funeral procession was passing through.

Ferdosi died penniless and heartbroken, but is revered as the hero who saved the Persian language. Ferdosi had written in Farsi at a time when the language had fallen out of fashion.

The Arab invasion meant that Arabic was the preferred language of the educated elite. Ferdosi built a fortress around his native tongue with sixty thousand lines of verse. Without him, Farsi would have been lost. *Shahnomeh* is more than a mythical history of a people. It is a treasure of their identity.

I climbed up the steep steps to the platform. The midday sun reflected off the white monument and warmed my face with its heat. I placed my palms on the hot stone, then turned away and glanced down at the expanse of the park below me. Iranian families picnicked under shade trees and children floated paper boats in the fountains. A photographer took photos of children dressing up in mock warrior armour. They brandished plastic swords and frowned at the lens from beneath miniature helmets trying to look as fierce as Rostam. Ferdosi's mythical pahlevans, created centuries ago, were the children's heroes.

A tall marble statue of Ferdosi sat above a reflecting pool in a corner of the garden. The poet wore a turban and a dignified white beard and stared with sadness upon the monument that marked his burial. His face looked weary.

The shrine was built in 1933. It was renovated in the 1960s by the last Shah as part of his campaign to glorify Iran's Persian past and suppress its Islamic character. The Shah spoke widely of the glories of pre-Islamic Iran as told in *Shahnomeh* and encouraged Iranians to name their children Rostam or Sohrab rather than Reza or Mohammed. The Shah's supporters were quick to quote the line from *Shahnomeh* that reads:

> Damn this World.
> Damn this Time.
> Damn Fate,
> That uncivilized Arabs have come to force me to be
> Muslim.

This quotation, however, is from one of Ferdosi's characters, not the poet speaking in his own voice. Ferdosi himself was a devout Shia Muslim, and would have resented the Shah for using his masterwork to prop up a Godless political system. He certainly would have been saddened at how the design of his burial place ignored his faith. The tomb was devoid of anything Islamic. Oddly, the only religious motifs were the Zoroastrian carvings that decorated the top of the monument.

After the Islamic Revolution in 1979, when secularism gave way to enforced Islam, anything associated with the Shah's regime was anathema to the ruling ayatollahs. Khomeini reserved special venom for Ferdosi. In 1980 a group of extremists stormed Ferdosi's garden with the intention of destroying the shrine. Tempers eventually cooled, and the monument suffered only minor damage, but even its complete destruction could not have erased the poet from the Iranian soul. Ferdosi was carved from marble, etched on the flesh of men, and inscribed in the heart of a people.

As I walked through the park, I felt I was missing something. It was hard to imagine Ferdosi's import. For most Westerners, poetry is little more than a grade-school affliction. Still, the veneration of an ancient scribe seemed wholly civilized. I thought back to Babak and Azad reciting poetry in Qazvin's darkened streets, and for the second time I felt jealous of the Persians and their poetry.

Back in Mashhad I went in search of bachoukheh. This style of wrestling is native to Khorasan Province and was the most popular of the traditional Iranian wrestling styles. The annual national championship in Esfrayin features wrestlers from around the country and draws thousands of eager fans. Musicians play songs on traditional instruments inspired by Rostam's adventures in *Shahnomeh*. Most sports centres in

Khorasan host Friday-night matches to hone the skills of the local bachoukheh heroes.

A man at the wrestling federation in Tehran gave me the address of a sport centre in Mashhad, but when I gave the slip of paper to my taxi driver the address turned out to be incorrect. "Don't worry," he said. "There are many places for bachoukheh." He pulled a U-turn in the middle of the highway and dropped me at a nearby varzeshga.

Inside, I introduced myself to an official, Issa, who led me into a poorly lit gymnasium. There was a ragged wrestling mat on the floor and about a dozen spectators in the bleachers. Issa allowed me to sit at a table near the mat and offered me tea. Barefoot men milled about, some with their arms crossed, others softly running in place. They looked by turns tough and nervous. All wore a durable cotton shirt called a *choukheh*, the garment for which the sport is named. The wrestlers also wore tight shorts and a strip of cloth, or "shawl," tied around their waists like a belt.

The first match of the evening was about to begin and the two wrestlers took their places. One man wore a tight armband holding bits of paper inscribed with verses from the Quran, and each wrestler, as he stepped on the mat, first bent to touch the mat with his fingers then touched his lips and forehead. "The mat is a holy place," Issa explained. "It is a surface of Allah."

As the referee checked each man's choukheh, making sure that it was tucked properly into his shorts and that his shawl belt was tight, a man at the side of the mat led the crowd in a shouted prayer that called for Mohammed's blessing upon the athletes. Then the two wrestlers kissed each other on both cheeks and shook hands. The referee waved at the timekeeper, a pudgy man wearing three watches on each wrist. The timekeeper raised his arm, looking like a small-time criminal trying to fence watches, and blew the whistle.

At the signal, an ancient ritual started anew. The men stepped forward, each one reaching for the back of his opponent's neck. From the sidelines it seemed a gentle gesture, cradling the skull at the base, but I knew this position. I'd felt a man's hands dig into my own neck like a climber on a rock wall, seeking a place to pull and hold. This was no tender embrace. The wrestlers' forearms were tight and strained. They pushed into each other, necks bulging, and already they had begun to sweat. "You see how difficult is bachoukheh?" Issa said to me. "Wrestlers must be very strong. In bachoukheh, strength is 70 percent. Technique is only 30 percent."

Each man had his opponent by the head and upper arms. One man dropped his hand and grabbed at his opponent's choukheh, twisting a handful of the fabric into a knot around his fist. The other man reached down and gripped the tight hem of his opponent's shorts. It looked like roughhousing at first, these grabs of cloth, but each move was deliberate. Every grip, every tug, was a fight for position and a shift of balance. When men are this close, close enough to breathe each other's breath, not even the slightest flicker of muscle is unintended.

Suddenly, one man turned and hopped forward, and hooked his calf around his opponent's leg. The energy of the crowd surged; they sensed a fall. The caught man tried to sprawl his leg back, but his attacker was all over him now. Trapped in this tangle of limbs, he teetered and fell on his back, his rival on top. The air moaned out of him and his eyes searched the rafters for what went wrong. The crowd hollered and cheered *mashallah* as the victor stood. The two warriors hugged, kissed each other's cheeks again and the match was done.

There were four more matches that evening. The crowd grew more excited with each bout and the air became thicker with the dull stink of sweat. By the time I left the gymnasium I was spent. My early arrival in Mashhad was lying heavily on me, but more than this, I was tired from watching the bouts. A wrestler knows the efforts on the mat. He can sense the pulls and twists and strains. He needs only to witness them. As I walked into the street I rubbed at sympathetic pains in my shoulders. The night's battles were not my own, but I could feel them in my muscles. This is the wrestlers' empathy, a bond between men.

I travelled to Torqabeh that night for dinner. The town was just outside of Mashhad in a picturesque valley filled with fruit trees. Torqabeh is renowned for its open-air garden restaurants and there were dozens along the main road. I chose one set in a birch grove with a pathway that wound its way through the trees. There were no tables or chairs. Diners sat cross-legged on raised wooden benches called *takht*s laid with carpets and cushions. Each takht was large enough to accommodate an entire family and I felt self-conscious dining by myself. I found a free takht at the back of the restaurant, kicked off my sandals and sprawled out on the soft cushions.

The menu was entirely in Farsi, but I was able to decipher enough of the text to order. As in most restaurants I'd seen in Iran, most of the choices were kebab dishes. I opted instead for *abgusht*, which means "meat water" in Farsi, a dish I'd never tried.

A tray of appetizers preceded my abgusht. There was fresh bread, some soup, a salad with a thick pink dressing and a platter of *torshi*, or Iranian pickles, that included tasty cloves of pickled garlic. I was nearly full by the time my abgusht arrived. A cylindrical clay vessel held a brothy and aromatic stew made of lamb, potatoes, carrots, chickpeas and a chunk of jiggling lamb fat. I couldn't wait to start, but paused when I saw the utensils I was given. There were an empty metal bowl, a spoon, a slab of bread and, curiously, a metal pestle. I didn't know what to do.

I summoned a waiter. "This is my first abgusht," I said. Sighing, he tore off a piece of bread to use as a pot holder and lifted the hot clay vessel over the bowl. He poured out only the broth, holding back the meat and vegetables with the spoon. Then he ripped some of the bread into small pieces, dropped them into the soup and handed me the spoon. "Eat the soup. When you are finished, I will return."

The soup was rich and salty. I saved the sodden chunks of bread for the end. My man returned when the bowl was empty. "Finished?" he asked. I nodded. He lifted the clay vessel and dumped the remaining contents into the bowl. He took the pestle from the tray and used it to pound the lamb, meat, vegetables and chickpeas into a chunky mash. "Now eat with bread," he said and walked away. I could not conceive of a more laborious way to eat stew, but the abgusht was tasty and filling. It was finished by the time the waiter returned. I ordered an orange-flavoured qalyun and a pot of tea, and flopped against the cushions.

Four young Iranians were dining at the takht next to mine. There were two men and two women. One of the men leaned over to me, said something in Farsi and pointed at one of my cushions. "Go ahead and take it," I said, assuming he wanted to borrow the cushion. He was surprised at my English. "You are a foreigner?" he said. "This is very fortunate. I am an English teacher. Would you like to join me and my friends?" They shuffled to make room for me.

His name was Amir, and he and his friends lived in Mashhad. They were avid mountain climbers and spent much of their free time in the Alborz Mountains north of Tehran. I assumed that the two women were the wives of the men, but as we talked I discovered that they were all just friends. This surprised me. I thought that in Iran, and especially in the holy city, there would be little socializing between unmarried people and members of the opposite sex.

I was also surprised at the headcovering of one of the women. She wore a narrow red scarf that was draped over the top of her head and tucked behind her ears. Most of her hair was visible. I couldn't help but stare. I knew that only religious women wore the sort of all-encompassing chadors that my Farsi teacher wore in Canada, but I never expected to find such liberal dress here on the outskirts of Iran's holiest city. I had imagined black-on-black conservatism.

"I like your headscarf," I said to her. "My girlfriend in Canada would like something like that. Is it from Mashhad?"

"No. There is nothing good in Mashhad." She pinched the corner of the fabric between her fingers. "I bought it in Kish. Do you know the island, Kish? In the Persian Gulf. You should go there. It is very beautiful. Big bazaars. Excellent shopping."

The five of us chatted for a while before their waiter arrived with four long swords of saffron-scented chicken kebabs. "You will eat with us?" Amir offered. I told him that I'd already had a dinner of abgusht. "Abgusht? Do you have abgusht in Canada?" I shook my head. "Then how did you know how to eat it?"

"My waiter taught me."

"Do you like Iranian food?"

"It is all right, but I am getting sick of kebabs." I bought an Iranian cookbook before I left Canada and read about the blend of sweet, sour and savoury that characterizes Persian cuisine: stews that feature dried limes, tart cherries or blanched orange peel. Duck flavoured with pomegranate juice and walnuts. Pistachio-stuffed leg of lamb. Rice with apricots. I dreamed of this food, and was disappointed that nearly all of my meals in Iran were variations of skewered meat.

Amir laughed. "Yes, Iranians love kebabs. Have you tried *qormeh sabzi*?"

"No, not yet."

"You must come to my house tomorrow. My mother makes the best qormeh sabzi." His friends groaned. Obviously this was not the first time Amir had bragged about his mother's cooking.

"You see how much we laugh?" Amir said. "We laugh because living in Iran is a joke."

One of the women looked up at him. "And Mashhad?"

"Mashhad? Living in Mashhad is a serious joke," he snorted. His friends nodded. "I will tell you a popular joke here. To show you the Iranian sense of humour. As children we learn about a very famous martyr called Hossein Fahmideh. Fahmideh was thirteen years old and a suicide bomber. During the war with Iraq he sacrificed himself by crawling under an Iraqi tank and exploding a bomb. In school, every child learns about Fahmideh and we are told to admire his sacrifice for Iran. Khomeini said that Fahmideh was our leader. There is also a postage stamp with his face.

"But now there is a joke about Fahmideh. The joke says that they have found the 'black box' from the tank that Fahmideh blew up. Now we can hear the last words of the martyr before he died. It turns out his last words were, 'Hey buddy, don't push me in front of this tank!'"

I chatted with Amir and his friends for a little while, then excused myself. "Thank you for the conversation," I said, "but I am very tired. I'd better be heading back into Mashhad."

"You do not want to stay? I would give you a ride back into Mashhad, but we are waiting for some more friends to join us. They are late, but we are not surprised. They are newlyweds. They were married yesterday."

"Yes, they are still *gahrm*. Still hot," the woman in the red scarf added.

Amir walked me out of the restaurant and helped me find a taxi. He gave the driver instructions to my hotel, and wrote his phone number on a piece of paper. "You call me tomorrow. We will arrange a night when you can come over for qormeh sabzi." Then he shook my hand. "*Khoda hafez.*"

The next morning I made my way along Mashhad's main street towards the haram. Like the multitudes of the faithful I was drawn to the dual domes of the shrine, one as gold as the sun, the other sky-blue. The light of morning shimmered off the golden dome and the streets smelled of saffron.

I paused for water at one of the public drinking fountains that were common in most cities. Many Iranians carried plastic bottles or cups with them to fill up at the gleaming stainless-steel fountains, but there were usually tin cups or shallow dishes hanging on a chain. I met travellers who refused to drink from the public fountains. They were worried about the purity of the water, or the cleanliness of the hanging cups. But these fountains were one of my favourite things about Iran. This was the quintessence of hospitality in a desert land. To refuse it would be like refusing a handshake.

Metal detectors and a baggage search greeted me at the entrance to the shrine. Not long ago this noble sanctuary was defiled by violence and the splatter of blood. The security at the gate was a reminder of the grim day in 1994 when a five-kilogram bomb exploded in the women's section of the Imam Reza mosque. The attack coincided with Ashura, the day Shiites mourn the martyrdom of Imam Hussein, and the shrine was packed with pilgrims. The blast littered the ground with twenty-seven shattered bodies. No group claimed responsibility for the attack but the Iranian government found a convenient scapegoat in the MKO, a secular terrorist group bent on overthrowing the regime. It is more likely, though, that the bombing was the work of anti-Shia extremists based in Pakistan.

Inside, the scale and wonder of the shrine complex is testament to the reverence Iranians feel for Imam Reza. The faithful believe that in the ninth century, the Sunni caliph Mamun, who feared the growing popularity of the Shia Imams, fed Imam Reza a dish of poisoned pomegranates. Over the centuries his burial place has grown in scale to its present glory, and further expansion is ongoing. Millions visit the haram every year. Each pilgrim earns the respected title of *mashti*.

The shrine has long been believed to perform miracles. For centuries, devotees carried or wheeled the sick and infirm to the haram in hopes that the spirit of Reza could heal them. A more whimsical miracle occurred in 1973, involving a herder named Hussein Zadeh and his pious camel.

Zadeh brought a herd of camels to a slaughterhouse in Mashhad. One of the camels escaped, made his way into central Mashhad and entered the haram. According to a gatekeeper at the time, the camel walked through the inner courtyards, circled a sacred water fountain three times, then approached the centre of the shrine. There he laid his head on the stones in front of Reza's tomb and wept. The gatekeeper, moved by the animal's miraculous devotion, wrapped a green shawl around the camel's neck. The custodians of the shrine summoned Hussein Zadeh. "Your camel has implored Imam Reza's protection. What do you want us to do for you in exchange for this animal?" Zadeh asked to be made a gatekeeper to the shrine.

I spent most of the day wandering the vast complex. The place was achingly beautiful. The high *iwans*, arched gateways leading into the inner courtyards, were inlaid with dizzying patterns of mosaics, or lined with pure gold. Arabesque calligraphy swirled on high walls. Golden minarets strained towards heaven. Marble fountains burst forth clear water that shone like diamonds. Everywhere was the shine of mirrors, the softness of turquoise and the gleam of gold.

My awe grew into an unexpected exhilaration. As a non-Muslim, I was restricted to the outer areas but in the face of such majesty, and surrounded by this community of believers, I did not feel like an outsider. So I stepped inside. As I passed through the lofty gateways into the inner courtyards, I dragged my fingers along the huge wooden doors as I'd seen the faithful do. I hid my guidebook in my pocket and sipped from the golden dishes at the fountains. Awash in splendour and faith I felt like a believer. I wanted to be a part of whatever philosophy created such marvels, if only for these few moments. I wanted to know this God.

I did not, though, enter the very heart of the holy shrine where Imam Reza lay. The inner sanctum was the holiest of places. My outsider's religious feelings did not belong there. Instead I sat and watched the pilgrims float in and out of the shrine. Some were joyful, others solemn, but each gave the already dazzling scene the extra gilt of faith.

I left the haram and browsed the saffron stalls and religious souvenirs at the *bazaar-e Reza* before calling Amir. He told me his mother would not be able to have me over for dinner until the following night, but I was welcome to join him and his friends that evening. "I lost a bet with some friends about the World Cup. I said France would win and now I owe some pizza. Tonight I will pay. You can come along."

Amir picked me up that night in his car. An electronically enhanced Cher sang of her belief in "life after love" from a bootlegged disc on the stereo. Amir's friends lived on the other side of town, and we drove through the traffic underpass below the shrine complex. "My father is buried here," Amir said. It is considered a mark of distinction to be buried near Imam Reza, and the purchase of burial plots under the haram helps to pay for the ongoing construction of the shrine complex.

"That is quite an honour, isn't it?" I said.

He shrugged. "It was very expensive."

Amir and I picked up two of his friends, Ali and his pregnant wife Mahtab, and we found a seat in a crowded pizzeria. Amir told me that pizza was very popular, especially among young Persians. I practised my Farsi with them until the food arrived, then watched in horror as my friends squirted ketchup on their pizza. They were surprised that I didn't want any.

"I'm Italian. If I put ketchup on pizza I will lose my inheritance," I said. They didn't understand my joke and offered me mayonnaise instead. I ate my pizza unsullied. We drank orange sodas and discussed the meaning of the movie *The Shawshank Redemption*, a film Amir had just seen. "I didn't know you could get American movies here," I said.

"Only movies that are approved by the government. I have a friend, though, who rents out unapproved movies. He cannot have a shop, but when I call him he comes to my house with a suitcase filled with videos."

"That's better service than I get in Canada. What happens if your 'dealer' gets busted?"

"I don't know. Maybe a fine. Maybe he gets flogged. He would probably just pay a bribe. He is not worried."

We finished our pizza and drove back out to Torqabeh for saffron tea. Amir laughed at my poor Farsi when I ordered a qalyun. I wanted to order strawberry-flavoured tobacco but accidentally said the word for tomato. "I thought you didn't like ketchup," he said. When my pipe arrived I took one of the new qalyun mouthpieces I'd bought that day in the bazaar and slid it into the hose. Amir and Ali laughed, calling me a qalyun professional, but Mahtab shook her head. "Smoking those things will give you nothing but trouble."

For centuries, Persians have quarried for turquoise from the mines at Neishabur. The stones grace the fingers of rich men, and inspired the pale blue domes of countless Iranian mosques. Neishabur's poets, though, were more precious than any stones. Omar Khayyám and Farid al-Din Attar made this dry desert town their home, and I travelled to Neishabur to visit their garden tombs.

Omar Khayyám is one of the most renowned poets in the world, though in Iran he is revered more for his study of astronomy and mathematics than his poetry. He was born in 1048 and died in the early twelfth century but did not earn the world's attention until over 700 years later, when the English poet Edward Fitzgerald published an English version of Khayyám's *Rubáiyát.* The book, more of a paraphrase than a faithful translation, became an international bestseller. Only the Bible has sold more copies. The poems of the *Rubáiyát* are odes to wine and courtship; it is poetry for lovers. Fitzgerald's version includes these famous lines:

> Here with a little Bread beneath the Bough,
> A Flask of Wine, a Book of Verse—and Thou
> Beside me singing in the Wilderness—
> Oh, Wilderness were Paradise enow!

Khayyám's and Fitzgerald's lives were separated by centuries and geography, yet each man was responsible for the other's renown. Without Fitzgerald, the *Rubáiyát* would have vanished into time like most of Khayyám's poetry. And Fitzgerald was known more for his rendering of Khayyám than for any of his own verse. It is fitting, then, that the roses on Fitzgerald's grave in Suffolk, England, grow from seeds gathered at Khayyám's tomb.

Turquoise shops and souvenir stands line the street near the Bagh-e Mahrugh, the pleasant garden that envelops Khayyám's gravesite. The men at the entrance were napping when I approached to buy my ticket. They didn't notice the flaws in my Farsi and charged me the Iranian admission price, a tenth of what I was supposed to pay. The error was due less to my language skills than their grogginess and the fact that I was in disguise. My Italian features look Persian enough that most Iranians do not automatically peg me as a foreigner, but my clothing often gave me away. My blue, long-sleeved T-shirt always betrayed me as an outsider. So did my glasses, for some reason. I learned early on in the journey that if I wanted to pass as a local and enjoy the cheaper entry fees, I needed to wear my contact lenses, black trousers and a plain buttoned shirt. Socks with sandals completed my Persian disguise.

The garden was filled with flowers, and greenery lent freshness to the rose-perfumed air. I found Khayyám's simple tombstone, placed my hand on the centuries-old slab and frowned up at the *art moderne* structure added to the grave in 1962. Once warmed by sunlight, Khayyám now lies under a chunky, domed gazebo made of concrete and painted tile. I wondered what the poet would have thought of this awkward memorial. As he neared his death his only request was that "My tomb shall be in a spot where the north wind may scatter roses over it."

I left the Bagh-e Mahrugh and followed a shady street to the grave of Farid al-Din Attar. Attar does not enjoy the fame of his fellow Neishaburi, but in Iran Attar is far more revered. He was born in 1130 and lived for a hundred years before being killed by Mongols during their invasion of Neishabur. The Mongols beheaded the entire population of Neishabur, and Attar was likely among them, though more colourful accounts of his death are suspect. One historian wrote that Attar's freshly severed head continued to recite poetry and composed the *Bisar-nama*, or "Book of the Headless One," before falling forever silent.

The poet's name suggests that he was a perfumer or an apothecary, responsible for distilling the attar of flowers and herbs into fragrance and remedy. According to one of his own poems, Attar tended to five hundred customers a day. One day, a poor and dishevelled ascetic came into Attar's shop and marvelled at the wealth of items on the apothecary shelves. Attar became nervous and, fearing the man was a thief, told him to leave the shop. The man pointed to his own ragged clothes and said, "With only this, I have no trouble leaving." Then he gestured to the well-stocked shelves of Attar's shop. "But you, with all of this, how are you planning to leave?"

Attar was moved by the ascetic's question and soon gave up his store to travel with a group of mystics. His journeys led him to Mecca, Damascus and India, where he studied with a Sufi order. He eventually returned to Neishabur, reopened his shop and, inspired by the wisdom gained on his travels, began to compose poetry. He used to write in his shop between tending to the ills and fevers of his clients. I could picture the poet dispensing vials and powders, testing pulses and tongues, with a notebook of verse resting on his lap.

Attar's garden was as grand as Khayyám's and abloom with pink flowers. His tomb was simple and charming. A hexagonal chapel, decorated with intricate mosaics and crowned with a sky-blue dome, stood over the poet's bones. As I approached the tomb I heard a voice coming from the shrine. Inside, a professor was speaking to a class of female students.

Attar wrote scores of poems, but his masterwork is the *Mantiq al-Tayr*, "Conference of the Birds." The poem is an allegorical search for God in the tradition of the Sufi mystics. In the *Mantiq al-Tayr*, the birds of the world gather and decide to travel the Seven Valleys to find their king, a fantastic bird known as the Simorq. Only thirty birds remain at the end of the journey. Instead of a king, they are shown a gigantic mirror made of a thousand molten planets. The birds discover that they themselves are the *Simorq*. (The word *Simorq* is a pun in Farsi; *si morq* means, in fact, "thirty birds.") They find God in their own purified reflections and dissolve into the mirror.

> A hundred thousand centuries went by,
> And then those birds, who were content to die,
> To vanish in annihilation, saw
> Their Selves had been restored to them once more,
> That after Nothingness they had attained
> Eternal Life, and selfhood was regained.

Sitting under a window I listened to the professor recite poetry. As the verses took wing from the shrine and, afterwards, when the chador-clad students, their lesson complete, came like blackbirds into the sunlight, I thought of Attar's birds. Three of the women noticed me sitting in the shade. I heard them practise English phrases in preparation for coming to talk to me. Unfortunately, their collective shyness prevailed and they only waved at me from across the garden.

I went to Amir's for dinner that night, taking a taxi to his home in a leafy Mashhad suburb. We snacked on sunflower seeds and pistachios in his room while waiting for dinner to be ready. On the floor was a green and yellow rug. It looked familiar.

"Where did you get that rug?" I asked.

"I bought it when I went to Dubai. The name of the store was IKEA." I laughed; I had the same rug on my bathroom floor in Canada. Not even Iran is safe from the plague of cheap Swedish home furnishings.

Two more of Amir's friends arrived, Kaveh and his wife, Pari. Kaveh was the head of the English school where Amir taught. He had a wide, kind face and smiled from behind a fat moustache stained with tobacco. Pari removed her overcoat and headcovering in the doorway. She immediately lit up a cigarette. She was wearing a cake of makeup and a black lace bra visible through a knit tank top.

Dinner was ready and Amir's mother summoned us to the kitchen. Dishes crowded the table. There was a crisp salad, a roast chicken stuffed with slivered almonds and dried barberries that looked like tiny rubies, and the much-lauded qormeh sabzi. This was a stew made of fresh fenugreek leaves, parsley and coriander. Cubes of lamb and red kidney beans gave the stew some bulk, and the addition of dried limes added a distinctively Persian tartness.

The rice was a masterpiece. Amir's mother mixed the rice on the bottom of the rice pot with butter and yogurt before cooking. This allowed a golden crust to form while the rest of the rice became perfectly tender. The crust, called *tahdig*, was broken into pieces and served as a crunchy side dish. A second plate of tahdig was flavoured with saffron and sweetened with honey. It saddened me that the next day I would be back to eating meat-on-a-stick at the kebab houses.

Kaveh had spent several years in London. His English was flawless, though he spoke it through his nose and was enamoured of obscenities. Pari didn't talk much, focusing her breath on her endless string of cigarettes, but when she did speak her voice was like sandpaper.

After dinner we retired to the salon for tea and fresh fruit. Amir turned on the television and slipped a cassette into the VCR. It was footage from a Chris de Burgh concert circa 1987. I laughed.

"You don't like Chris de Burgh?" Amir asked.

"I do. I mean, I did. Years ago he had a big hit in North America. 'The Lady in Red.' I used to play it on the piano when I was fifteen. My mom loved that song."

Amir pointed at the television. "I know that song. He plays it at this concert. He is very popular in Iran."

"He's popular *now*?"

"Yes."

"You're kidding."

"No. We love him." I wondered if Chris de Burgh had any idea.

Amir left the room and returned with a bottle of raisin araq. I was surprised. Drinking from a plastic bag with Azad and Babak was one thing, but I didn't expect to find home-made alcohol in an upper-class home in a suburb of Iran's holiest city. Amir's mother brought out a tray of delicate glasses with ice for the araq, but she didn't drink any herself. Pari, though, was enthusiastic, tipping back long shots between drags on her cigarettes.

Amir asked me if I'd tried araq before. When I told him about my visit to Qazvin, he and Kaveh looked at each other and giggled.

"You should not go to that fucking place," Kaveh squeaked.

"Why not?"

"*Bacheh-baz*," Kaveh said. "They play with children."

"There is a story about the men in Qazvin," Amir explained. "They have a reputation for sleeping with small boys." He told me a popular joke about Qazvin. It was difficult to translate but involved some sort of sports contest where the prizes were young boys dressed only in red ribbon.

I asked Amir if the men in Qazvin were really pederasts. "I don't know. I don't think so," he said, "but it is something we say about Qazvin. Every city in Iran has a bad reputation. For example, we also say that the Shirazis are lazy, Esfahanis are very cheap and greedy, and men in Rasht have wives that cheat on them."

This time Kaveh told the joke. "One day a Rashti returns home from work and finds a crowd of men lined up to get into his house. He asks the man at the end of the line what is going on. 'We are queueing up to fuck your wife,' the man says. 'You really should divorce her.' The husband replied, 'I can't divorce her. Then I will have to go to the back of the line.'"

"There are good stereotypes, too," Amir said. "The Tabrizi Turk women are the best cooks in Iran. Yazdis are very honest. Kermanis are nice. And the women in Mazanderan are the most beautiful."

"But their husbands are *babus.* Stupid villagers," Kaveh added.

"What do they say about Mashhadis?" I asked.

Amir looked at Kaveh and they both shrugged. "They say we are cheaters and frauds."

Amir's mother eventually went to bed, but the rest of us discussed politics until very late. "George Bush has the Ayatollahs scared shitless," Kaveh said. "They see what is happening in Iraq and are afraid that Iran is next." Then he turned to me and joked, "You are not CIA, are you?" It was two in the morning before Kaveh and Pari stood to leave. Amir said it was too late to take a taxi back into town, and let me stay the night in his guest bedroom. I lay half drunk on the bed and laughed. I never thought my nights in Iran would include booze, black bras and Chris de Burgh. Or that I, in the land of Persian carpets, would step on my own IKEA rug.

I was on my way to the bus station the next morning when I saw a poster pasted to a wall. I couldn't read the Farsi, but the photo depicted two actors in warrior armour. One was collapsed on the stage. The other was standing over him, his arms outstretched and crying. It looked just like the famous scene of Rostam and Sohrab from *Shahnomeh.*

I asked a man on the street if he could explain the poster to me, but I struggled to understand his Farsi. Then I heard a voice behind me. "Excuse me, do you speak English?"

I nodded, relieved to have a translator.

"Excellent. Please, how do you spell 'midget'?"

"Midget?"

"Yes, please."

"Midget is *m, i, d . . .*"

"One moment." He reached into his bag and lifted out a pen and a ragged notebook. He opened the book, poised the pen on a page and looked back at me. "Yes, please. Start again."

I spelled the word for him and asked him to translate the poster. There was to be a play based on *Shahnomeh* the next night at a Mashhad theatre. I smiled at my good fortune.

"Where are you going?" the man asked.

"I was headed to the bus station. I am going south to Yazd but I will stay in Mashhad for another day or two if I can see this play."

"It is very fortunate that I found you today. My name is Arash. I will make a deal with you. You can come to my home and we will have conversations in English. You can help me translate an article from a journal. Then I will serve you lunch and let you stay at my home for two nights."

"That is very kind, but I am happy in a hotel."

"It is no problem. If you like, you can pay me two thousand tomans to stay."

Arash was a scarecrow of a man, thin with long lanky arms. He was in his fifties but had a childish look to him, perhaps imparted by the newsboy-style cap he wore that was too big for him. Arash eyed me with an eagerness that I mistook for the hospitality I was used to. I shook his hand and accepted his offer.

"Excellent," he said. Arash called his wife at a payphone and asked her to prepare lunch for us. Then he bought a dozen eggs from a nearby shop and we boarded a bus to his home.

It was my first time on an Iranian city bus. The bus was segregated: men up front and women in the back. Women were forbidden to step into the front of the bus even to pay their fare. They had to hand their ticket to the bus driver through the front door or an open window before walking along the outside of the bus to the back door. Even families had to be separated. Husbands at the front. Wives and children at the rear. In order to speak husbands and wives had to shout at each other from across the bus.

When Arash and I boarded the bus, the men's section was full. Passengers jammed two to a seat and stood in the aisle. Meanwhile, the back of the bus was nearly empty. I spent the trip eyeing those empty seats with claustrophobic longing. I was lucky to find a place to stand near the back door, right on the frontier between the men's and women's sections. There was space here to lay my rucksack and Arash's eggs.

A few minutes into the ride a beggar caused a commotion on the bus. He entered through the front doors and pushed his way through the crowd of men. He was moaning and crying and the men were annoyed. When he reached me I could see he was a teenaged boy. His body was too thin to fill his filthy jeans. His skin was pale and blotchy, and marked with wet red sores. He held out his arm to me to show me a gruesome three-inch gash in his flesh. I felt ill and turned away. The boy collapsed on the floor in front of my feet, and Arash moved his eggs for fear the boy would crush them. A few people tossed money to him, and he swept the bills off the floor and into his pocket, but most of the passengers just shouted at him. Arash helped two men push him out the door at the next stop.

I asked Arash about the boy. "He said that he needed money for an operation to fix his arm," Arash explained. "But he is a liar. He is a drug addict. An opium addict. One of the men said that he saw him on this same bus just yesterday with a different story. He is acting."

"Does this happen often?"

Arash shrugged. "We have buskers in Iran, too."

Arash's place was on the edge of town and took nearly two hours to reach. We rode three different buses, then unlocked Arash's bicycle from a tree at the last stop and walked it another two kilometres to his house. Once we arrived, Arash yelled a greeting to his wife through the door but did not open it right away. "My wife is a serious Muslim. We must give her a moment to put on her hejab." After we entered he asked me to give the money for my stay to his wife. "She thinks that non-Muslims are stingy," he said, then he barked at her to serve our lunch. She appeared in the living room a moment later. She smiled shyly at me and laid down a bowl of lentil stew.

While we ate, Arash handed me a copy of *The Journal of Persian Carpets and Islamic Arts* and asked for my help understanding an article about carpets from Baluchistan. The journal was a scholarly publication I could barely understand, much less explain. Arash demanded I pause at each troublesome word, explain its meaning, then write my definition in his notebook. Each time he cross-referenced my meaning with his English dictionary, then checked a Farsi dictionary. Once satisfied with the definition, Arash had me explain each sentence and decipher the formal language into words simple enough for him to understand. This took two and a half hours. I was exhausted by the time we were done.

Arash hollered at his wife to bring us tea, and then at his son, Khalid, to come and join us. Khalid, who was about twelve years old, sat in front of me on the floor. Arash turned to me. "Now, talk to him in English," he commanded.

I exchanged a few basic pleasantries with Khalid, asking him about his school and his family. Arash was pleased. "Khalid needs someone to practise English with. Maybe I will send him with you to Yazd so you can talk to him on the bus." I started to protest—I had no desire to baby-sit an Iranian boy on a long-distance bus trip—but then Arash turned his head towards the kitchen and bellowed, "Where is my tea?"

Seeking some sort of escape, I told Arash I was very tired and would like to take a nap. He showed me to a spare room. "You can sleep for two hours, then I will take you to a small village and show you my orchards." He closed the door behind him. I would have fled the house right then had I not already paid Arash for the next two nights, and if I had had any idea how to get back into central Mashhad. I started to regret knowing the spelling of *midget.*

When I woke, Arash and I took a shared taxi to a village just outside Mashhad. The place was charming enough, and the mud-brick buildings reminded me of my time in the African Sahel. Arash's "orchards" were meagre, just a few small plots with some immature apricot and mulberry trees. We stopped for tea at a dusty *chaykhune*. Arash knew all of the men inside and made a show of introducing his Canadian charge. Speaking in English he pointed out which men in the tea house owed him money, and which were opium addicts. "This is a real traditional tea house," he said. "Not like those fancy places in Mashhad which are just for tourists." He told all the men what I paid for tea in Mashhad and they all laughed at me.

On the way back to Mashhad, Arash said to me that perhaps sending Khalid to Yazd with me would not be a good idea. "It would be good for him to practise speaking English, but I am afraid he will want to smoke qalyun with you." I was relieved, but then Arash said that I must pay him another five hundred tomans for every meal I had in his house.

I raised my eyebrows at him. "You never mentioned this before," I said.

"Are you pissed off?" he asked.

I lied and told him I wasn't. "I don't think I will stay with you a second night, though," I said. "I thank you for your hospitality but your house is too far from the centre of Mashhad. I'd like to be closer to town." I couldn't imagine spending another day on Arash's leash, translating English for him and listening to him order his wife around.

Arash didn't seem perturbed by my decision, which was a relief because I didn't want to argue. "Okay," he said. "I know what we will do tomorrow. We will have breakfast in the morning, then I will take you to a carpet shop where you will listen to a lecture about traditional nomad carpets. You will find it very interesting because you are a writer—"

I interrupted him. "A lecture about carpets? You mean a sales pitch." I couldn't believe I let myself be taken in by a carpet tout. I felt angry and embarrassed. I thought I was a better traveller than that.

"No, no, no. A lecture. You will learn about history and culture and . . ."

"Thanks, but I am not interested in carpets."

"Really?"

"Not at all."

"Well, I know a man in the bazaar. We can go there and he can show you traditional turquoise polishing. Maybe you might want to buy a small turquoise for your mother or your girlfriend."

"I am not interested in turquoise either. Sorry."

"Okay, then we will go to the post office."

"Why would I want to go to the post office?"

Arash paused for a moment. "How can I say this? I would like you to send a carpet to Ireland for me. I will pay for it, of course. Do not worry. Last year my friend from Ireland bought a carpet from me and I need to send it to her."

"Why do I have to do it?"

"I am permitted to send only a small number of carpets abroad every year. It is an export law. Since you are not interested in carpets for yourself you could send this carpet to my friend in Ireland."

"Your friend was a tourist?"

"Yes. Like you she stayed in my home."

"You sold a carpet to a traveller last year but you haven't sent it yet?"

"That is correct. That is why I want you to do it."

I shook my head. "No. I'm not going to do that."

At his house, Arash demanded dinner and his wife, obedient, delivered a bowl of vegetable soup and bread. It was excellent. Arash agreed, and commented after every spoonful. "Mmm, this is delicious. *Slurp.* Mmm, this is tasty. *Slurp.* Mmm, this is delightful. *Slurp.* Mmm, this is scrumptious." I wanted to throttle him. After dinner and tea I was ready for bed. Arash said he would be leaving very early the next morning, but Khalid would help me get back into town. He insisted I meet him the following evening so we could go to the play together. "I will be your guide so I can get in for free," he said. I nodded but I had no intention of seeing him again. In the morning, after returning to town with Khalid, I escaped into the busy Mashhad streets.

I arrived at the theatre early, an hour before the box office even opened. I met the assistant director of the play in the lobby. He was excited to have an audience member from abroad and brought me into the theatre to meet some of the cast.

The actors lounged in the theatre seats. They were a Bohemian-looking group, not unlike my actor friends back in Canada. The actors offered me a chair and welcomed me to Iran, then scolded me when they heard I purchased a ticket. "You should not pay. You are our guest." After enduring the faux hospitality of Arash for the last couple of days I was happy to be back in the company of genuine Iranians once again.

The star of the play was the actor playing the hero Rostam. He was a lion of a man with thick arms, a black moustache and a mane of stringy hair: a perfect Rostam. He asked me if I'd been to Qazvin, his hometown. I told him

I had, and that I knew what was said about men from Qazvin. The actors hooted.

After a last preshow cigarette, the cast went backstage to get into costume. I wandered through the theatre building. There was a ladies' aerobics class going on in an auxiliary room. I could hear the generic dance music, the commands of the instructor and the rubber-soled footfalls of the women. The windows, though, were papered over lest a man catch a glimpse of a woman in spandex.

I took my seat in the nearly empty theatre. By the time the house lights went down there were only about a dozen people in the audience. Still, one man, a friend of the cast, sat in the seat next to mine.

The play dramatized stories from *Shahnomeh* and scenes from Ferdosi's life. All the dialogue was in Farsi so most of the play was a mystery to me. I recognized the warrior kings who clanked around the stage in gold-coloured armour and, of course, the famous scene when Rostam, after much wrestling and swordplay, slays Sohrab. The Qazvini Rostam knelt over the body of Sohrab, discovered the medallion that identified him as his son, and stretched out his arms to wail at the sky.

The scenes from Ferdosi's life were also familiar. The poet was played as a dignified but cheerless old man wearing a beard and turban. The Turkish Sultan was a villainous boor whose royal entourage consisted of a fool, a cripple and a giggling, pink-clad homosexual. Each was played without a shred of nuance.

Near the end of the play I saw, again, the Persian love for Ferdosi. When the poet died on stage, penniless and betrayed, the man sitting next to me started to cry. There was no shame in his tears. His hero was dead.

5

THE CRUCIBLE OF GOOD MEN

Pahlevan Kuchik did not want to wrestle the woman. It was the end of the nineteenth century and the king at the time, Nassir-din Shah, was a great patron of the pahlevans. The king had awarded Yazdi Kuchik the Pahlevani armlet and named him Iran's official pahlevan. It was a fabulous honour and when a female wrestler from Russia challenged him to a bout, Yazdi Kuchik could hardly refuse. He owed it to his shah.

Still, the great pahlevan was hesitant. It wasn't defeat he feared. Kuchik was a fierce warrior and his skills in the gohd were legendary. He was afraid, instead, for his soul. Kuchik was a devout Muslim and such closeness with a woman's flesh was forbidden by his faith. How could he wrestle a rival he could not touch?

Nassir-din Shah's advisors respected Kuchik's dilemma, but they weren't about to forfeit the match and lose face to the Russian wrestler and her tsar. The officials swiftly designed a special uniform for the woman to wear. The coarse leather garment covered her entire body like a second skin, and none of her flesh was exposed. Yazdi Kuchik met his challenger in the ring, he in his embroidered bastani trousers, the Russian shrouded in leather. Their battle was short-lived. Kuchik quickly tossed her to the ground, his title, reputation and virtue still intact.

Pahlevan Yazdi Kuchik was born Mohammed Abdul but was given the name Yazdi Kuchik, which means "Little Yazdi," to distinguish him from one of his contemporaries, Pahlevan Yazdi Bozorg, or "Big Yazdi." As a small wrestler myself, I doubt Yazdi Kuchik appreciated the moniker but it was the curse of sharing a town with a Goliath. Yazdi Bozorg was as big as they come. He stood over seven feet tall and weighed nearly five hundred pounds. When Nassir-din Shah travelled to Europe he made the mistake of placing Yazdi Bozorg in the front of his entourage. The colossal wrestler stole the crowd's attention and nobody noticed the king.

I found portraits of the two legendary pahlevans hanging in a zurkhane in Yazd, their hometown. I arrived in Yazd that morning after spending two days travelling through the Dasht-e Kavir and Dasht-e Lut, Iran's great eastern deserts. I'd traded Ferdosi's epic poetry in Mashhad for epic desert landscapes. I was happy. I had been looking forward to desert days.

Ever since my first visit to the Sahara years before I'd been enamoured of deserts. That a terrain blessed with such soft curves could be so unforgiving intrigues me, and the solitary traveller feels most pleasantly alone when surrounded by such an expanse. I find the desert towns the most beguiling, though. Like caravans of travellers before me, I seek comfort in the oases that defy the nothingness with their green promise. The surrounding emptiness brings each detail of these places into high relief; each flash of colour, every old man's smile, seems more vibrant when juxtaposed with so much nothing. I feel closer to everything.

As the vastness presses in, goodness blooms. Generosity is the desert's child. In this harsh landscape, to offer a stranger a glass of tea, or a night of shelter, is more than mere kindness. It is life. The desert urges men to look inwards, to think of virtue, character and God. It is the crucible wherein good men are forged.

I left the zurkhane and walked along Imam Khomeini Street, the major traffic artery that leads into the Old City. The streets of Yazd wore a modern veneer. Shopfronts had glass windows, electric-lit interiors and curvy neon signs. Inside, brand new televisions flickered with the day's news. The traffic outside, too, was wholly contemporary: noisy, fast and dangerous.

This modern façade, though, was thin. I walked a few steps off the main road and watched the urban terrain change. The asphalt dissolved into dust beneath my sandals and the wide avenues narrowed into a web of alleys called *kuches*. There was no steel, no glass and no windows. Buildings were made of bricks and mud plaster, and guarded with heavy doors. What was most immediately noticeable about the Old City was the quiet. The plaster absorbed sound like a sponge. Just metres from the blaring traffic was a landscape of sepia-toned silence.

At first, the quiet made the Old City seem abandoned, but this was a living city. I walked past a work crew laying new plumbing in a trench dug into a side street. A man spread fresh plaster over a crumbling wall. Power lines hung like afterthoughts from hooks along the mud exteriors and disappeared over walls. There were Farsi graffiti, skeletal television antennae and the odd illegal satellite dish.

The Old City may have been alive, but the life occurred beyond my view. Once in a while I could hear a muffled sound. The clank of tools. The laugh of a child and a mother's scolding. A radio or television; I couldn't tell which. But only the call to prayer brought the life out into the street, at least during the hot afternoon hours. As the call echoed over the city, women ambled past, their brightly coloured trousers emerging from beneath their black chadors. A mullah stepped out of a doorway in front of me, nodded a greeting, and I followed him through the alleyways to the Jomeh Mosque.

The building was huge and boasted a lofty entrance portal and the tallest minarets of any mosque in Iran. The mosque was like the desert itself. Its scope was best appreciated from a distance, but apprehending its detailed beauty—its swirling calligraphy, elaborate brickwork and rosette mosaics—required closeness. I stepped softly past the men who slept and prayed on the worn carpets, and felt the tiles with my fingertips. Yazd's Jomeh Mosque was a marriage of size with intricacy. I stared up at the thick minarets and imagined Yazdi Bozorg, his arms raised, with poetry tattooed on muscle.

I left the mosque and became lost anew in the narrow kuches of the Old City. I found a man sitting in the shade of a doorway, his face as sunbaked as the mud bricks. He could tell I was a foreigner somehow and, without smiling, stood and beckoned me to follow him. He led me to a set of steep stairs leading from a courtyard. He pointed at the stairs, then walked away. He wanted me to see his city from the rooftop. "*Merci*," I said to his back.

I climbed the stairs and the city stretched out below me. Aside from the blue-tiled domes, and the occasional flash of green from a tree growing out of a courtyard, this was a sand-coloured world. There were dozens of *badgir*s, wind-towers that acted as ancient air conditioners by directing and cooling the slightest of desert breezes. My eyes were drawn to the high ornate minarets of the Jomeh Mosque. Beyond the city lay the desert. I sat on the rooftop until sundown. Then, realizing I would be hopelessly lost in the labyrinthine Old City once darkness fell, I made haste to the lights of Imam Khomeini Street.

I went to Ardekan in search of camel kebabs, desperate for anything to vary my diet of Iranian burgers and skewered lamb. I never found the camel kebabi promised by my guidebook and wandered the Ardekan streets instead.

The dusty streets of Ardekan reddened my sandalled toes. I passed old archways and the domes of mosques. The city was an odd combination of the fresh and the forlorn. Some walls had crumbled from neglect, and exposed interiors collected the stink of trash. Other buildings boasted new plaster. Often, one of the renovated homes shared a wall or an archway with a building that had collapsed.

Ardekan was made lonelier by my poor timing. I arrived at the height of the day's heat when locals, wiser than I, abandoned the streets for shady interiors. I walked, alone and sweating, seeking signs of life. The soft voices of women, the songs of children and the smell of animals drifted so faintly from behind the closed doors they seemed like rumours. Only four young boys had decided to defy the heat. They were flying a yellow kite over the city.

The former Iranian president Mohammed Khatami knew these streets. He was born in Ardekan. Although a cleric, he was a moderate and a reformer. His surprising rise to the presidency in 1997 imbued the populace with a sense of hope. They could feel the grip of the conservatives loosen a little, and newspapers around the world heralded a new dawn in Iran.

The promise remained unfulfilled. Little reform ever occurred during the eight years of Khatami's watch. Regardless of the desires of Iranian voters, the conservative religious council held the real power in the Iranian government. This committee of clerics judged most of Khatami's ideas to be an affront to Islam and the Revolution and struck them down.

Foreigners usually liked Khatami. It was hard not to. He seemed well spoken and modest, a man with ideas whose failures were the fault of his political superiors. Iranians, though, were less forgiving. For them, Khatami was the man who promised change but delivered none. To them, he became just another of the ruling elite. They had few kind words for

Khatami, and twirled their fingers over their heads when they mentioned his name. In 2005, once Khatami's two terms as president were finished, reform-minded Iranians were too disillusioned to vote at all. The non-cleric hardliner Mahmud Ahmedinejad, Khatami's opposite, won the election easily.

I returned to my hotel in Yazd and found the manager, Taslim, drinking tea in the courtyard. Taslim was a tiny man of about fifty who always wore a dusty black suit and white shirt. He invited me to sit with him and ordered one of his staff, most of whom were staring glassy-eyed at a television, to fetch me a glass. The hotel, called the Kohan Koshane, was lovely, but business was slow. I was grateful for the solitude, but Taslim was hoping for clients. Each day as I left the hotel he said to me, "If you see any new travellers on the street can you tell them about this place?"

As we drank tea, Taslim asked what was my favourite thing about Yazd.

"I like wandering in the Old City."

"Yes, but what is your favourite thing? Is it the Jomeh Mosque? The old bazaar?"

"No. I just love walking through the small streets and kuches."

"Have you seen any kuche *ashti konan*?"

"I don't know. I don't think so."

"I will show you."

We left our tea and I followed Taslim into the maze of streets. I was lost within minutes. As we walked Taslim pointed out a poster plastered to a door, and we stopped to look at it. There was a faded image of a man. "Do you recognize this man?" he asked. I didn't. "It is me!" The poster was for a recent civic election. Taslim had run for public office, but did not win.

"You want to be a politician?"

"Yes. I want to be the politician for this neighbourhood." Taslim pointed to a house at the end of the lane. "I was born there," he said. "And over there is my sister's house. My father's house is also near to here. Now I live only fifty metres away. All my life I have been in Yazd. In this neighbourhood. I think I will be good politician. Very good."

"Why is that?"

"Because only I tell true. Always I tell true."

We turned a corner into a very tight kuche. It was too narrow for me to outstretch my arms. "Here it is," Taslim said. "It is called ashti konan. This means 'be friendly' in Farsi. If two enemies come through the street, and one is going this way and the other is going that way, they must touch each other when they pass. It is too small, so they must touch. For that time they cannot be enemies. They must be friendly." The alleyways, like the desert, press in and compel men to intimacy.

The pahlevans in Qazvin suggested the zurkhane rituals were the dying art of a few nostalgic old men. In Kerman, down a dark unpaved street, beyond the Imam Zeman Mosque and behind an unmarked door, I was pleased to discover the old Qazvinis were wrong. The zurkhane seemed like a gangster den from the outside, but once I stepped past the piles of running shoes and propped-up bicycles I found a room filled with children.

Boys between the ages of eight and twelve jogged in place and swung mils in unison. There were so many young athletes in the room that they could not all fit into the gohd. Some had to perform their exercises on the floor outside the pit. There was one man in the room, who acted as a coach, but the morshed who led the proceedings was a twelve-year-old boy. He kept the time on his drum and sang poetry for Imam Ali. He had a beautiful voice and lent the rite both a boy's playfulness and a mature solemnity.

My arrival distracted the boys from the ritual, but the coach barked at them to pay attention and fetched me a chair so I could watch. The exercises were identical to those I saw in Qazvin, only with miniature athletes and without the sour odour of manly sweat. Most of the participants wore traditional red loincloths. One boy, though, had a pair of intricately embroidered bastani trousers similar to Vakili's prized pants in Qazvin. Led by the terse commands of the coach and the young morshed's song, these tiny pahlevans swung mils the size of bowling pins behind their backs, did push-ups, jogged in place and, when the ritual reached its climax, spun like dervishes in the centre of the gohd.

In the spinning, the boys were superior to the older pahlevans. They whirled at startling speeds, their feet rotating beneath them and their arms a blur at their sides. Some were better than others, and I tried not to laugh as one of the chubbier boys spun out of control and careened into his friends, but those who perfected this feat were proud of their skills. I could see it in their revolving smiles as they spun towards becoming noble young men.

After the ritual, once the strict discipline had eased, the boys mobbed me. Some tried out the English words they knew. "Do you have any identification?" one boy asked. Others asked to see my notebook or into my bag. The young morshed sent a boy to prepare tea for me, and watched the crowd to make sure I was treated respectfully. When one boy started tugging on my shirt to get my attention, the morshed barked at him and banished him to the other side of the room. The boys would not let me leave the zurkhane until I shook their hands. Then one of their fathers drove me back to my hotel in his rattling truck through the night's heat.

Kerman is the largest of Iran's desert cities, and the Kermanis have a reputation for being pleasant and harmless. Unfortunately, I found scarce evidence of this. I squabbled with every taxi driver and argued with my hotel manager for twenty minutes to get a fair price on a room. When I finally heaved my pack onto the bed it became apparent at least one female traveller had stayed in my room before and enjoyed little privacy. Scrawled on the wall of my room, in English, was the warning: "Beware of the peeping men."

Afterwards, I had lunch at a kebabi manned by a twelve-year-old boy. When I sat to eat, he and his friends joined me at the table and made sexual gestures with their fingers. "Mister!" they cried. "Do you do this in Canada?" They thought this was hilarious. I tried to ignore them and read my three-day-old *Iran Daily.* "Mister!" one of the brats called again. I looked up. "Do you know what this is?" He had bent his thumbs and forefingers into the shape of a vagina. Again, his friends roared. I finished my meal quickly and walked away from their taunting. I thought back to the zurkhane boys. I wanted to believe that the young pahlevans, taught respect and humility in the gohd, were above such vulgarity.

I sought invisibility amid the press of bodies in Kerman's grand bazaar. Shoppers and vendors clogged the passageways amid the televisions, sport socks and underwear on offer. Motorcycles compounded the crowding by jerking through the mobs, honking incessantly and trailing a stink of exhaust.

The Kerman bazaar is a marvel of elegant arches and coloured tiles that belies the rather banal merchandise sold within. Most of the bazaar is covered, its ceiling a series of small brick domes, and the interior was cool and dark. Narrow shafts of light charged through portals cut into the apex of each dome and painted evenly spaced discs of light on the ground. Strategic merchants used these spots of light to illuminate their goods. Women sat in front of tiny bags of henna while nut-sellers allowed the light to pour into sacks of pistachios. In another part of the bazaar I saw a beggar sleeping catlike in one of the beams of light. His shirt and trousers were rolled up to expose his blotchy Appaloosa skin, and a small cup collected coins.

The covered bazaar ended where the open-air food market began. I met an unlikely quartet of female travellers there: an Italian, a Greek, a German and an Iranian-Canadian. Their presence caused a commotion among the men in the bazaar who followed after them in large packs. I introduced myself to the women, thus upstaging the men who tried to get their attention by shouting "I love you!"

The four women had met at an international nursing school in Holland. They were celebrating their graduation with a two-month trip through Iran. It was the Iranian-Canadian's idea and she was their unofficial guide and translator. I talked to the Italian while her friends bartered for peaches. She was tall, fair-skinned and very pretty. She would have trouble being inconspicuous on the streets of Europe, much less in an Iranian bazaar. "What's it like travelling as a woman in Iran?" I asked.

"You can see the attention we get," she said, turning to face the mob of men who had gathered on all sides of us. I laughed; the women effectively halted the day's commerce. "I feel safe, though. We are having a wonderful time. Aside from the occasional pinched ass we have had no troubles."

"And you're Italian," I joked. "You should feel at home getting your ass pinched."

She smiled. "Yes, but in Italy I know what to do."

In Sirch, a village of orchards near Kerman, I found a family in a fig tree. A father and his three children had climbed the branches to pluck free the sticky fruit. The youngest son prowled the highest branches where the ripest fruit hung. His mother, standing on firm ground to catch the falling harvest, shouted up at him to be careful.

I had travelled to Sirch for a little solace from the city. The highway passed through a flat desert plain into the Payeh Mountains. Nomads' tents made spots of darkness on the mountainside, and shepherds' trails snaked across the greyness. After the noise of Kerman, however, the freshness of the land and the rural quiet was like a balm.

I expected no poetry in Sirch, but I found it surrounded me. Apricot trees grew in ordered rows like *qazals*. A stream, fed by distant desert springs, murmured past the orchards. I walked through vineyards, past animal pens made of mud and thatch. The fruit on the pomegranate trees was still young and green, but scarlet blossoms, freshly fallen, lay in the shade like tiny bursts of flame. It was little wonder this country inspired men to verse.

I came upon a farmer napping on a blanket beneath a canopy of grapevines. My footfalls woke him, but instead of scolding me for my trespass he beckoned me closer. Without saying a word he filled my rucksack with sweet green grapes and went back to sleep. Suddenly I was awash with a familiar envy; I wanted his life. In that moment I would have given all I had for a vineyard, a donkey, his farmer's calluses on my soft writer's hands. I wanted a grove of date palms. I wanted to live in a green village surrounded by desert, or in a nomad's black tent. These brief imaginings of other vocations are one of travel's greatest gifts. When the envy passes, and it always does, it leaves admiration in its wake, and the urge for less, not more.

After my visit I stood on the side of the road to flag down a passing taxi. I waited for an hour, sitting on a cinder block across from a chaotic thatch of roadside sunflowers. When I returned to Kerman I plunged my grapes into a pitcher of water and ate them chilled for my next morning's breakfast.

It is an immutable law of travel that the procedures required for obtaining visas and visa extensions must be irrational. When I was travelling in Africa, the Nigerian embassy in Accra required me to make three visits to their office before deciding I was ineligible for a tourist visa, and I had to "dash" the gatekeeper with a few coins each time or he would not let me in. In the same city, I received a visa for Togo in mere minutes, only because the visa official developed an immediate crush on the woman I was travelling with. At the immigration office in Cairo, extending my visa meant standing in line in front of six different windows on two different floors to gather the necessary forms, stamps and photocopies, and pay the requisite fees.

Extending my Iranian visa in Kerman would offer the same frustrations. I followed the map in my guidebook to the immigration office, only to discover that the office had moved. I asked policemen and taxi drivers for directions and followed their pointed fingers for two hours before I found the new building. The woman behind the visa desk seemed tired and didn't smile as she handed me a set of forms to be filled out in triplicate. I completed the forms and handed them to her along with some passport photos, then reached into my pocket to hand her the money for the extension fee. She shook her head.

"I do not take the money. You must go to these banks." She wrote the names of two banks on a slip of paper and instructed me to deposit a portion of the fee into two separate accounts.

"Why can't I just give you the money?" I asked.

"We cannot take it. You must go to the banks."

"All right, but why two *different* banks?"

She shrugged. "This is Iran."

"Are these banks nearby?"

"No. You must take a taxi. When you are finished, come back here."

I was fortunate to find a kindly taxi driver outside the visa office who was willing to ferry me to the banks, wait as I made the deposits, and drive me back to the immigration office. After an hour of driving, standing in line and being shuttled to and from various tellers I returned to the woman behind the desk. I handed her my deposit slips. "Now sit and wait," she said and left the room.

I sat in the lobby for half an hour drumming my fingers on the glass coffee table and glancing at the clock. The wait was not without some anxiety. According to regulations, travellers must wait until the last minute before applying for an extension, and my first visa would expire the next day. If my application was denied I had less than twenty-four hours to leave Iran. I would have to leave Iran at the Turkish border, which was far from Kerman, and it was unlikely that I could make it to the border in time.

The official came back. She allowed herself a slight grin when she handed me my passport. A new red stamp had been added granting me another six weeks. "Enjoy your time in Iran," she said.

I spent the rest of the day in the nearby town of Mahan, the final resting place of Shah Nematollah Vali, a fifteenth-century dervish who founded one of the most popular Sufi orders in the world. Vali had a mystic's flair for wandering, poetry and longevity. His travels led him from his birthplace in Syria to the holy city of Mecca, and through much of Central Asia. He lived for over a century and left behind nearly fourteen thousand poems. His verses celebrated the intoxication of faith and spiritual devotion. The mythical pahlevan Rostam marched through the sage's poetry as a symbol of the idyllic man made flawless by God:

> Since we have laid our hand in your hand,
> We are like Rostam, more powerful than whoever . . .

My minibus dropped me at Vali's mausoleum. I walked through a pair of antique wooden doors into a courtyard filled with flowers and tall cypress trees. A reflecting pool caught the image of the large blue dome with its tile pattern of eleven-pointed stars. The caretaker spotted me in the courtyard and offered to let me climb one of the two minarets that towered over the complex. A staircase wound its way up the inside of the minaret in a tight spiral. At the top, my guide warned me not to lean on the loose tiles on the railing. My view stretched into the unfriendly desert where rocky hills looked like sand dunes hardened by bad moods. My guide offered to take my picture. He told me to wait at the top of the minaret, then took my camera down the staircase, walked across the roof of the tomb and climbed the other minaret. I shouted camera instructions to him and smiled like a dolt as he snapped a photo.

For most tourists, the shrine is just another of Iran's architectural jewels, a brief stop on most guided tours and an opportunity for a cheesy minaret photograph. But for the thousands of adherents to the Nematollahi order it is a place of devout pilgrimage. For the faithful, Shah-e Vali's spirit resides here. Unfortunately, the mystic sage has an uneasy relationship with the contemporary Iranian government. In the spring of 2002, hundreds of Shah-e Vali's followers were due to gather in Mahan for a symposium. The event was delayed, then cancelled, due to protests from ruling clerics who declared Nematollah was a Sunni Muslim. This was a dubious claim. In the sixteenth century, Nematollah encouraged Iranian leaders to formally adopt Shiism as the state faith. The cancellation of the conference had more to do with the uneasy alliance of religions in Iran, even among different Islamic sects, and the suspicions of clerics who did not like the idea of hundreds of foreign Sufis descending on Iran.

A taxi waited for me in front of the tomb when I emerged. "Shahzade?" the driver shouted. I nodded. Obviously I was following the regular Mahan tourist circuit: going from the Aramgah-e Shah Nematollah Vali to the famous Shahzade Gardens. The driver was used to tourists, and though the ride was less than five kilometres he demanded an extortionate fare. I argued with him for ten minutes in my lousy Farsi before relinquishing the money. I felt foolish for not walking.

I walked into the garden still fuming at the taxi driver, but there was something immediately calming about the sound of fountains and falling water. Water tumbled down a series of stepped pools. At the top, a nineteenth-century palace had been converted into a restaurant and tea house. I wanted to enjoy a quiet smoke at one of the tables, but three young men, including a soldier officer whose job it was to guard the garden, decided to join me. They wanted to talk about sex. I endured their locker room discourse as I finished my tea, then made my way towards the garden exit. The soldier put his hand on my shoulder. "Wait," he said. "You must come with me first." I sighed and readied myself for a mild interrogation. Instead the guard led me off the garden path into a grove of fruit trees. He plucked two handfuls of fresh apricots and cherries, gave them to me and wished me a pleasant stay in Iran.

I met a Spanish traveller at the entrance to the gardens. He was chatting with the gatekeeper and his Farsi was excellent. He had been staying at the hotel that existed within the garden walls for a few days and befriended the gatekeeper. While we spoke, an Iranian woman came up the road with two of her friends. She handed the Spaniard a letter written in English. "Please, sir, can you read this letter for me?" The letter was from a doctor, an eye surgeon, who had examined the woman. The doctor prescribed her a drug that might alleviate some of her eye problems, but said that even with the medicine, it was unlikely her vision would improve. The woman would go blind.

The woman listened carefully as the Spaniard translated the letter. When he finished he said, "I am sorry." She nodded sadly, said thank you in a soft voice, then walked back down the road. Her friends laid their arms across her shoulders.

I needed to find a ride back to Kerman. There was one taxi in front of the gate. I walked towards it and girded myself for another battle over the fare. The driver was old and dishevelled, his mouth a mumble of pale green teeth.

"You want to go to Kerman?" he said.

"Yes." I was surprised he spoke English. "How much will that cost?" I gritted my teeth. He quoted me a price that was suspiciously low, less than what I paid for the five-kilometre trip from Shah-e Vali's shrine. "You will bring me all the way to Kerman for that price?"

"Yes."

"All the way to Kerman? That is very cheap."

"It is okay. Let us go."

When we reached the outskirts of Mahan my driver turned to me and asked, "What is the most important thing for my wife and for my children?"

I faced him. He was serious. "I don't know. What do you mean?"

"How can I be sure that my wife and my children will not go hungry?"

I raised an eyebrow. "I don't know."

"How can I be a good father to my wife and to my children?"

"I don't know, for sure."

"How can I be a good man?"

"A good man?" He was making me nervous, and spitting a lot as he spoke. "I'm not sure."

"Am I a good man because I have money, because of the Quran or because I am clever?"

"I don't know. I'm not sure if any of those things will make you a good man."

"Why not?"

I laughed. “I don’t know.”

“Am I a good man because I have a taxi?”

“No. I don’t think so.”

“Why not?”

“I don’t think that having a taxi makes you a good man.”

“Why not?”

“I don’t know.”

“How can I be sure that nobody will take my taxi away from me?”

“I don’t know. Try locking the doors.”

“How can every person in the whole world say that I am a good man?”

“I don’t know.”

“How can every person in the world trust me?”

“I don’t know.”

“How can every person in the world like me?”

“I don’t know. I think everyone has these questions. I’m not sure if there is an answer.”

“Why not?”

“There just isn’t.”

“Why not?”

“I don’t know,” I said, exasperated.

He paused for about a minute. This gave me a chance to wipe the spittle from my face. Then he asked, “How can I become the president of Canada?”

“You want to be president of Canada?”

“Yes.”

“Well, you have to be Canadian, first of all. Why do you want to be the president of Canada?”

“If I want to be the president of Canada, do I need money? Do I need to be clever? Or do I need to have knowledge?”

“I think you will need all of those things.”

“Which is the most important? Money, knowledge or to be clever?”

"I'm not sure."

"Do I need to be a good man?"

"You mean to be president of Canada, or in general?"

"In general."

"Yes. It is good to be a good man."

"How many kinds of 'good' are there?"

"I don't know."

"Is there one kind of 'good' or many kinds?"

"I suppose there are many."

"What are they?"

"I'm not sure."

"How many kinds of 'clever' are there?"

"Many."

"How many kinds of 'rich' are there?"

"Many."

"How can I be sure that I will not go to prison?"

This interrogation continued the entire ride to Kerman. My driver proceeded at a crawl, as if the taxi itself was mired in the muck of his inquiries. Twice, when the question at hand was particularly weighty, he stopped the car altogether. I first thought his endless rhetorical questions were an elaborate preface to something else. I thought he might try to convert me to Islam, or ask for money to keep his wife and children from going hungry. Travellers learn quickly to distrust the motives of taxi drivers. But my driver never asked for anything and, as it turned out, his questions were not rhetorical at all. This philosopher hoped for answers.

It was dark by the time we reached Kerman. I paid the driver the paltry fare and shook his hand. He held tight and smiled his green grin. He asked me if I thought he was a good man, and didn't let go of my hand until I said that he was.

6

TRAVELLERS TO BAM

Bam, an oasis city southeast of Kerman, didn't match its name. "Bam" is a ham-fisted noise. The sound of a slammed door or a gunshot. But when I arrived in Bam, after passing from Kerman through two hundred kilometres of yellow desert, I was overcome by the quiet. The eucalyptus-lined streets were almost abandoned. Aside from the clatter of the occasional motorcycle, usually piloted by a pair of teenaged boys in mullet haircuts, there was only heat and hush.

I found a bed at Ali Akbar's guest house. Akbar was relaxing in the shade at the front gate when I arrived. "Welcome to Bam," he said, rising from his chair. His English was flawless. "You can pay me whatever you like for your dorm bed," he said, blinking at me from behind his thick glasses, "but take off your shoes before entering the house. And, please, try to take only one shower per day." Three scruffy backpackers looked up and nodded at me from a picnic table in the courtyard as Akbar led me to the dorm.

Since 1979, Iran hasn't been a popular destination for Westerners. The Revolution closed the Shah's bars and discos, and insisted foreign women cover their heads and dress modestly, even on the newly segregated beaches. Then came the hostage crisis and the eight-year war with Iraq. In the late 1990s, travellers were beginning to return to Iran, but after September 11 and the ongoing wars in neighbouring Afghanistan and Iraq, Westerners stayed out of the Islamic Republic. Muslims, it seemed, made too many white people nervous.

A trickle of backpackers, though, still make their way along a defined circuit that curves through Iran. The trail links Iran's borders with Turkey and Pakistan and includes most of Iran's major cities and tourist sites. The trail itself isn't new; it follows one of the southern Silk Road routes. Instead of caravans of camel-borne traders, contemporary travellers are Western tourists following their *Lonely Planet*s east from Istanbul or west from Kathmandu.

I don't like backpackers much. I find their culture hypocritical. These travellers often laud the merits of independent travel and ridicule package tourists, yet they rarely stray off the paths set out by their guidebooks. They may eschew materialism, but well-worn passports are flashed like diamond jewellery—status symbols. Backpackers trade in passport stamps as their currency. The most bothersome among them will rattle off lists of the places they've been as if they were boasting about a new sports car.

What disturbs me most, though, is that many of the backpackers I have met are not remotely interested in the places they visit or the people who inhabit them. These are the young travellers who eat Kentucky Fried Chicken in Cairo, seek out Irish pubs in Ghana and crowd the backpacker bars in Istanbul in search of other travellers to bed down with. Insulated from the cultures around them, they hole up in hostels with others of their ilk, share beers and sex, then move on to their next outpost.

Iran's strict policy against alcohol, though, makes it an unlikely destination for the worst of these travellers. At the very least it tempers their behaviour. There are no backpacker bars where Westerners can pound back beers until they are nearly blind. No drunken mosquito-net sex in hostel dormitories. The backpackers I met in Iran were genuinely interested in the country, and were typically older than their kin in more party-friendly locales.

That said, there were a few irksome travellers who came west from India and Pakistan and complained Iran was not "traditional" enough. One German tourist bemoaned the modernity of Iranian cities. "Iran is too developed," he said. It took a special breed of Western arrogance to claim Iran was not poor enough to be interesting.

Akbar hosted nearly every backpacker who passed through Iran. His guest house was immensely popular with the overland tourists and Akbar was patient with their non-Iranian sensibilities. Soon after I laid my rucksack in the dormitory a group of Koreans came in. There was one female in the group. Akbar told her she was free to remove her hejab inside the guest house. The woman went into her room and returned wearing a skimpy T-shirt, a pair of tight cotton pants and a smile of relief. Akbar, though, shook his head and laughed. Later he said to me, "I told her she could take off her headscarf. I didn't think she would come out in her underwear. If the authorities see this I will be in trouble. They will think I am running a brothel."

I woke the next morning at sunrise and made my way to the Arg-e Bam, an enclosed mud-walled old city that for centuries had been a stopping point for travellers. In the Silk Road days, traders paused here to fill the bazaars with merchandise, water their camels and find respite from dusty days in the desert. The Arg fell into disuse once the overland trade diminished. The Iranian army used the old city as a barracks for some time, then the Arg was abandoned for over forty years. In the 1970s the Iranian government turned the Arg into an open-air museum, and restoration was ongoing.

The early-morning air was cool and the Arg nearly deserted. After passing through the tall gatehouse I hiked up the crenellated city walls and I wandered the streets in search of ancient mosques and bazaars. I paused at a chaykhune where an unfriendly woman served tea and breakfast. She charged a ransom but I was too ravished by the setting to care much. Then I climbed the citadel, the fortress that dominates the Arg. From that height I had a panoramic view of the entire city. I could see through the broken roofs and into buildings with the thin brown walls of gingerbread houses. Restored domes resembled bubbles of mud. Aside from the occasional tree reaching out of a courtyard, the Arg looked like a vast sepia photograph. Beyond the walls was the opposite view. The modern city of Bam hid beneath the date palms. Only the immense Jomeh Mosque emerged out of the green canopy.

The Arg encompasses less than two square kilometres, but the twisting passageways held me for hours. I wandered past the old synagogue and through the arches of the bazaar, pausing to take an occasional photograph. I came upon an ancient zurkhane. The dome on the rooftop was smoothly restored but the inside was in ruins. I imagined the ritual inside. The room would have been lit with lanterns. There would have been no photos on the walls, only portraits of Imam Ali. Stacks of shields and mils would fill the corners. There would be the resonance of bells and drumbeats and songs of mythical battles. Here, surrounded by battlements and in the shadow of the citadel, men made fortresses of their bodies. I jumped down into what was left of the gohd where the sweat of pahlevans mingled with age-old mud.

I moved slowly through the city, afraid of missing details. In my head, though, I wished I were ten years old again and had my cousins to chase through the mud-brick labyrinth. We'd climb through windows and over ramparts. We would imagine armies and battles and, with sticks as swords, lay siege to the citadel. We'd play until we were breathless, then our mothers would tell us it was time to go home, turning our brave battle cries into tears.

The renewal of the city was so complete that many of the buildings looked brand new. The bazaar and citadel, in particular, seemed recently abandoned rather than centuries old. The mud plaster was smooth and flawless. Akbar said the Arg was too perfect, that the restoration had robbed the city of its character and antiquity. It was true. There was something artificial about such smoothness in a place so ancient. Sometimes the restoration smacked of cosmetic surgery. For all its fresh lines the Arg lacked the fragrance of age. A traveller does not need every wall rebuilt and every crack repaired. Our imagination is an able enough bricklayer.

I found authenticity, though, in a whiff of wet earth. Near the Friday mosque a man was quietly rebuilding the city. I watched as he turned a heap of dust collected from a fallen building into fresh mud. Each spadeful became a new brick and was laid to harden in the heat. Old walls—crumbled, moistened and reformed—became new walls. I was relieved that the city's renewal was no fibreglass illusion, but the ancient merging of mud and hands.

I met Mirabelle and Frans at the guest house. They were a pair of Dutch travellers who had spent the last two and a half years seeing the world on their bicycles. They cycled through Asia, India and South America. They braved Brazilian downpours that washed away the roads beneath their tires, rode through the Himalayas twice, and had recently come from China where Western travellers were suspected carriers of the SARS virus. (I had to laugh when Mirabelle told me that, in China, SARS was known as "the Canadian disease.") I envied their experiences as much as their resolve. I don't possess the stamina, nor even the inclination, to pedal myself across the world.

As Frans tended to his laundry, Mirabelle and I walked to a sweet shop down the road. The shy girl behind the counter sold us a box of date cookies and cups of saffron ice cream garnished with strawberry gelatin. Then we sat to eat next to a guitar-shaped fountain in the courtyard. Mirabelle told me that she and Frans were nearing the end of their travels—their insurance policy was about to expire—and were headed home through Iran, Turkey and eastern Europe. I asked her how she felt about going home.

"I am scared," she said. "Last year we flew home from Thailand when Frans's mother died. After the funeral we stayed in Holland for two months, but we could not handle it. We tried to get jobs, but all we wanted to do was travel. So we packed up our bicycles again and flew back to Thailand.

"Now we have to go home, and I am nervous. All my friends will have new jobs, new homes, new babies. We will have nothing. We will be starting at zero. I don't know what we are going to do."

"Do you regret it? Travelling for so long, I mean?"

"Not at all. Not for one second," she said, looking over my shoulder and into the desert darkness. "We have seen so much."

On my last day in Bam, I hired a car and driver to visit the tiny villages in the surrounding desert. Single-storey mud homes stood at the side of vast date plantations. The dates of Bam are reputed to be the world's finest, but the fruit was unripe at the time and hung in green bunches from the base of the palm fronds. Families invited me into their homes and showed off prized sheep in mud pens. Children waved at me from the backs of donkeys. Cattle strolled untethered through the streets and past heavy wooden doors. My driver showed me the *qanaat* system, an ingenious web of underground canals that brings water from the desert springs to the date gardens. There was a break in the qanaat outside the village of Kork. Three young boys splashed in the canal, their skin slick with water and shining in the sun. As we returned to Bam from the east, we could see the Arg in the distance. For weary Silk Road traders it must have been a welcome sight, but for all its magnificence, the Arg paled in beauty beside the charms of those who wrestle life from its shadow.

I left Bam, and the intimacy of the desert, at first light. Akbar accompanied me to the bus station and helped me find transport west to Shiraz. Written on the side of the bus was the message: "We go to trip goodbye." It seemed a happy omen, but I felt sad to leave Bam. In four days, the city had claimed me. I shook Akbar's hand and told him I would return one day. It was a clichéd traveller's promise, but it expressed a true wish, and Akbar said, "I have a feeling I will see you again."

There are few places that truly become part of us. Our home does so, of course, but home always has the luxury of time. The world's true wonders are the places that affect us immediately. After a short visit we feel their streets and faces etched upon our bones. They are the places that are generous with their secrets. And when tragedy befalls such a place, we feel a lopsided sorrow.

7

THE CITY INSIDE THE CHEST

By the time I arrived in Shiraz I had little time to do anything but find a room and have a parakeet read my fortune. There were street vendors all around Iran who, for a small fee, lifted parakeets from cages and allowed them to pluck at a wooden box filled with coloured bits of paper. There was a fortune written on each, usually a quotation from one of the great Persian poets.

My oracle was a turbaned old man; parakeet diviners were always either old men or young boys.

"How much does this cost?" I asked.

"Fifty tomans."

My parakeet selected a pink fortune. The vendor handed me the paper.

"I cannot read Farsi," I said. "What does it say?"

The man squinted at the paper. "This is very good," he said. "It is wisdom from Imam Reza."

"Thank you," I said, but I was mildly disappointed. I had hoped for Hafez.

A woman climbed the steps of the mausoleum. She knelt at the head of the gravestone and laid her palms on the cool marble. Then she touched the stone with her forehead. I could hear her whispered prayers from the foot of the stairs.

She stayed in that position for nearly twenty minutes; I couldn't take my eyes off her. Eventually she kissed the stone, rose and walked away.

I knew of the Iranian veneration for the poet Hafez before I visited his tomb. When Khadije, my Farsi tutor, spoke of Hafez she always smiled, closed her eyes and recited his poetry from memory. Her voice grew soft with reverence. In Iran, Hafez is everywhere. His poetry, centuries old, colours the everyday speech of Iranians. Nearly every city has a street or square named for him, and no home is complete without a copy of his collected works, the *Divan-e Hafez*. I knew the tradition of *fal-e Hafez*, or "opening Hafez." Iranians believe that the solution to any problem can be found by opening the *Divan* at random. The answer you seek will be hidden among the verses on the page you have chosen. The parakeet diviners are a version of this tradition.

Still, the devotion I witnessed at his tomb surprised me. I watched as Iranians crowded the garden and wept for a poet who died six hundred years ago. Some posed for photos next to the pillared gazebo that shades the monument. Others laid roses on the grave. One man stood before the stone, a thin volume in his hand, and read Hafez's poetry back to him from across the centuries. Their devotion reminded me of the pilgrims at the tomb of Imam Reza. It was a different brand of piety, but with the same sincerity of emotion. They celebrated the poet as a saint.

Hafez was born in Shiraz in the early part of the fourteenth century. His full name was Shams-od-din Mohammed, but he took the pen name Hafez when he began writing poetry. The name Hafez means "one who knows the Quran by heart," and some claim Hafez memorized the holy book fourteen different ways. Hafez learned the Quran from his father, a coal merchant who died when Hafez was in his teens. He and his mother moved in with an uncle and Hafez left school to find work. One day, while working in a local bakery, Hafez was sent on an errand to deliver bread in one of Shiraz's wealthier neighbourhoods. There he spied a beautiful woman walking on the street and fell immediately in love in the way only poets can. Hafez made inquiries and learned her name was Shakh-e Nabat, but he never met her. He would later raise and lose a family—some of his poems mourn the deaths of a wife and son—but he never forgot Shakh-e Nabat. Many of his most beautiful poems are dedicated to a woman he had seen only once, and only for a single moment.

Hafez's truest love was for the city of his birth, which he called the "city inside the chest." Celebrating Shiraz was his favourite theme:

> Breezes blow from Isfahan
> And flowers from Jafarabad, which is made of flowers
> Yet both are only halfway to Shiraz.
> No need to import Egyptian sweets.
> Shiraz honey flows in Shiraz streets!

Hafez was no wayfarer and spent almost his entire life in Shiraz. Only once was he tempted away from his beloved city. Hafez accepted an invitation to become a court poet in India, and his patrons sent him a sum of money to cover his travel expenses. When Hafez arrived on the Persian Gulf to board his ship he met by chance an old friend who had fallen on hard times. Hafez gave the man all of his money. The crew on the India-bound ship were so charmed by Hafez they decided to let him travel gratis, but before they could sail, a fierce storm blew in. Hafez looked at the churning sea and, fearing either seasickness or homesickness, turned around and went home. He wrote:

Seawater seemed a bargain to cross
When your offer came.
Then a storm blew in,
And the ration changed
Between the Indian Ocean
And its pearls!

Hafez's poems mean different things to different readers. Verses that celebrate love, wine and nightingales are read literally by romantics. The devout see metaphors for piety. In the West, his status as a Sufi sage is exaggerated, and questionable translations of his poetry are tailored for New Agers shopping for the next fashionable mysticism. Most Iranians would scoff at this. For them, Hafez is enduring and infinite.

After taking lunch in the walled chaykhune I walked through the garden of orange trees that surrounds the tomb. Everyone held books of poetry. Families were picnicking and reciting favourite passages aloud between bites of dried apricots. Some people sat alone near the fountains and whispered verses to themselves. Others penned their own rhymes in small notebooks. Four college-aged men took turns reciting verses from memory, while across the park in a discreet corner a pair of young lovers read poetry to each other.

I wanted to be part of the phenomenon. I went to a bookshop near the tomb and bought a small English translation of Hafez's poetry. I sat amid the slender cypresses to read but the translation was clumsy. Misspellings and words that were not words filled the text. I put the book aside and reached into my rucksack for a volume of poetry I had brought from home, written by Rajinder S. Pal, a friend from Calgary. I mimicked the Iranians and read the words softly aloud. The verses floated from my mouth into that sacred garden.

I left the Hafezieh at sundown. I felt exhilarated, as if I'd been a witness to some sort of miracle. To be immersed in their sacred culture, and to breathe in the same verse-sweetened air, was the closest I had felt to the Iranians.

I took dinner in the Hamam-e Vakil, a bathhouse dating back to the 1700s that had been converted into an opulent restaurant. Once my eyes adjusted to the soft lights inside I could see the centuries-old frescoes of hunting scenes and floral motifs that covered the arched ceiling. An oven in the corner filled the interior with the smell of fresh *sangak* bread.

It was Saturday night and the hamam was throbbing with diners. Iranians tend to eat out in groups and the manager was reluctant to give up a table to a single guest, but he found me a small bench near the door. From there I had a view of the entire room. Families sat cross-legged on takhts laid with red carpets. They ate metre-long swords of kebabs and piles of saffron rice. Children leapt into the dry central fountain and ran up and down the corridors making the waiters nervous. Women with faces half hidden behind camcorders documented the scene. A musician wearing thick glasses performed folk songs on a dulcimer. As his delicate hammers tapped out the melodies people clapped and sang along. Everyone knew the lyrics and the music filled the room right to the painted ceilings. This was the Shiraz that Hafez loved. It was a city of music, gaiety and startlingly beautiful women. I dined slowly, wanting to be part of the Shirazi *joie de vivre* as long as I could.

There were two women at the table next to mine. They had an English-language guidebook with them. I leaned over and introduced myself. The younger woman was an American from Chicago. "I am in Iran visiting my mother," she said, indicating the older woman, who smiled and nodded at me. They asked me if I was enjoying my time in Shiraz and

I told them I spent much of the day at the Hafezieh. "We went there yesterday," the daughter said. "It is my favourite place in Shiraz. Maybe in all of Iran."

"Why is Hafez so important to Iranians?" I asked her.

She seemed startled by the question, as if the answer was too obvious to express. "I'm not sure," she said, after some thought. "He just is. I guess it's because Iranians, in general, are very literate people. We grow up reading poetry and literature. And not just Hafez. Also Ferdosi, Attar, Sa'adi. And not just Persians, either. We read translations of Shakespeare and Tolstoy and Dumas. Everyone."

"People in the West are literate, too," I said, "but writers, even ones we love the most, are not revered as they are here. I doubt anybody brings the family to Tolstoy's tomb for a picnic, or cries at Shakespeare's grave."

"That is true," she said. "I don't know why Iranians are so different." She turned to ask her mother. The mother responded in Farsi and the woman laughed.

"My mother says that going to see the poets is important because, in Iran, we have nothing better to do."

I spent much of the next day wandering around Shiraz. I stood inside the serene interiors of old mosques and cooled my face in the water of reflecting pools and fountains. Families lined up for absurdly tall cones of soft ice cream and milkshakes made with carrot or melon juice from streetside shops. Under the high ceilings of the Vakil Bazaar I browsed sacks of dried petals and herbal medicines, snacked on greasy samosas, and avoided the souvenir peddlers and carpet dealers. Market stalls overflowed with the Shiraz grapes so prized by wine-drinkers in the West.

I left the bazaar and entered the Madraseh-ye Khan, an Islamic school decorated with floral motifs typical to Shiraz. Orange trees and date palms crowded the courtyard and goldfish swam in the central pool. Mullahs gathered under the main iwan to listen to a lecture from a teacher. They sprawled out on the rugs, and their shoes lay scattered on the stones below. Each man's turban matched his beard. They were either dark and neat, or white and unruly. It was a solemn, holy place. I was grateful to be received with nods of greeting rather than chased away.

Outside, near the entrance to the bazaar, a guide introduced himself. "I Mohammed Mehdi. I guide for you in bazaar. Bazaar Vakil. No pay me now. Maybe after. You say price."

"Thanks, but I don't need a guide."

"Maybe tomorrow maybe?" He handed me his "card." It was a piece of cardboard cut from a tissue box, with a message handwritten in red ink:

> SHIRAZ IRAN THE
> GATE OF THE VAKIL MOSQUE
> ONE MOHAMMED MEHDI
> THE MOST INTERNAL
> THE SECURITY TALENT
> GUIDE 39 YEARS OF FIVE
> OF THE CURRENCY THE
> LANGUAGES OVER THE WORLED
> AGE 44 UNMARRIED NO
> SMOKED A CIGARAT LIFE NO
> HOLIDAY

I slipped the card into the envelope where I kept the rest of my Iranian poetry.

Takht-e Jamshid, at the foot of the Mountain of Mercy, has seen little mercy itself over the centuries. The city was plundered and burned by Greeks, vandalized by Arabs, defiled with pomp by the last shah, and nearly bulldozed by Islamists.

The ancient city, known as Persepolis to less limber Western tongues, dates back to the fifth century BC when the Persian Empire was at its height. The Achaemenid kings ruled over much of Central Asia and the Middle East, and held nearly thirty ethnicities under their sway. They built Persepolis as a venue for No Ruz, a festival celebrating the first day of spring and the Persian new year. It was the custom at No Ruz, as the chill of winter eased, for delegations from around the empire to be invited to Persepolis to pay homage to their king. Stone carvings at the site depicted lions devouring bulls, a symbol of the return of summer to the land. Others showed ambassadors from subject nations bearing gifts to the Persian sovereign.

I hired a car to take me the fifty kilometres from Shiraz to Persepolis. I climbed the staircase that led to the main gateway, passed between the massive winged bulls that guard the Gate of all Nations, and tracked my fingers along the curls of stone that formed the beards of carved men. The city was a temple of ancient Persian masculinity. There was not a single female form to be found in the carvings. All were bearded men, bulls and lions with manes.

The No Ruz celebrations at Persepolis would have been male affairs featuring drum-beating warriors and men in iron helmets. There would have been wrestlers here, too. *Dast-e baghal*, a wrestling style as old as Iran itself, originated on the southern slopes of the nearby Zagros mountains. Dast-e baghal matches were part of the No Ruz festivities. Here amid the pillars and palaces stone-muscled men welcomed the spring thaw and visiting nobility with battles in the dust.

The annual gathering of nations ended in 330 BC when the Greek armies of Alexander descended on the city. Alexander loaded its treasures onto the backs of twenty thousand mules and five thousand camels, and left the city aflame. For the ancient Persians, Alexander was not "the Great."

Persepolis would wait two thousand years for the world to return. This time, though, the celebrations would be an affront to the ancients and an insult to Iranians. In 1971, Shah Pahlavi announced that he was a descendant of Cyrus the Great—a dubious claim—and planned a gala at Persepolis to celebrate the 2,500th anniversary of Iran. Royalty and leaders from around the world accepted their invitations to the event, many, I suspect, with a sense of morbid curiosity. Both Richard Nixon and Queen Elizabeth II declined to attend. He feared terrorism and she feared tastelessness. It turns out the monarch was right.

Bemused guests watched a procession of mock battleships, armaments and warriors in various Persian costumes. Although ostensibly staged to honour Iran's past glories, the gala was in reality not much more than a display of imported excess. Two hundred and fifty red Mercedes sedans shuttled dignitaries to and from a newly expanded Shiraz airport. The Shah erected a Golden City made of air-conditioned tents built of European cloth and surrounded it with a "forest" of trees imported from France. Guests drank thousands of bottles of French champagne from Bohemian crystal. The organizers coaxed a Parisian chef out of retirement to prepare the gala dinner. He brought a staff of 160. Alka-Seltzer tablets wrapped in gold foil were flown in in case the delicate stomachs of the visiting royals did not appreciate the chef's talents.

The event cost nearly three hundred million dollars, and deeply angered the Iranian people, who were suffering through a drought at the time. It was small wonder that, after the Revolution, some of Ayatollah Khomeini's more energetic followers drove bulldozers to Persepolis with the intention of tearing the entire site down. They claimed that the Zoroastrian origins of the ruins were an affront to Islam, but undoubtedly many of them associated Persepolis with the egomaniacal Shah and his shameful display of wealth.

The bulldozer activists were persuaded to let Persepolis stand, and in 1992 a visit from then-president Akbar Hashemi Rafsanjani gave Persepolis the blessing of the ruling mullahs. It shows that the Iranians have dignity, he said. They are a people with a history.

My arrival at the varzeshga in Arsanjan caused a sensation. I came from Shiraz looking for dast-e baghal, in hopes the ancient style was still practised. As soon as I stepped into the office, everyone dropped what they were doing to help me. Someone found a man, Abbas, who spoke a little English. Old wrestlers appeared to shake my hand and a teenage boy brought me tea. My welcome was more than hospitality. It was an expression of the only thing we had in common. We were all wrestlers, cauliflower-eared men versed in the collision of flesh.

The men assured me that dast-e baghal was not dead. It was popular in rural areas, especially in Fars province, where it originated. The men plucked yellowing photos from cracked frames showing a dast-e baghal competition in the 1980s, and there had been a tournament just the month before. I cursed my poor timing.

"If you like, you can see dast-e baghal today," Abbas said. He picked up the phone on the desk and before I finished my tea two teenaged wrestlers arrived at the office. Abbas led me and our growing entourage of men into a gymnasium that smelled like a high school chemistry lab. He helped fit together pieces of a thin green mat on the gym floor while the boys stripped out of their jeans and donned traditional dast-e baghal wear: long-sleeved shirts, loose pyjama-style trousers and black fabric belts. Abbas told me that the wrestlers were supposed to be wearing knit slippers called *givehs*. There were none available in the sports centre so the boys would fight barefoot.

The wrestlers stretched and jogged around the gymnasium. When they were ready, they stepped in the centre of the mat. They reached around each other and each bound his hands together in a curl of knuckles behind his opponent's back. The rules of dast-e baghal demand that both wrestlers stay in this rigid embrace for the duration of the match.

Abbas checked their grips, shouted at them to wrestle, and I watched their fingers turn pale with strain. The boys bent forward and sprawled their hips back, trying to get their bodies as far away from each other as their clinch would allow. Their heads were on each other's shoulders and their ears rubbed together. One of them twisted his forearm into the other's side and tried to wrench him to the mat, but couldn't get a good position because his opponent was taller and his arms were long. Frustrated, the first wrestler let his arms relax for a moment, and the tall boy sensed opportunity. He took a long stride forward and hooked one of his legs around the back of his opponent's knee. The first boy tripped and fell backwards, his lanky opponent landing on his chest. Only then did the wrestlers break their grip.

They stood and Abbas ordered them to try again; in dast-e baghal, a wrestler must win two out of three bouts to be declared a victor. The wrestlers clinched and fought again. This time the smaller wrestler, no match for his opponent's long limbs, was tripped back to the mat in a few seconds.

"I am sorry," Abbas apologized when the boys lifted themselves from the mat. "We have no professional dast-e baghal wrestlers for you. These are just boys."

"Can I try?" I asked.

"You want to wrestle? Yes, of course." Abbas beamed and the two small boys who were watching clapped their hands. Abbas pointed at the shorter wrestler, who was still breathing heavy. "Give him your clothes," he commanded. I pulled the sweat-wet shirt over my head and fastened the belt to my waist before doing a few rudimentary stretches. I met my opponent, the winner of the match I had just watched, in the centre of the mat and we locked our arms around each other. His sweaty sideburns were cold against my temple. I curled my hands together and pressed my fingertips into my palms. Abbas ensured my hands were in the proper position, then, shackled to each other by our own limbs, we began to wrestle.

Both of us sprawled our legs back. The boy was so tall his body seemed a mile away. I felt my arms stretch and strain. The boy's grip was surprisingly loose, though, and his muscles lax. I could tell he was going easy on me. His Persian instinct for hospitality was at odds with his wrestler's itch for combat: only a bad host would topple a foreign guest. Still, he didn't have to spend much effort to bring me down. I tried to mimic his success in the previous matches. I stepped forward to hook his leg but the boy was out of range and my long stride put me off balance. He took advantage of my wobbly position, trapped my forward leg with one of his and lifted my foot off the mat. I struggled to keep my balance but I was tangled. I squirmed in his embrace until he diplomatically eased me to my back.

The boy helped me to my feet. He smiled at me, his face soft and contrite, and we walked back to the centre of the mat. We clinched again, and I chose a new tactic. I dragged my tightly clasped hands down my rival's spine, my knuckles rattling down his vertebrae to the small of his back. He winced and tightened. The unexpected pain froze him in place. I lowered my stance and jerked him forward onto one knee. I squeezed my forearms into the bottom of his ribs and, using all my strength, powered him over onto his back.

It was an inelegant manoeuvre, more roughhousing than wrestling. I was stronger than he was, that was all. The boy stood up without his conciliatory smile. He didn't appreciate being muscled. When we clinched for our final bout he butted the side of his head against mine. The welcome was gone and the dance with the foreigner finished. Wrestling took over. Abbas tapped our shoulders and the boy lunged forward, his foot seeking the back of my knee and a chance to trip. I kicked my leg away and the boy shot his other foot forward. He was all arms and legs. I felt like I was wrestling a spider. His aggression, though, was clumsy. When he lunged a third time I stepped aside, spun on the balls of my feet, plowed my hips into his and lifted him off the mat. There are few sensations more satisfying than hoisting a foe into the air and throwing him on his back. We landed hard. The thin mat was merciless.

Afterwards we shook hands and posed for a group picture. I couldn't help but grin. I had no reason to gloat about my victory. After all, my opponent was just a smooth-eared boy. I was happy just to have stepped onto the mat: for the first time since my arrival in Iran, I was more than an observer. There was joy in that first collision of flesh. My sore rib throbbed pleasantly all the way back to Shiraz.

That evening I made my way to the Darvazeh-e Quran at the edge of town. There was another poet buried here, Karju-e Kermani, but he was not the reason for my visit. An old Quran rests atop a gateway near the tomb. According to tradition, a traveller should pass beneath a Quran before embarking on a journey. I'd already been travelling for weeks, but I reasoned that a blessing, however belated, couldn't hurt. I passed under the gate a couple of times, just to be sure.

8

HALF THE WORLD

The façade of Esfahan's Sheikh Lotfallah Mosque breaks the unadorned arcade around Nagsh-e Jahan Square with a shock of blue-painted tile. A short flight of steps brings the faithful to a high entranceway framed with turquoise coils. The intricate decoration is stunning, but the mosque is best known for its ceramic dome. Cream-coloured and decorated with floral motifs, the dome is famous for the way it changes colour in the day's shifting light. In a country blessed with exquisite mosques, the Sheikh Lotfallah is the most shimmering jewel.

The day I arrived, Nagsh-e Jahan Square was raucous. It is the heart of Esfahan, and every visitor to the city is, at least in a small way, pulled within its orbit. Horse-drawn carriages were clopping along the smooth paving stones while Iranians lined up for souvenirs, soft ice cream and cubes of Esfahani nougat called *gaz*. Polyglot carpet sellers patrolled the old stones and guessed at my nationality. "Français?" "Deutsch?" "Engleesh?" At the northern end of the square taxis battled, with all the stink and temper of aggravated goats. This was the only place where cars were permitted—cement barriers stencilled with "Down with USA" kept the cars penned in—but teenagers on motorcycles screamed up and back the length of the square for lack of anything better to do.

Inside Sheikh Lotfallah, though, the square's clamour filtered into silence. Through the door a dim hallway led me to the main sanctuary. A bend in the passage gently turns each visitor westward, a nudge towards Mecca. The interior of the dome is a marvel. Lemon-shaped mosaics, surrounded by unglazed brick, narrow towards the centre of the dome, giving the illusion of infinity. Latticed windows ring the base and give the sanctuary its only illumination. I visited at sunset when the dance of light was just reaching its end. I sat on the smooth stones and heard chanting float up through the floor from the basement prayer chamber that was still in use. The devotion swirled around me. I felt tiny there, surrounded by the endlessness.

The shrine was named for a fifteenth-century Lebanese sheikh, but was built exclusively for women. An underground passage once led from the Ali Qapu Palace across the square to the mosque. This allowed the women of the palace to go to prayers without being seen in public. There is a femininity about the place. Compared to the bravado of the nearby Imam Mosque with its sharp edges and piercing minarets, the Sheikh Lotfallah is gentle and contemplative. It opts for softness over scale. The vastness of the Imam Mosque challenges the heavens, but here a cream dome yields to the light of day.

I'd been looking forward to Esfahan since I first arrived in Iran. The Iranians I met urged me to visit and repeated the ancient rhyme *Esfahan nesf-e jahan*: "Esfahan is half the world." But for all Esfahan's promised pleasures, my moments within the Sheikh Lotfallah told me that I was missing something. Until then, I felt that Iran had revealed itself fully to me. The men I met were generous with their culture, their politics, their stories and their secrets. I had expected reticence and found only openness. Standing amid the feminine curves of the Sheikh Lotfallah Mosque, though, reminded me that my trip had been utterly devoid of women. My experiences, rich as they were, had neglected half the world.

I did not expect to encounter women in the sweaty wrestling halls or dingy male-only tea houses, but even outside these preserves of men—in restaurants, buses and gardens—I hadn't exchanged more than a few words with Iranian women. It was not because I couldn't find them. To suggest that men and women are treated equally in Iran would be preposterous, but at least here women are not hidden behind burqas or secluded in purdah. Women are everywhere. They crowd the streets and bazaars and work in shops and offices. In Iran, women can drive, vote and hold political office. They are highly educated—far more women than men attend Iranian universities—and seemed sophisticated and clever. When they talked to each other they laughed often and their eyes danced with intelligence. I wanted so much to speak with them, to learn something of their lives, but I didn't know the protocol. I didn't want to offend. A stone wall separated me from the women of Iran.

It was dark by the time I left the Sheikh Lotfallah. On the square, the central fountain had been turned on. It freshened the air and caught errant balls from impromptu football games. I walked past the arcade of souvenir shops and climbed a steep staircase near the entrance to the bazaar. The Qeysarieh tea house was at the top.

In Esfahan I began to measure my time in tea-house hours. I sucked on sugar cubes and water pipes and watched my days go up in fruit-scented smoke. The finest of Esfahan's chaykhunes were well known and very popular; some were so busy they enforced a time limit on their customers. Still, each seemed like a secret. They were concealed in alleyways and under bridges. Finding them meant navigating narrow stairwells. They were deliciously clandestine.

The Qeysarieh tea house felt less secret than most places. Its view over the Nagsh-e Jahan Square granted it some cachet, and the place was nearly always full. Despite its hectic commerce, the staff started to recognize me after only a couple of visits. They brought me a pot of tea and an orange-flavoured qalyun before I ordered. No one learned my name but the old man who never strayed from the front desk called me "the Canadian." I was flattered. There was something immensely rewarding about having a haunt in a foreign land, about being a regular amid the irregular.

I found sensual joys inside as I unbuckled my sandals and crawled up on the carpet-laid takhts. I placed my fingertips against my tea glass to test the heat, then slurped from the saucer and felt a sugar lump dissolve between my teeth. I carried an ornate qalyun mouthpiece in my pocket, slipped it into the water-pipe hose and drew in long breaths of smoke. The embers glowed orange. The bubbles rumbled on the metal table. I smoked until the embers cooled, then called out for more "fire." A second glass of tea. A third.

I always arrived alone but rarely suffered much solitude. Chaykhunes were social places and before long affable Esfahanis joined me and wanted to chat. They welcomed me to Esfahan first, but initial pleasantries always led to talk of politics. By the time I reached Esfahan, my misgivings about discussing affairs of state had vanished. Few Iranians in the tea houses wanted to talk about anything else. This was tradition. Since ancient times, the tea house has been a venue for dissent. Shah Abbas the Great, the sixteenth-century king whose portrait graces much of the tourist junk for sale in Esfahan, worried that rebellion was fomented in the tea houses. Instead of closing them down he sent dervishes to entertain the customers with poetry and stories. He hoped to distract them from political discussions, but his plan failed. The recitation of Ferdosi's *Shahnomeh* fanned their nationalism and further inspired dissent. Centuries later, in the days before the 1979 revolution, rebellious poets gathered in tea houses to recite verses critical of their shah.

The voices of defiance against the current regime are rather less poetic than in the past, at least when dumbed down for anglophone travellers. "Mullahs fuck you!" was a common phrase. They were also less optimistic. Men shook their heads and clicked their tongues when they spoke of their government. Sadness blackened the cheer of their welcome. I would hear this over and over in Iran, the gloom in the voices of those who'd lost their country to stern, turbaned men.

Political discussions frequently led to talk of sex, and at this men would brighten. Often, sex and politics were united, especially for young men. They revealed their frustrations with the mullahs, proclaimed, "I love George Bush," then inquired about the price of a prostitute in Canada. Some asked me if it was true that women in the West walked around the streets nearly naked. Often it appeared that the freedom Iranian men desired had less to do with democracy than with short skirts. There was no chivalry or poetry in this foolish discourse, and it made me want to know the women of Iran all the more. Surely they were too clever for such vulgarities.

I met Benjamin at Qeysarieh one evening. He was a thin man in his mid-twenties, who spoke English with an accent I could not place. Benjamin worked as a tutor in Esfahan and taught English to wealthy Iranians, most of whom planned to emigrate to Canada or the United States. Nine months previously, he had been in Afghanistan translating for Médecins Sans Frontières. He said that the Afghans were very kind.

I told Benjamin about my interest in Iranian poetry and wrestling and he gave me directions to the nearest zurkhane. He also had translated some of Hafez's poetry into English and offered to show it to me. We talked for about half an hour when Benjamin paused and looked at me hard. "Are you Jewish?" he asked.

I didn't know how to take this question. Israelis were regarded as enemies by many Iranians, or so I had heard. The

Iranian parliament reserves a seat for one Jewish member, but I didn't know how Iranians on the street felt towards Jews in general. I wasn't sure if Benjamin asked the question out of curiosity, or whether it was some sort of insult. Or threat. "I'm not Jewish," I said. "My parents are Italians and I was raised Catholic. Why do you ask?"

"Because you look Jewish."

"Do I?" I took a pull on my pipe.

Benjamin sensed my discomfort and smiled. "*I* am Jewish," he said.

I relaxed. "You're kidding. I didn't know there were any Jews left here."

"There are not many. A few here in Esfahan, and a small community in Tehran."

"Have you ever been to Israel?"

He shook his head. "I would like to go."

"Are you allowed? I know if I had an Israeli stamp in my passport I would not get a visa to enter Iran. But are Jewish Iranians allowed to visit Israel?"

"I can go, but then I can't come back."

"Would you like to go?"

"Yes, of course. I am Jewish."

I paused. "I've been to Israel," I said, lowering my voice a little. "I lied on my visa application. My passport is new. I went a few years ago."

Benjamin lowered his voice a little more. "So have I. But if we are going to talk about it, let's call it Disneyland. You don't know who might be listening."

The sun set over the square as we talked about our time in Disneyland. Benjamin told me how he returned to Iran illegally through Jordan and Syria. He talked about the difficulties of being Jewish in Iran. A few years ago he told some of his Muslim friends that he was Jewish and they stopped talking to him. They refused to shake his hand. Now he tells no one.

Despite this, Benjamin held all religions in high regard, especially Islam. His few Jewish friends couldn't understand this and were uncomfortable with his interest in the Quran. When Benjamin heard I had come to Iran via Turkey, he asked if I'd been to any of the Sufi gatherings there. I told him all I'd seen were men whirling in touristy Istanbul restaurants. He told me stories of his time in the Turkish dervish halls of Konya, his visit to the tomb of Sufi poet Molanna Rumi and his meditations in a Syrian Christian monastery.

"I feel an emptiness," he told me, with surprising candour. "I try to fill myself with faith." He reminded me of the travellers of old. The sort of men who trod the earth with rucksacks and walking sticks in a genuine search for God. It was refreshing to meet a man whose search was honest, for whom faith was not a fashion. There was a sincerity about Benjamin and, above all, a goodness.

We talked until the darkness over the Zagros Mountains was complete. When I mentioned that I'd run out of English books to read he offered to lend me his copy of Amin Maalouf's *Leo the African.* He also said he wanted to show me his Hafez translations. "We will meet here tomorrow?" he said.

"Yes. Eight o'clock?"

He suggested seven. "Then we can watch the sunset."

I was staying at the Amir Kabir Hostel on the Street of Four Gardens, a tree-lined thoroughfare with a pretty walkway forming the median between opposing lanes of traffic. My timing was lucky. I had arrived in time to claim the last dormitory bed. "This is the first night we have been full since eleven September," Shapur, the hotel manager, said as he happily recorded my passport details.

The hostel was crowded with foreigners. This was the first place in Iran, other than Akbar's guest house in Bam, where I found myself in the company of other travellers. The inner courtyard was perpetually crowded with European backpackers. Each clutched the same *Lonely Planet.* I introduced myself and we engaged in the brief set of greetings that travellers seem obliged to exchange: name, nationality, where we are travelling from and where we are going next. Then I retired to my dormitory's lumpy mattress.

I was up early the next morning thanks to a pair of chatty Japanese travellers. I left the hotel and wandered in the covered sixteenth-century Bazaar-e Bozorg. Most of the shops were still closed and the corridors were empty but for the merchants busy sweeping their shopfronts. The rising dust sharpened the shafts of sunlight that poured through the vaulted ceiling. Spice sellers heaved canvas sacks of dried flower petals, sumac berries and herbal medicines. Metalsmiths crouched in tiny workshops surrounded by the gleam of iron and copper. It would be an hour or so before the stores selling plastic kitchenware, ceiling fans and underwear would open. Cheap televisions and alarm clocks would fill the bazaar with modern clamour. Until then, the centuries-old bazaar was acting its age.

I made my way to the Jomeh Mosque and cringed at the hefty entry fee. The woman at the entrance did not fall for my Farsi and charged me the tourist price. My Iranian disguise never worked in Esfahan. I recalled a story about an Australian couple who feigned pious indignation at having to pay to enter a mosque. "Isn't Allah for everyone?" the woman implored. The Iranians at the mosque nodded, impressed with the foreigners' surprising devotion, but charged them the full admission nonetheless.

Inside I photographed the mosaics and minarets. A guide opened up the interior doors for me and showed me the dark colonnaded interiors. Light filtered in through stained glass and a pane of translucent marble. The place was lovely and serene, especially in the morning before the tour buses unloaded, but my visit was half-hearted. I'd seen so many mosques and shrines I was starting to confuse them. I knew I'd return to Canada with a stack of photos of buildings whose names I would not remember. I wondered why I even bothered.

I returned to the hotel after lunch. The manager and his brothers huddled in the lobby. They were staring at something on the front desk and looked completely befuddled. One of the men saw me enter and called me over.

"We found a box of these things in one of the rooms today." He showed me the little white object in his palm. "Do you know what this is?"

I laughed when I saw it. "Yes, of course."

"What is it?"

"I don't know the word in Farsi," I said. "It is for women."

"For women?"

"Yes," I said, and pointed between my legs.

He raised his eyebrows and quickly returned the tampon to its box.

Two lions, carved from grey stone, faced each other across the Zayendeh River near the Khaju Bridge. Examined up close, the sculptures were unremarkable: simple figures with cold stone eyes. However, when I went to the bridge after dark and stood next to the lion on the southern bank, the eyes of the lion across the river glowed with some mysterious light. It was only from this vantage point that its eyes appeared to shine.

This bit of Persian magic was just a mysterious trick of reflection, but the old bridges of Esfahan conjured genuine enchantment. Every night, and especially on the Friday holiday, the riverfront became a playground for Esfahanis. Families with prams and camcorders monopolized the pathways on each side of the river. They came to drink tea in the open-air tea houses under the Si-o-Seh Bridge or cook kebabs on tiny portable grills. Women sat on the lower tier of the Khaju Bridge and dipped their feet in the river while their children begged for ice cream. Vendors sold roman candles, whose green glare reflected off the water. Cameras flashed in the darkness. There were picnics, swan-shaped paddleboats and other wholesome Persian delights.

I discovered more illicit pleasures beneath the Khaju Bridge. Not drugs or alcohol, but dancing. Public dancing was forbidden in Iran, but in the softly lit underside of the bridge, men sang and danced and laughed. The scene was spicy with disobedience, and I joined the throngs of Iranians who gathered to clap along to the outlawed joy.

The riverbanks were quieter in the daylight. Nearly every afternoon I walked along the riverside path that links the Si-o-Seh, Chubi and Khaju bridges. The bridges were hardly architectural marvels, at least not when compared to the wonders of Nagsh-e Jahan Square, but prompted slow strolls along the Zayendeh. Following the green riverbanks, passing back and forth across the water, and, more often than not, pausing for qalyun in the chaykhune under the Chubi was one of Esfahan's greatest pleasures.

Each evening I met with Benjamin at the Qeysarieh. One night we were both distracted from our conversation by three girls sitting on the women's side of the tea house. They were laughing loud and sharing a water pipe. "Persian women are beautiful," I said. I missed Moonira.

Benjamin nodded and seemed proud. "Yes. Iranian women can make even the hejab sexy. Have you seen the beads they wear with their manteaus sometimes?"

"I love those things," I said. Most Iranian women wore an overcoat called a manteau. The garment is long-sleeved and purposely shapeless. It was designed to be loose and modest and in accordance with the laws governing female dress. Many women, though, tied leather strings decorated with wooden beads around their waist overtop the manteau. The strings of beads rested on the wearer's hips and tightened the manteau just slightly at the waist to give a hint of the shape of her body. It was a fashionable rebellion, and was surprisingly attractive.

"Iranian women are sometimes very vain," Benjamin said. "Appearance is very important to them. Many get their noses fixed."

"You mean plastic surgery?"

"Yes. Haven't you seen the young women on the street? With the bandages on their nose?"

I'd seen plenty. "Those are nose jobs?"

"Of course. What did you think they were for? Nose jobs are very popular in Iran," Benjamin said. "Especially in Tehran and Esfahan."

"Aren't nose jobs expensive?"

He laughed. "Not here, but these are not the best plastic surgeons. These doctors perform the surgeries in one or two hours. In their offices. Sometimes the noses come out looking terrible. Very unnatural. But many people get them. Both women and men."

"Men, too?"

"Yes. Many men. There was a woman that I liked very much. Very pretty and smart, but she said she would not be with me unless I get a nose job. It is so stupid. I like my big nose."

Our talk of surgery led to a discussion of Laleh and Ladan Bijani. Their side-by-side faces filled that day's newspapers. The conjoined twins, twenty-nine years old and fused at the head, had died in surgery the night before, when doctors in Singapore had attempted to separate them. The procedure was risky, even the chief surgeon had advised against it, and their deaths surprised few. Every newspaper cried out condolences. One of the English headlines was: Laleh and Ladan: Conjoined Again in Heaven, which, if true, would surely be a particularly cruel joke.

Their death replaced politics as the talk of the tea house. It was cause for sadness, surely, but many questioned the wisdom of such an operation after twenty-nine years. Others derided the skills of the Singapore doctors. Benjamin was less affected and scoffed at the attention the women received. "People in Iran die every day. Every hour. Why should we care so much about these two?"

A few days later another woman's death became the talk of the tea house. I was at the Qeysarieh when a man asked me, "You are 'the Canadian,' yes?"

I nodded, grinning at my nickname.

"Did you know the woman who was killed?"

"No," I said, my smile gone. "I did not know her."

The news had broken that morning. I read about Zahra Kazemi's death online and in the *Tehran Times*. Her face, taken from a blurred passport photo, replaced the doubled smiles of the Bijani twins on every front page. Kazemi was a photojournalist with dual Canadian and Iranian citizenship. Iranian police arrested her for taking photos in front of a Tehran prison and she died in custody. Officials claimed Kazemi suffered a stroke and that she was hurried to a nearby hospital where she passed away. The Canadian government, and every Iranian I spoke to, believed she was beaten to death.

Tense days followed. A second autopsy revealed that Kazemi died as a result of a blow to the head, but a conservative (government-allied) newspaper reported that Kazemi died of a pre-existing health condition and that her doctor in Canada had advised her to quit journalism. Kazemi's rushed burial in Iran raised the ire of the Canadian officials and, especially, of Kazemi's son, who demanded his mother's body be returned to Montreal. Some Iranian officials accused Kazemi of resisting arrest and refusing to hand over her camera to police. Canada recalled its ambassador and threatened sanctions.

Then came an ill-timed tragedy back in Canada. A police officer shot and killed an Iranian teen who threatened him with a machete. The conservative press in Iran jumped on the story and wondered how the Canadian government could claim the moral high ground in the Kazemi case when Iranians were being shot to death in Canada. For the first time I felt nervous about being in Iran. I called my embassy. An official assured me that the embassy would remain open in the absence of the ambassador, but he couldn't guess how things might play out. "This is a country of many surprises," he said.

In the wake of the tragedy I questioned my own travels in Iran. I had been charmed by the Iranians I had met, but now I wondered if the affection I felt for them amounted to a betrayal of my own people. My experiences suddenly felt superficial. I had found Iran to be a place of beauty and hospitality, with a culture of poets and pahlevans. Yet these people had bludgeoned a fellow Canadian to death in an Iranian jail. A conservative newspaper called Kazemi a spy. It said that those who considered her death suspicious were "spokesmen for the enemy." Did it matter that the pomegranate trees were in bloom?

I worried, too, whether the locals' reaction to me would change. As a Canadian, I'd never been the enemy. I thought of the hateful murals I saw in Tehran and wondered how far the crisis would go. I was hesitant to discuss the matter with the men in the tea houses. I was afraid of seeing my own flag burning on television.

I had nothing to fear. When men found out I was Canadian they extended their sympathy for Kazemi's death.

It was as if my being a Canadian made Kazemi and me members of the same family. They wanted me to understand that under the current regime this sort of tragedy was all too common. They knew better than to trust the state-run newspapers and did not doubt that Kazemi had indeed died beneath fists and batons.

I never knew Zahra Kazemi, and had never heard of her before seeing her face in the newspapers. I could feel only the most general sort of sadness for her death. The Iranians, though, saw the link of our common nationality. To them, I had lost one of my own to their hated regime. This connected me to them, as if now I could have some understanding of their plight. "Bad things happen here," one man said, before refilling my tea. "Now you know what it is to live in this country." It was a bond, wholly unwanted and sealed with someone else's blood, but a bond just the same.

9

THE ZAGROS MOUNTAINS

The air chilled and my eardrums swelled as the bus eased its way up the alpine highway. I was seeking out *koshti maghli*, a wrestling style indigenous to the slopes of the Zagros Mountains near Esfahan. Surrounded by jagged slabs of stone, it was not hard to imagine this landscape as the dwelling of wrestlers. The mountains stood against the sky with the presence of immense stone-muscled men.

The highway ended at Shahr-e Kord, Iran's highest city. At the bus station I hired a taxi driver to take me to a sports centre. The official in the wrestling office told me that maghli was not practised in Shahr-e Kord any more. "You should go and talk to Rahim," he said. "He is a wrestler who knows all about maghli." He gave Rahim's address to my driver.

We drove into a quiet residential district of whitewashed houses and knocked on a few doors before finding Rahim. He was a well-built man in his forties, balding, and wearing tinted eyeglasses. Rahim was surprised by the arrival of a foreigner at his home, and I'd interrupted his lunch, but he immediately offered his help. "Come," he said. "We will go speak with my father at his carpet shop." My taxi driver drove off and I jumped into Rahim's rattling Land Cruiser.

Rahim reached over and pinched my cauliflower ear. "Are you a wrestler?" he asked.

"When I was younger," I said.

"National team?"

I laughed. "Not quite." I eyed Rahim's massive arms. "Were you a wrestler, too?"

"No," he said. "I *am* a wrestler."

"Maghli?"

"No. I wrestle freestyle. Nobody does maghli any more. But my father wrestled maghli many years ago."

When we arrived at the shop, Rahim's father, Shapur, was napping on a pile of red kilim rugs. Like his son he blinked at me with surprise but seemed pleased by the interruption. Shapur stood and demonstrated maghli positions with Rahim. He showed me how both wrestlers grip their opponent's belt with their left hand. The right hand remained free and could be used to attack. Shapur said that maghli bouts had no time limit. The first wrestler to bring his opponent to the ground was the winner. "Sometimes the matches went on for hours," he said.

Maghli, like dast-e baghal, used to be performed on special occasions such as weddings and No Ruz. "We wrestled in a field just outside of Shahr-e Kord. There was a patch of ground next to a spring. This is where all the wrestlers and spectators used to gather."

Rahim drove me to the site. There was little left to see. The spring, Rahim said, dried up years ago and an apartment building now stood in the place where the wrestlers used to battle. It was difficult to picture the field swarming with belted warriors and boisterous fans. "We stopped doing maghli in Shahr-e Kord twenty years ago," Rahim said. "Many traditions in this country are fading away."

Afterwards, Rahim served me kebabs and rice in his home. Between bites, I returned the smiles of his five-year-old daughter Qazelle who sat across the table. As Rahim drove me back to the bus station he asked if I could send him some body-building magazines when I returned to Canada. Before I entered the terminal, he shouted from his truck, "You should go to Kuhrang. It is a small town. Maybe you can find maghli there."

Kuhrang is built with stone and mortar and sits deep in the Zagros Mountains surrounded by dry rocky hills. The town itself encircles a patch of fields and grazing land where shepherds grow feed for sheep and goats. Kuhrang contained little more than the essentials for a rural Iranian town: a police post, a post office, a mosque, a bakery and a varzeshga. I arrived via a minibus. Roadworks were under way and the main street was dug up and muddy. There was a small strip of shops on one side of the road, a few general stores loaded with canned goods and baskets of fly-buzzing fruit, and three sandwich shops. I ducked into one of these for lunch.

Three men were eating kebab sandwiches inside. They wore round black caps and woollen shawls decorated with vertical black and beige stripes that reminded me of piano keys. They were Bakhtiyaris, an ethnic group that occupies the alpine landscape in this part of Iran. The Bakhtiyari have their own language and are traditionally nomadic.

Each of the men in the sandwich shop had an antique-looking rifle propped up on the floor next to him. They seemed gentle, though, in spite of their weapons. They smiled up at me with curious kindness from behind their trim white beards.

"Are you hunters?" I asked, hoping they spoke Farsi.

"Shepherds," they said. "The guns are to protect against wolves."

"Are there many wolves in the mountains?"

"Some."

I asked them if they knew anything about maghli wrestling. They didn't, but recommended I visit the varzeshga on the hill overlooking the village.

"Is there any place to stay in Kuhrang?" I asked.

"We have one hotel. Behind the hill. Very expensive."

"Do you know how much?" He gave me a price that was ten times what I normally paid for a hotel room. I didn't understand why such a tiny village would have such pricey accommodations.

I finished my kebabs and made my way up the hill to the sports centre. Two girls in chadors swatted at a ping-pong ball at a table in the lobby. Some ratty wrestling mats lay on the floor in an adjacent room. I found the main office and asked the man at the desk about maghli wrestling. "You are too late," he said. "Two weeks ago there was a major maghli competition in Kuhrang, but the season is now over. Tonight there will be a practice here in the sports centre. Maybe the maghli wrestlers will come."

"Do you know where I can sleep tonight? A man told me that the hotel is a little pricey."

He opened his eyes wide and whistled. "Yes, yes. It is too much. You can sleep here." He showed me to an adjoining room. There was no bed, but a few thin foam mats were stacked against a wall.

"This is perfect. Thank you."

I dumped my rucksack and walked into the street, making my way back towards the town centre. Children kicked footballs in the gravel roadways, while old men waved their sticks at herds of goats. A man tended to the corpse of a sheep in front of an abattoir. He blew into an incision he'd made in the animal's skin and inflated the hide like a morbid balloon to make removing the fleece easier.

By the time I reached the main street, the entire town knew that a foreigner was visiting. I sat in a tea house and attracted a crowd of young men. I answered the same questions over and over again. "Where are you from? Are you married? What is your job? How much money do you make?

Are there Iranians in Canada?" The repetition sharpened my Farsi, but only for these few introductory phrases. Beyond the basics my grasp of the language was still clumsy.

A man named Omar offered to give me a tour of the surrounding mountains. First, I helped him unload a stack of empty soda bottles from the bed of his truck. Then we picked up his four-year-old son and drove up a dirt road. Omar punctuated his sentences by reaching over and poking me in the arm. "These are the Yellow Mountains." Poke. "There is always snow on them." Poke. "You see that spring?" Poke. "It is where the Zayendeh River begins."

The beauty of the alpine landscape, though, made up for Omar's tedious jabs. Nomad tents dotted the rocky slopes. Some were made of crisp jet-black fabric while others, worn by seasons of mountain winds, seemed a thousand years old. Stacked stones formed pens to house goats and sheep. I watched a man drive a flock of goats across a ridge while women bent over streams to collect water and wash clothes.

Then a young nomad woman appeared alone on the hillside. Her red dress was alive with wind and she glided along the hillcrest like a spirit. My chest swelled. She embodied all the splendour that surrounded her. The black tents on green hillsides, the short, goat-nibbled grass, the icy water that fell from grey stone. All were contained in the fleet steps of this nomad woman who looked back at our truck before disappearing like a ghost over the hillside. Sights like this, these momentary distillations of beauty, are the reason I travel.

A busload of Kuwaiti tourists heaved expensive-looking luggage from beneath their bus in the parking lot of Hotel Kuhrang. The men wore smart robes, white turbans and designer sunglasses. The women were veiled; only their eyes showed through a narrow slit in their headcovering.

The hotel was bland but modern. White walls held photos of mountain scenery and a mannequin in the lobby wore Western ski apparel. In the lounge, a large television flickered with the BBC World Service. Tempted by an English-language newscast I sat in front of the television and ordered tea. At the front desk, the crowd of Kuwaitis struggled to make themselves understood to a receptionist who spoke little Arabic.

Eventually a spry man in his fifties came to sit next to me. He introduced himself in flawless English as Hassan, the owner of the hotel. "I enjoy meeting Westerners," he said. "Are you American? I used to live in America."

"Canadian."

"Very good. I like Canadians." He sat down but the receptionist called out and interrupted our conversation. He nodded at her and turned to me. "I must go now and take care of these Kuwaitis, but please join me for dinner tonight." I told him I would return after I met with the maghli wrestlers.

I arrived at the sports centre just as a large group of young boys started practising for a stern coach. Most of the boys were about ten years old. While they warmed up I asked the coach about maghli wrestling. "I am sorry," the coach said. "There are no maghli wrestlers here tonight. But we can show you." He fetched two black belts from a box in the corner. He pulled two boys from the practice, tied the belts around their waists and urged them to demonstrate maghli wrestling for me.

The wrestlers faced each other and gripped their opponent's belt with both hands. When the coach barked at them to begin, they tugged and pushed on each other, their chests butting together, until the stronger of the two boys hoisted his opponent from the mat by his belt. The lifted wrestler stretched his toes towards the mat, trying to get at least one foot on firm ground: in wrestling, there is no more vulnerable place to be than in the air. The attacker knocked his opponent's leg aside with his knee and the two crashed down. The boys stood, shook hands and returned to practice.

This was different than the maghli wrestling that Rahim described. "I thought in maghli only one hand stays on the belt and the other is free," I said.

"No, no. It is always two hands. Who told you this?"

"A wrestler in Shahr-e Kord."

The coach scoffed. "They know nothing there."

I watched the rest of the boys' practice. It was identical to the hundreds of practices I'd attended during my time as a wrestler. After their warm-up, the coach led the boys in some stretching exercises. Then he instructed them on how they should arch their back to prepare for a throw. The boys practised these back-bending throws over and over. They hurled their bodies backwards with the sort of fearlessness that makes men envious of boys. Afterwards, each found space in a corner of the wrestling room to skip rope and lift weights.

Being in the room and watching the boys' training inspired a sort of visceral nostalgia. I was itching to get on the mat and was happy when two men approached me and asked if I wanted to wrestle. "We will not do maghli. We can wrestle freestyle." They found me a pair of shorts to wear, then we slipped off our shoes and walked barefoot onto the mat. One of the men was short but had the build of a gorilla and outweighed me by thirty pounds. His thick cauliflower ears were scabby from recent battles. The other man was tall but slender, and close to my weight. I invited him to wrestle but Gorilla poked me in the chest. "I want you," he said.

I gave a half-hearted protest in my simple Farsi—"I am very small and you are very big"—but he would not be put off. The boys in the corners put down their dumbbells and skipping ropes and sat around the mat. The foreigner was about to take on the local behemoth. Gorilla took off his shirt to reveal his mountainous physique. He had a bulging chest and arms as big as my legs. He flexed his biceps and the boys applauded. I pulled my shirt over my head and someone snickered. We shook hands and began to wrestle.

Gorilla and I circled each other on the mat. He was smirking at me from below his thin moustache. I wanted to keep my distance from his huge arms. Instead of tying up with him I shot my body at his right leg. I pinched his knee with my wrists and pressed my chest into his thigh, but I couldn't uproot his tree trunk leg. Gorilla gripped me behind my triceps, tore me off his leg and pulled me into a body lock. I tried to back away but his arms were tight around me and getting tighter. I could smell his breath and feel his stubble grate across my cheek. I didn't want to be this close. This was the position I feared. He could have knocked me to the mat then, but Gorilla straightened his legs and pushed his hips forward. He didn't want a simple takedown. Gorilla wanted to show off to the boys in the room. He wanted to throw me. I could feel it. I reached down for his leg. Tied up in his bulk I knew my attack was useless, but I wanted to distract him. He forced his leg back and charged his entire body into me.

There, on the edge of balance, came the moment that every wrestler knows. It comes with a subtle shift of flesh, the certainty of physics and the sudden revelation that something has changed: one man, the wrong man, is about to come crashing down. I let out a cry of effort and, using Gorilla's own forward momentum, twisted him off his feet. For a crumb of a second we were both airborne, our chests merged, his back turning in air down, down, down. He hit the mat like a meteor, and I on his chest, grinning like a madman an inch from his face.

The boys cheered. Gorilla rose meekly, passed a hand through his hair and said, "This man is difficult."

We continued wrestling, both of us growing slimy in the heat of the wrestling room. Our first battle had cracked open the scabs on Gorilla's ears and they glistened with fresh blood.

He grabbed me by my head and neck and planted my face into the ground. I breathed in the dirty mat. Gorilla pounced on my back and coiled his arms around my midsection to apply a gut wrench. My rib cage compressed like an accordion, wheezing out my breath. My cracked rib flashed. His hands were clenched together beneath my chest. I rolled forward on his hands to grind apart his grip with my sternum, but with a brief grunt he flipped me over as if I were made of nothing.

We stood and continued to wrestle. I got clobbered. I scored a few counterattacks, but Gorilla had me picking myself up off the mat over and over. I surrendered. Hunched over and gasping, I waved at the thinner wrestler to take my place.

I collapsed on the edge of the mat. My pulse pounded inside my skull and my lungs ached. In my nostrils was the smell of sweat: mine, his, the stale stink of the boys' practice. I knew the next morning would greet me with aches and heavy legs. Still, in spite of my exhaustion, my mood shone. Shaking hands and engaging in a few minutes of friendly combat inched me closer to the Iranians. And I'd tossed the Gorilla.

·

My heart rate had just begun to slow by the time I reached Hotel Kuhrang. I didn't have the time to shower before leaving the sports centre and hoped that Hassan couldn't smell my efforts at the varzeshga. He received me warmly, brought me to his restaurant and ordered us two plates of fried fish with rice.

I asked Hassan about his clientele. "Most of our guests in the summer are Arabs from the Gulf, like the Kuwaitis who came today. They are easy to please. They rarely leave the hotel. They just want a place to sleep, eat and make love. In the winter we are busier. We run skiing trips in the mountains. The chairlift for the main resort is near the hotel. Then we get some Europeans. Mostly Germans. Still, the hotel does not make much money. I have already made my money in this life. The hotel is more a hobby for me than a business, and it is a good place to house my horses. I have ten horses now." He pointed out the window. One of his staff was hosing down a grey stallion next to a paddock.

"Business is very slow. The Arabs still come, but since eleven September we get very few Westerners. And now that America is in Iraq we will get even less. They are afraid to come here. The American media is run by Zionists and they like to scare people. George Bush, too, is a puppet of the Zionists. They want people to hate us." He paused to take a bite of pickled greens, then pointed at me. "And you? Are you afraid in Iran?"

"No. Iran is the safest place I have travelled. People said that I must be brave to come here, but I feel safer on the streets of Iran than I do back in Canada."

"That is because you *are* safer here. Iranians are taking care of you. You never have to worry. I feel so sorry for the Americans. They are good people, but they are cursed with such a man for a president."

We finished our dinner and Hassan sent a waiter to fetch us tea. "If you want to learn about Iran, I know the place you must go. It is a small village near Kuhrang called Saragh-Seyed. The road is closed for half of the year because of the snow. You cannot use the roads. But now it is all right. The people are very simple. Shepherds, mostly. They are famous because after the Revolution, Khomeini asked them what they wanted from the new government. They asked him to send them a king." Hassan laughed.

According to Hassan, only one minibus headed to Saragh-Seyed each day. It left Kuhrang in the morning, stayed the night in the village and returned the next morning. Hassan called the minibus office to reserve a seat for me on the next day's bus, and he invited me back to the hotel for an early breakfast. "There is no hotel in Saragh-Seyed," he said. "But the people are kind."

I woke early and stepped out into a perfect Persian dawn. The early light dyed the landscape pink and softened the rough edges of the surrounding mountains. The air was fresh and cool, cold enough for me to see my breath, and the chill gave relief to my wrestling-weary muscles. A pair of rough dogs and a few early-morning chickens wandered the otherwise empty streets. I walked slowly through the reddish glow and decided that I see too few sunrises.

I walked to the minibus office after breakfast. The man behind the desk pointed to a red van parked out front. "This bus will go to Saragh-Seyed," he said. "You can put your bag on a seat right now, but the bus will not go for two hours." I dumped my rucksack on one of the seats. A few minutes later a driver with a bushy moustache started up the van.

"Is it leaving now?" I asked.

"It is going to Shahr-e Kord first. It will come back and go to Saragh-Seyed."

"But my bag is in there."

"It is fine. It will come back." As the minibus sped away with all of my belongings, I hoped that Hassan was right about never having to worry.

I napped for an hour and a half on the floor of the minibus office. Another hour passed before the minibus returned. It held no passengers, but now there were bags on most of the seats. I climbed aboard, claimed my seat and we clattered up the road towards the edge of town.

It looked as if I would have the minibus all to myself, but the bus stopped only a kilometre up the road from the office. A crowd of elderly Bakhtiyari were waiting on the street. They swarmed the bus as soon as it stopped and pushed their way in, elbowing each other aside to find themselves a seat. I was relieved that I was the first aboard since it was unlikely the entire crowd would fit into the van.

A haggard old woman shoved her way to where I sat. She poked me in the shoulder and howled at me. "This is my place!" She pointed to a straw bag on the floor under the seat. "That is my bag and you are in my seat!" The woman's face was shattered with wrinkles and only three teeth made a home of her mouth. Two thick braids of black hair snaked out from under her headscarf and were tied together where they mingled with her considerable beard. Two other women, also hideous, began shouting at me too. I couldn't understand much of their Farsi, but it was clear they wanted my seat.

I protested. "I put my bag on the seat this morning. Mine was the first bag here. This is my seat." But my bearded rival poked me again and the rest of her coven continued berating me. I was battling the witches from *Macbeth*.

At first, the other passengers were too busy struggling for their own seats to notice, but once they settled in they turned their attention to the foreigner and the witches. I tried to appeal to some of the others in the van, but they just smiled; I could tell they knew better than to war against these three women. Finally the driver came in, heard the ruckus and told the women I had claimed that seat in the morning. The women turned their ire on him and heaved curses until a vendor selling Zam Zam arrived at a window and distracted everyone with cold orange soda.

Once we left Kuhrang, the narrow gravel road skirted the edges of mountain cliffs and alpine meadows. After a half hour, our driver stopped at a mountain spring so we could take a drink. The van was so jammed that only a few passengers at the front left to fetch water for the rest. Empty bottles, tin cups and plastic bowls were passed out of windows and returned filled with icy spring water. Back on the road, the minibus rattled over a particularly narrow and dangerous mountain pass. Only inches of dirt separated the bus from the cliff. A man led the rest of the passengers in prayer. My witch, who was seated on a stool in the aisle beside me, pinched my arm and asked me why I wasn't praying. Another man answered for me. "He is not a Muslim. Leave him alone."

Two hours later the minibus arrived at the top of Saragh-Seyed. I was amazed. The village clung to the angles of the mountain like mushrooms to a tree trunk. Houses were made from stone and mud; fences from sheets of recycled tin, twigs and flattened wooden crates. Stout branches supported overhanging mud roofs. Woven mats hung in front of doors and windows, or formed the pens that housed sheep and goats. There were no roads, just twisted passageways that wormed through the village and disappeared around corners. No space was wasted; the roofs of the lower buildings were the walkways for the level above. It was ramshackle, pieced together with bits and scraps, but ingenious and elegant at the same time.

A mountain stream tumbled through the village from a pipe sticking out of a stone. The women of the village gathered around this spout to fill basins, scrub clothes and wash dishes. Wandering chickens jerked their heads into the tiny puddles. Drying animal feed was piled on rooftops. The alpine air intensified every scent: the goats and fresh-cut hay, cooking fires and tobacco from the cigarettes all the men smoked. The Zagros Mountains hovered around and above all of this like overprotective parents.

The minibus driver instructed Ali, a boy who stood nearby, to lead me to the village *imamzadeh*. Imamzadehs are burial shrines built for the twelve Shiite Imams and their seemingly infinite number of descendants. Nearly every town and village had an imamzadeh. Some, like Reza's haram at Mashhad, were grand complexes. Most, though, were modest domed structures holding the tomb of a holy man. Saragh-Seyed's imamzadeh acted as the village's mosque. "You can sleep there,"

Ali said. I followed Ali down a central pathway to the imamzadeh gate where I met the one-eyed mullah. He welcomed me to the village without smiling, and sent Ali to prepare tea. I marvelled, again, at the hospitality of the Iranians and how effortless it was to slip into the warmth of their welcome.

While we waited for our tea, another man joined us. He introduced himself as Hossein. He was a mathematics teacher from Shahr-e Kord and spoke some English.

"Why did you come here to Saragh-Seyed?" he asked.

"I like mountains," I said. "I come from a mountain city in Canada. And I wanted to see the village. Hassan at Hotel Kuhrang told me this was a beautiful place."

"Yes. I know Hassan. How long will you stay?"

"I was planning on leaving tomorrow, on the morning minibus back to Kuhrang, but it is already late. I think I'd like to stay longer. May I stay for two nights?"

"Two nights. One week. One month. Stay however long you like."

"I will pay you something, of course."

Hossein shook his head.

"I must give you something."

"No. Nothing."

"May I make a donation to the imamzadeh, then?" I asked, gesturing to the mullah.

"No. He will not take your money. Never. You are guest."

It was nearly dusk by the time we finished our tea. Hossein suggested we take a walk around the village. Shadows lengthened over the uneven walkways and I had a hard time finding my footing. Young girls in bright-coloured headscarves peered out from behind blankets draped across doorways. Old men in piano smocks and black caps waved greetings, and teenaged boys with T-shirts and puffy haircuts followed us around. Women, their backs bent under impossible loads of hay, smiled up at us from underneath their burdens. We went into a shoe shop, where we sat on the floor with Hossein's friends and drank orange sodas.

A small boy appeared at the doorway. He was breathless and rushed his words. His eyes were frantic. Hossein grew solemn. The boy spoke Bakhtiyari and I couldn't understand anything, but I sensed tragedy in his tone. Hossein nodded, took a deep breath, then turned to me. "There was an accident. A man fell down from the mountain. He is my uncle. They are now looking for his body."

We left the shop. The darkness was complete. I followed Hossein through the alleys, up the stone stairways and across narrow bridges. We reached his home and sat on the edge of a terrace looking over the village. I could see nothing aside from the distant yellow glow of candles and kerosene lanterns. I listened to the living blackness. Voices called out to each other from across the village. There were children singing and the occasional donkey's lament. Behind me, Hossein shared a sombre conversation with one of his relatives. A woman I had not been introduced to appeared from a darkened doorway, placed a platter of scrambled eggs with tomatoes and bread in front of me, then disappeared without saying a word.

I ate, not knowing how to reconcile my feelings of wonder with feelings of vicarious sadness. Hossein sat with me and shared the meal. He didn't say much, only urging me to eat. When we were finished the woman appeared again to clear away our plates, then returned with tea. A young girl came out of the house and, with an impish smirk, leapt from the terrace and disappeared into the darkness. We could only hear her giggle and her footfalls on the rooftop below.

As we walked back down towards the imamzadeh, I had difficulty navigating a steep set of stairs in the darkness. Then I felt a wrinkled hand on my arm. A woman in a black chador, nearly invisible in the shadows, guided me down the stairs one step at a time. "Ya, Ali," she said, invoking the help of the

Imam with each step. "Ya, Ali." At the bottom I turned to thank her. It was my witch from the minibus.

Hossein and I laid blankets outside the imamzadeh. The sky was flooded with stars. Hossein and Ali made their beds next to me. I protested, telling them that I would be fine on my own and they should return to the comfort of their own homes, but they would not listen. Their hospitality dictated a visitor should not be left alone. Then we went to sleep.

Wailing voices woke us in the middle of the night. "Those are women," Hossein whispered. "They found my uncle's body."

A minibus blared its horn into the early morning. The sound penetrated the entire village, briefly interrupting the rustic peace with reminders of traffic. I rolled out from beneath my blankets. "I think they are honking for me," I said to Hossein. "The driver thinks that I am going back to Kuhrang today."

"Yes."

"Should I run and tell him I am staying behind?"

"It is okay. He will not wait."

The honking continued for another minute before an engine growled and faded into silence.

I spent the morning accepting the countless offers of tea from villagers, sitting in the shade of mud roofs and meeting old men. In one house, I chatted with a man while his children stood behind him, staring at me over their father's shoulder. He asked me if I was married and I told him I was. Too often, when I mentioned I had a girlfriend, Iranians reacted as if I had told a dirty joke.

"Is your wife Iranian?"

"No, she is Indian. She is a Muslim."

"Sunni?"

"Shiite." He seemed impressed. "Do you have a wife?" I asked him.

"Of course. I have two wives. And five sons."

"Any daughters?"

"Yes." He reached over his shoulder and poked his little girl in the cheek. She snorted and hid behind his back. "Have you phoned Moonira? You can phone her today. We have a phone in the village now. It is beside the police post."

"No, thank you."

Most of the day's conversations were the same. The curious locals asked me whether I was married, if I had any children and whether I was enjoying my time in Iran. The villagers also seemed especially proud of their new phone. Nearly everyone told me about it and asked me if I would like to call Canada.

After lunch Hossein suggested we hike into the surrounding mountains. I walked back to the imamzadeh to change out of my sandals. The mullah was there, and he was angry with me. "Where did you go? Some policemen were here looking for you."

"Police?"

"Two police from Shahr-e Kord. They wanted to talk to you."

"Why?"

"I don't know." The mullah glared at me through his good eye as if I were a criminal hiding out in his imamzadeh.

"Where are they now?"

"They couldn't find you so they left. Where did you go?"

"I was in the village. I was here all day." He frowned at me. "Agha, I have done nothing wrong."

He said nothing else. I couldn't understand what police officers from Shahr-e Kord could want from me, and the mullah didn't seem to know. Perhaps Hassan was worried that I did not return to Kuhrang. Hossein just shrugged. He told me not to worry. I was more curious than concerned, and there was something exciting about being a fugitive.

I changed into my hiking boots, left my sandals next to my rucksack at the imamzadeh and followed Hossein out of the village. We walked down the mountain from the village, passing green pastures, grazing sheep and clouds of menacing bees that hummed over white bee boxes. We came upon a tiny waterfall where three teenage boys were washing their clothes and themselves. "This is the Saragh-Seyed shower," Hossein said. One boy asked if I knew any women in Canada who would marry him. Then, as Hossein and I walked away, the boy called out to me and flashed his penis. Hossein was embarrassed. "These boys are very bad," he said.

Along the pathway that led out of the village we found a man and his two young daughters tending a field of green animal feed. Hossein showed me a tree on the edge of the pasture. Beneath the tree were blood-red splotches and the trunk and branches were smeared with red handprints. It looked like a crime scene. Hossein pointed to the juicy berries that hung from the trees. "These are red *tut* berries," he said. They looked like large, oblong raspberries. "Do you have these in your country?" I shook my head. "They are very delicious. We can pick some."

We both climbed into the tree. The farmer and his daughters left the field to join us. The ripest berries were at the top, and only the two girls were light enough to climb the upper branches to reach them. They passed handfuls of the berries down to us. Our hands, lips and tongues grew incarnadine with the tart juice, and my shirt was smeared with red. By the time we climbed down I had tattooed the tree with my own crimson fingerprints.

Hossein and I continued our hike along a dry riverbed. Narrow trenches built of piled stones lined the sides of our rocky path. In the rainy season, when the river was high, the trenches were the irrigation canals that led river water to nearby pastures and gardens. We followed a course of sharp switchbacks from the crest of a cliff down the mountain face. In the valley, a turquoise river snaked along at the base of the high mountain walls. We walked upstream, crossing on rustic wooden bridges and admiring the waterfalls that decorated the cliffs like tumbling lace. A mountain spring seeped out of one rock, making the stone shine and soaking billowy balls of green moss. We pressed our faces against the cool wet stone and sipped the fresh water.

Then came the long hike back up to the village. My shirt was wet with sweat and spring water, my boots blanched by white dust. We paused midway up the cliff face to catch our breath and allow two men and their burdened donkey to pass. It took two hours to reach Saragh-Seyed. I collapsed on the mats in front of the imamzadeh. My exhausted bliss ended when I pulled off my filthy hiking boots and reached for my sandals. They were gone. A pair of dirty white sneakers was in their place. "Hossein, my sandals are missing." He helped me look in my rucksack and underneath the blankets where we slept the previous night. They were not there. Someone had stolen my shoes.

The mullah came in and Hossein told him what had happened. "The gate was locked most of the day," he told Hossein. "Only Ali was here."

"Ali stole my sandals?" I asked. I was getting angry.

Hossein put a hand on my shoulder. "Do not worry. Your shoes will return. We will go and drink tea. And my friend has a qalyun we can smoke. You said yesterday you like qalyun."

"I don't want to smoke or drink tea. I want to find my shoes. I want to find Ali."

"Okay. Okay."

Hossein and I walked through the village and asked everyone if they had seen Ali. Each time Hossein explained what happened my predicament was met with grins rather than genuine concern. I could not blame them; it was hard not to smile at the idea of a furious little Canadian stomping around barefoot in search of his missing sandals. The news that the foreigner lost his shoes spread quickly and became the village joke. I was not laughing, however. I felt betrayed, but my fuming made the whole ordeal even more comic.

Eventually we spotted Ali coming up the path. I marched towards him and asked if he had seen my sandals. He could tell I was angry. "I didn't take them," he said and a crowd of curious children gathered around to see what I would do next.

Then I heard the mullah call out from down the pathway. He held my sandals in his hand and waved them over his head. He handed them to me. "Where were they? Who had them?" I asked, but the mullah just smiled down at me and said something to Hossein in Bakhtiyari. Hossein looked embarrassed.

I turned to Hossein. "Who had my sandals?"

"I will tell you after."

I apologized to Ali and shook his hand, then followed Hossein to his friend's shop. Six of us sat on the floor, drank tea and smoked a qalyun while two boys smirked at me from outside. I was embarrassed and wanted to know what had happened to my shoes, but the cool apple smoke curled in my lungs and calmed me. I didn't want to let my anger stain the day black.

"Do many foreigners visit Saragh-Seyed?" I asked Hossein.

He laughed at the thought. "No. Very few, but last week there were two. One man and one woman from Holland."

"Did anyone steal their shoes?" Everyone laughed.

I mentioned my interest in traditional wrestling. One of the men was a maghli wrestler in his youth and began to tell me how the style is practised, but a young boy jumped up and interrupted him. "You want to see maghli? I will show you." He tugged a friend outside and borrowed belts from two nearby men. The boys fastened the belts around their waists, kicked off their shoes and began to wrestle. The other men and I watched the pair pace back and forth in the street, their hands gripping their opponent's belt, trying to knock each other to the ground. Neither boy seemed to know what he was doing. They danced for ten minutes before one boy caught the other off balance and they both tumbled down into the dust. The winner stood and raised his hands in the air, but by then nearly everyone had stopped paying attention.

I spent the rest of the afternoon talking with the village men. They were interested in my opinions of Iran, my life in Canada and my travels. They were especially curious when I told them I'd visited Israel and Palestine a few years before. They asked whether I'd seen the Al Aqsa mosque, and wanted to know about the struggles of the Palestinians. My Farsi skills did not permit much commentary, but the men seemed satisfied when I told them that life for the Palestinians was hard.

At nightfall, Hossein said, "We are going to a gathering for the dead man." He led me to a large black tent erected on a terrace overlooking the village. The tent was laid with carpets and lit with candles and lanterns. Dozens of men, most old enough to have grey beards, sat in a circle inside the tent. I joined them. We were all silent. The night was thick and black, and the tent darkened by sorrow.

Attendants rushed in and laid plastic tablecloths in front of us. Then came trays of bread, plates of rice and bowls of simple lamb stew. "You must eat fast," Hossein instructed. We spooned up the solemn meal, then men cleared away our plates and served tea along with dishes of Iranian cigarettes for whoever wanted to smoke. A man in a corner led a brief prayer before we all left the tent.

I was an outsider, a tourist to this grief, yet their hospitality washed away any unease. Instead I found myself feeling sadness for a man I never knew.

At the imamzadeh that night I thanked Hossein for his company, and for bringing me to the funeral tent. "It was a very good day," I said. He said I was welcome. But there was one last thing I wondered about. "Hossein, what happened to my shoes?"

In the darkness I could hear him shift under his blankets. "A boy took them. He wanted to wear them for a little while. Then he brought them back. He wanted to see the difference between Canada shoes and Iran shoes."

I almost missed the minibus the next morning. As we rattled along the alpine road back to Kuhrang the driver shouted back to me. "You stayed two nights. You like Bakhtiyari people?" I told him I did.

He placed his hand over his heart. "Thank you very much."

I stopped into Hotel Kuhrang to thank Hassan for pointing me towards Saragh-Seyed. "I sent the police to look for you," he said. "I thought you would come back after one night."

I smiled at his concern and told him I was having a good time. "You were right, the people were kind."

"I know," he said. "I thought so. I just wanted to be sure you were all right."

10

WEAKNESS

A wrestler's body offers few perfect holds. The top of the wrist where the arm narrows before the hand is one. Catch a man here, compress his tiny wrist bones, and you own his entire arm. The back of the neck is another; wrestlers reach here first, finding purchase where skull meets spine. The peak of the pelvic crest, alive with nerve endings, seems designed to grip. So, too, the pad of flesh that hides behind the knee. There are champions and losers, small men and titans, but all wrestlers share the same flaws. The best a man can do is know where he is weak.

Three large circles, drawn with flour on a trash-strewn field, outlined the battleground for the annual *loucho* championships. Kamal, Jamshid and I arrived early from Babolsar and passed the time inside a ramshackle tea house assembled out of plastic tarps, chicken wire and scrap wood. A set of rickety bleachers offered reserved seating for officials and honoured guests in front of the wrestling field. A few men milled about setting up the judges' tables and PA system, while four fat sheep, one for the winner of each weight class, nibbled on the grass.

Spectators, all men, began to arrive and sit around the perimeter of the field on empty rice sacks and flattened boxes. Trucks and tractors, parked in a ring behind them, formed an impromptu second set of stands for those who climbed onto the hoods and roofs to get a better view. The men were farmers and labourers from the surrounding villages with stubbled faces and calloused hands. Before long, the crowd grew into the hundreds, and nearly everyone munched on long black sunflower seeds. A black circle of spit-wet husks formed a second, unofficial boundary around the wrestling field. Through the clouds of their cigarette smoke I could smell the Caspian Sea.

I had arrived in Babolsar the previous morning, after passing over the Alborz Mountains to the coast. As I walked along the beachfront road towards my hotel I was startled to hear someone call my name. A few metres ahead a young man was leaning out of a car window. I didn't recognize him until I'd walked up to the car. It was Kamal, whom I'd met on the Lake Van ferry in Turkey two months before. I couldn't believe he remembered my name. I shook Kamal's hand. "How are you?"

"I am well," he said. He pointed to the man driving the car. "This is my friend Jamshid. He speaks English."

"Hello," said Jamshid, an Iranian Rasputin with blue eyes and an unruly black beard. "Welcome to Iran."

Kamal unlocked the back door. "Come with us."

I climbed inside and the car lurched forward. I thought the men would drive me the rest of the way to my motel. Instead we turned off the road at the next junction and headed into town. "We are going to buy food. You will come and eat with us." I shared saffron kebabs and cold araq at Jamshid's father's home and smoked qalyun on the beach with Kamal's brothers. I spent all of my Babolsar hours with them, and was a willing hostage of their hospitality.

At the wrestling site, a man stepped forward from the officials' bleachers, rapped his finger on a microphone to test the volume and began to sing. His voice boomed with static from two large speakers, while three young boys cleared garbage from the wrestling field. An echo effect on the microphone garbled the man's voice. I asked Jamshid what he was singing.

"This is poetry," he said.

"Really? Is it *Shahnomeh*?"

"No. It is Mazanderani poem. But like *Shahnomeh*. It has warriors and heroes and wrestlers. It is a strong, fighting poem."

I couldn't understand any of the words, but the cadence of the verse managed to push through the static and echo. After a sung invocation to Imam Ali, there was another poem. Jamshid placed his hand on my shoulder. "This is *Shahnomeh*," he said.

I held my breath. This was what I'd been wanting to see for two months. I looked around me as Ferdosi's thousand-year-old poetry echoed over the landscape. The day's wrestlers, stirred by the exploits of the ancients, limbered up on the side of the field. Men of myth inspired men of flesh, and the epic verses promised a night of heroes.

Kamal explained the rules. Loucho is similar to Olympic freestyle wrestling. The rules permit holds to both the upper body and the legs, and unlike many of the other Persian styles, wrestlers do not have to maintain any sort of grip during the match. In loucho, though, there are no points scored. Each match consists of two seven-minute halves separated by a one-minute break, and the first man to lift his opponent off his feet or take him down wins the match.

The first pair of barefoot athletes stepped into the circle and the crowd applauded. I recognized one of the wrestlers. Farzad worked at the snack stall at the motel where I was staying. I had bought peanuts and tea from him the night before. The men shook hands, a referee blew a whistle and two wrestlers crouched into combat.

The men grabbed at each other's head and neck. They pushed shoulders and pulled on wrists. Both knew that the smallest break in their adversary's position—a tiny misstep, a stance a little too high or a crouch a degree too low—was an opening for an attack. The crowd searched the wrestlers for weaknesses and shouted encouragement to their favourite: "Raise your head!" "Farzad, his left leg is forward!" But from a distance, no fan can sense all that the wrestlers sense. That close, every detail is in high relief. Every chest hair, the speed and smell of each breath, the specks of dirt beneath a fingernail.

Farzad struck first. His attack was flawless and as fast as a spark. He bent his body into a tight crouch. A lesser wrestler might have flexed his knees, but Farzad simply allowed his knees to dip, relaxing the joints for a moment and letting gravity drop him smoothly down. At the same instant his right hand shot at his rival's leg as if fired from a gun, and his fingers found the soft patch of flesh behind the knee and dug in. His man tried to kick free, but Farzad had him in a perfect hold, immobilized with one hand. His victim spun and fell in the dirt with Farzad standing over him. Farzad's fans erupted and the referee raised his arm.

There were two more matches before Farzad took to the field again. This time he faced a wrestler from the town of Babol. He was a better match for Farzad than his first opponent. The Babol wrestler easily defended himself against Farzad's quick leg attacks, sprawling his target knee backwards and leaving Farzad with nothing but empty air to grasp. The wrestler, though, was not able to take Farzad down. For six minutes the men lunged at each other's legs and fought in and out of body locks. Their sweat turned to mud in the dirt ring.

Then the two men attacked simultaneously. Their limbs were a flurry and in the ensuing scramble of bodies, both men touched the ground. Each man raised his arms and claimed victory. The fans started to holler, but the referee was unsure which of the men had scored a decisive takedown. There was a pause while he reviewed a videotape of the match with the other officials; the electronic equipment seemed out of place alongside the prize sheep and barefoot warriors. The wrestlers waited on the field, their hands on their heads and breathing hard. The crowd became impatient.

The officials huddled around the television for ten minutes. At last, the referee returned to the centre of the ring, where he gripped the Babol wrestler's wrist and raised it above his head. Farzad had lost. The men from Babol cheered, but Farzad's fans foamed with rage. Five men charged the field to shout at the referees in spite of their friends' attempts to pull them back. Spectators from both towns shoved on the sidelines, and two men started punching each other. "Maybe we should go," Jamshid said as the mood blackened. "This is not good." Eventually three policemen appeared to break up the fights.

As we stepped back from the melee I looked up at the wrestlers. Farzad's face was dour, but he accepted the referee's decision and shook his rival's hand. Grace gilded his disappointment. The two warriors stood side by side on the field as their fans fought, watching their dignified contest be blemished by the tempers of weaker men.

The coast of the Caspian Sea is like another country. The landscape seems more South Asian than Persian. The northern slopes that lean into the sea are green with jungle and hung with mist. Farmers bend in the shin-deep water of rice paddies and tend lush tea plantations. The air is clean and in the hot summer months thousands of Iranian tourists, mostly Tehranis, ply the scenic alpine road en route to the seaside. Along the highway are kebab restaurants, open-air tea houses and the clusters of large, pre-erected tents that pass for campgrounds. Roadside stalls sell fruit, honey and jars of homemade pickles. Small boys wave oranges tied to sticks at passing vehicles; living billboards letting drivers know that oranges are for sale a few metres up the road. The major draw for these tourists is the beach.

The day after the loucho championships, Kâmal and Jamshid took me to the shoreline. The sand was crowded with excited Iranian tourists enjoying the Persian version of a seaside vacation. Nobody seemed to mind the overcast sky or the trash that fouled the sand; candy wrappers, plastic bottles and cigarettes were everywhere while yellow garbage bins were nearly empty. Everyone but the two sulking horses for hire was having a good time. Families bought beach toys from shaded stalls and posed for souvenir Polaroids taken by wandering photographers. Boys sold fresh figs and apricots from plastic pails. Men compared biceps and kicked footballs. The beach boys of Babolsar looked tanned and fit in sport sandals and faux Adidas shorts, like young men on beaches everywhere.

The women, though, were completely covered. By law, women had to wear full hejab, including their headcovering, even when in the water. I watched them splash and swim as best they could in their cordoned-off stretch of surf; they were forbidden to swim with men. They tossed beach balls and tugged on kite strings as their chadors floated up around them like pools of ink. I wondered how much fun they could possibly be having. Burdened by sopping clothes the women looked more like shipwreck victims than beach vacationers. Certainly they would rather be in bathing suits. Their laughter, though, divulged their joy. I found it difficult to feel sorry for women who were so clearly having a good time.

Kamal's brothers were there; Jamshid and I helped them heave a speedboat across the beach into the water. We pulled ourselves aboard and roared away from the sand with a stink of diesel smoke. Kamal bounced the boat over the incoming waves before anchoring a few hundred metres from the beach. I stripped to my boxer shorts, slipped off my sandals and dove into the dark green sea with the other men. The water was surprisingly warm but left the sour taste of pollution in my mouth.

I couldn't remember the last time I had swum and it was exciting to be in the water. The sea was rough, though, and fighting it drained my energy away after only a few strokes. While the others slipped in and out of the waves, I tried to swim back to the boat but the current kept pulling me farther away. Jamshid noticed I was struggling. He called out to me and asked me if I was all right. I told him I was fine—I didn't want to seem weak—but my voice betrayed my distress. Jamshid swam beside me to make sure I didn't drown. I scolded him for helping me, but by the time we reached the boat my lungs ached and my arms were limp. I would not have been able to pull myself into the boat by myself.

Soon afterwards the other men returned to the boat and we headed back to shore. Jamshid said everyone thought the water was too rough, but I suspect they would have kept swimming if I hadn't come up lame. I was embarrassed. I'd spent two months in Iran seeking out strongmen. I told people I was a wrestler. It was humiliating to be so feeble.

I was in Iran to seek out the best in men. I wanted to find noble wrestlers and wise poets, and learn from their masculine ideals. In Shulabad-e Sofla, though, I found the worst of men. And the worst in me. I disappointed myself. Instead of reacting with wisdom and nobility, instead of behaving like a pahlevan, I gave in to belligerence.

I left the coast and travelled south to Aligudarz. I was looking for a wrestling style called *jang* (a word that means "war" in Farsi), but no one I spoke to had heard of it. I decided to visit one of the villages in the vicinity and ask there. I looked at my map. The mountain town of Shulabad-e Sofla was nearby and seemed as good a choice as any. When I arrived at the terminal and asked for a car to Shulabad I was swarmed by men who thought I was mistaken.

"Shulabad? You mean Esfahan. Esfahan is very nice for tourists."

"There is nothing in Shulabad. You should not go there."

"You mean Khorramabad? You want to go to Khorramabad?"

Eventually, the babel of voices found me a minibus for Shulabad. As I waited for the bus to leave, a ten-year-old beggar girl in ragged clothes approached me. She had a dirty face, tangled hair and dark dancing eyes. She held out her hand and demanded a donation. When I refused she realized I was a foreigner. She gave me a puckish smile and pinched my arm. I frowned. She laughed and pinched again, this time twisting my flesh between her fingers as hard as she could. "Go away," I said, jerking my arm back. She snorted and walked to the next minibus. I should have taken her mischief as an omen.

The road to Shulabad passed through mountains dotted with tiny farms and nomads' tents. Shepherds led goats and sheep along rocky pathways, and wayward cows lounged on the roadside. The scenery was stunning, but half an hour into the trip a headache started to swell so badly behind my eyes I had to close them. By the time I reached Shulabad I was hot with fever. The sudden illness reminded me of a bout of malaria I had suffered through in Africa several years before. I couldn't tell if this fever meant a relapse, but I knew I needed to lie down. Fortunately, there was a rough *mosaferkhune*, a simple travellers' house, near the minibus stop. It consisted of a single room crammed with nine beds. I collapsed onto one of them.

I slept for an hour before the manager shook me awake. He had two police officers with him. "Get up," they said.

"I am feeling sick," I said.

"We will take you to the doctor."

I eased myself off the bed. My head was thumping and heavy.

"Take your bag with you," one of the men ordered.

"Can I leave it here?"

"No."

I heaved my rucksack over my shoulder and followed the officers to the town clinic. The doctor was out. "He will be back in an hour," an officer told me. "Come to the police station and wait."

"I am not feeling well. I would like to wait in my bed at the mosaferkhune," I said.

"No. You must come with us."

I followed them into the police post and lay down on the floor. One of the officers sat in the corner of the room and stared at me with a smile like a clown's smeared over his face. The other lit up a cigarette and turned on a television. My headache surged. "Please," I said. "My head is hurting me. Can you turn off the television?"

He ignored me. "Give me your passport." I handed it to him. "Now open your bag."

"Why?"

"Open it!" The man started to go through my rucksack. He pulled out a bottle. "What is this?" he asked.

"Shampoo."

"For your hair?"

"Yes."

Then he pulled out a tube of hair gel. "What is this?"

"It is also for your hair."

"Before or after shower?"

"After."

"Can I have some?"

"No."

"Why not?"

"Why are you going through my bag?"

"Because we are police." He kept picking through my things. Then he looked up. "Is it true women in Canada wear skirts to here?" the officer asked. He placed his hand on his upper thigh.

I ignored him. The man in the corner spoke a few words of English. "I see you no happy," he said.

"No, I no happy."

"You no happy, but I love you!" he shouted.

The search went on for two hours. When I asked about the doctor, the officers didn't respond. They were busy amusing themselves with my possessions. When the man found my book of Hafez he closed his eyes and opened the book at random to tell everyone's fortune. The officer in the corner laughed. I was furious. "Is this your job?" I asked.

"Yes," he said. Then he started speaking in a high-pitched nasal voice that was supposed to be an imitation of me. The other officer giggled.

"You are a child," I said in Farsi.

"What did you say?" He stopped smiling.

"I said you are a child." I held my hand a few inches from the floor. "A little child."

The officer regarded my fraying temper with a smirk. He picked up my passport and turned to my Iranian visa. He glared at me while he began peeling away the visa sticker.

"What the fuck are you doing?" I blurted out.

This needed no translation. "Fuck?" he said. "You say fuck? You say fuck to me?" His voice rose into a yell.

My muscles tensed and vibrated. I locked eyes with the officer. My aggression was foolish. Weakness disguised as strength. I should have backed down. I was alone and far from anywhere, with men who held guns and batons. This was a stare that risked too much but my fever turned to fury and charred my good sense. It was only luck that the officer returned his eyes to my rucksack, but the thought of what might have happened hung in the air like stink. He continued his search until he had examined everything: every page of every book and every scrap of paper. When he was finished he wrote out the details of my passport. This took another twenty minutes. I had been in custody for three hours when the man said I could go. "You want to go to the doctor?" he asked.

"No."

"Where are you going?"

"To the mosaferkhune."

"You should not go there. The men will slit your throat and steal your money."

"I'll take my chances."

"If anyone in Shulabad bothers you, come to the police."

"Right."

I stood but he refused to let me leave the room without shaking his hand, then he wouldn't let it go. He leaned his face into mine and kissed me on both cheeks. I smelled the tobacco on his breath and felt his unshaven face rasp against mine. It was the final humiliation. "Now you can go," he hissed.

My visa was about to expire again. I had heard that the immigration office in Tabriz was particularly generous when it came to granting extensions, so I took an overnight bus to Tabriz and walked directly from the terminal to the office. I waited on a stuffed leather chair while the visa official finished dealing with the pleas of a desperate Afghan family. I caught myself frowning at him across the office. My experience in Shulabad had put me on my guard. It occurred to me that I now had something else in common with most Iranians: a lingering distrust of uniformed men.

The visa official was in a foul mood by the time he called me forward. I forced a grin and tried to be charming, but he would not cheer.

"How long have you been in Iran?" he said.

"Ten weeks."

He raised his eyebrows. "Ten weeks? Have you had an extension before?" I nodded. He flipped through my passport. "Your first extension was from Kerman. You must go back to Kerman to extend your visa again." He snapped shut my passport and held it out to me.

I didn't reach for it. "In Kerman they said that they would not extend my visa again. They said I would have to go somewhere else."

"That is not true."

"It is true. That is what they said. And my visa expires tomorrow. Kerman is on the other side of the country. I could not get there in time. It is impossible."

"You can take an airplane."

"I can't afford that."

He shrugged.

"Please, why can't I get an extension here? What is the difference? I don't understand."

"It is the rules."

"Are the rules different in every city?"

"No. It is the same."

"Then why did the office in Kerman say that I would have to go somewhere else?"

"That is not true. They did not say that."

"It is true. I am not lying." I felt frustration rise in my head.

"It is not true." He handed me back my passport. "You must go to Kerman. If you cannot go to Kerman, you must leave Iran. You must leave tomorrow."

I felt powerless. Gut-wrenched. I slung my rucksack over my shoulders, trudged back to the terminal and boarded a bus. Sunflower fields along the highway faced east as I headed west towards the Turkish frontier. I found a hotel room in the border town of Maku, then sulked over my last Persian tea in front of a blue-tinged television at a nearby tea house. I searched for something poetic about my hurried exile but found none. I passed through the bazaar as I returned to my hotel. It was a shame to be leaving Iran just as the pomegranates were in season.

The returning traveller should not mourn the places he has missed. The voyage itself overtakes the best of itineraries, and the organic rhythm of travel is its own reward. I knew all of this. These are among the oldest of travel clichés. Still, I had a quest and it was not complete. I was searching for poets and wrestlers. I wanted the Iranians to teach me how to combine combat with art and literature with muscle. I wanted to be inspired. I'd learned plenty in my time in Iran, but I hadn't learned enough.

11

RETURN

I watched the Iranian passengers in the departure lounge. The men were slick and groomed and reminded me of the Italians I went to high school with. Nearly all of the women wore heavy makeup. They compared bottles of duty-free perfume until it was time to board. Then the airport officials berated them, one by one, because their hand luggage was too heavy. Inside the plane, the Iran Air flight attendants wore pillbox hats over their headscarves and welcomed me aboard with stern smiles. A screen played a safety demonstration in Farsi, English and German before we lifted into the sky.

It was September 2004. Thirteen months had passed since the abrupt ending of my first visit to Iran. I waited a year to return; for continuity's sake, I wanted to pick up my travels at exactly the same time of year as when I left. I was late by a month—a friend's wedding had pushed back my departure date—but I was happy to be returning at last to the Persians. I hoped I hadn't missed pomegranate season.

I'd spent much of that year watching Iran from afar. It had been a bad year for the Islamic Republic. A December earthquake shook the city of Bam to the ground. The disaster killed nearly thirty thousand people, and for a brief time Iran had the sympathy of the Western world. Attention spans for tragedy, though, are short. A few months after the earthquake

Iranians went to the polls for parliamentary elections in which thousands of reformist candidates were disqualified by the council of clerics who hold the real power in Iran. The election left the country even more firmly in the hands of hardline conservatives. Later, the United States accused Iran of aiding the insurgency against the occupation forces in Iraq, and of engaging in a clandestine nuclear arms program. Iran settled into its familiar role as international pariah.

In Canada, the investigation into Zahra Kazemi's death continued, but led nowhere. A police officer was charged with her murder and eventually acquitted in an Iranian court. The judiciary declared Kazemi's death an accident and closed the case. Canada objected but was ignored. The foreign ministry in Iran reminded Canada that Kazemi's death was an Iranian matter that had been settled, and warned the new ambassador that he would face trouble if he pursued the case. Iranian officials offered Kazemi's son, Stephan Hachemi, twelve thousand dollars as compensation for his mother's death. Hachemi, duly insulted, refused to accept the blood money.

The nightly news further cemented Western misconceptions about Iran. When I mentioned to people that I'd travelled to Iran they opened their eyes wide and suggested I must be an adventurer with some sort of extraordinary courage. My travels impressed them, but I was frustrated rather than flattered. I found myself defending Iranians to everyone I spoke to. I told them that I wasn't brave, that Iranians were gentle and welcoming, and that Iran was the safest place I'd ever been. I told them about the Persian love for poetry, about tea houses and gardens. They countered with talk of burqas, terror and the Taliban. Few believed that Iran was a destination for anyone but the truly heroic or reckless. I was ashamed that fellow Canadians held such an arrogant certainty about a place, and a people, that they knew nothing about.

So I sought out Iranians at home. I attended performances of Persian music. I became a regular at a Persian restaurant where I ate kebabs, drank tea and practised my Farsi with the staff. In March, Moonira and I celebrated the Persian New Year at a party put on by the local cultural association. It was a purely secular affair. The queues for whisky Cokes at the bar were long, and there were more cocktail dresses than headscarves in the banquet room. Men and women danced together to Persian pop songs.

I was surprised to find that even some of the Canadian Iranians I met were reluctant to travel to Iran. "I couldn't go there," my waiter at the restaurant said. "I have a problem with authority." They were all proud to be Persian and enthusiastic at my interest in their poetry and culture, but for many Iran was a place they were glad to have escaped. The excesses of the Revolution, with its secret police and summary executions, darkened their recollections of garden tea houses, picnics by the riverside and holidays on the Caspian Sea. They loved Iran, but not what Iran had become, and had no desire to return until the mullahs were out of power.

Only Khadije was homesick for Iran. I continued my weekly Farsi lessons with her as soon as I returned to Canada, except for a month in the spring when she had to stop to give birth to her second child, a son named Mustafa. Each week we talked in Farsi about the Persian poets and the Iranians in the news. Khadije envied my upcoming trip. She looked forward to the day that her husband finished his studies in Canada and they could return. Khadije was loyal to the mullahs and believed that everyone in Iran saw Khomeini as a hero and saviour. I never told her that my experiences in Iran, and among Iranians in Canada, suggested the opposite. This would have saddened her, I think, though I'm not sure she would have believed me.

I continued to wrestle and found a new training partner in an old friend. Most of my former teammates had hung up their wrestling boots; Jeremy was one of the few who had not. We met three nights a week, always outside of regular practice hours so we could have the mats to ourselves. I was no match for Jeremy's skills or fitness. We battled until I was spent, then retired to the sauna where we engaged in philosophical discussions about wrestling and art. Jeremy was a filmmaker. He knew about the disconnect between being a fighter on the mat and an artist behind the camera. Like me, he wanted to reconcile his creativity with combat. I was lucky that my wrestling-room foe was such an ally off the mat.

Tehran spread out below the plane like a sea of lights. It was four in the morning but the airport was packed. Excited Iranians crowded the arrivals terminal and waved bouquets of flowers at homecoming family members. I wanted to sleep for a few hours on one of the benches in the terminal, but there was no space to recline. I found a seat, leaned my head against the wall and tried to claim some slumber amid the happy racket.

At six o'clock I took a taxi to the same hotel I had stayed in the previous year. A teenaged boy with nose-job bandages took down my passport information and collected my money.

"The price has gone up since last year," I said.

He shrugged. "What can I do?" He led me up the stairs to my room. I stepped into a pair of slippers next to my bed and walked to the shower. Most hotels, even the most basic mosaferkhunes, provided a pair of pink rubber slippers for trips to the bathroom. They were my favourite feature of Iranian hotels, though the slippers were usually too big for my feet and often fell off as I clopped to and from the toilet. A few minutes after I returned to my room, the boy from the front desk knocked on my door. He had a flask of hot tea. "This is for you," he said. "No charge. Welcome back to Iran."

The next day was the annual National Day of Poetry and Literature. The occasion fell on the anniversary of the death of Mohammad Hossein Shahriyar, a poet whose tomb I planned to visit in Tabriz. In honour of the day, I visited the Reza Abbasi Museum where I rushed past the prehistoric pottery to view the illustrated poetry manuscripts. Sixteenth-century volumes of Sa'adi's *Golestan* and *Bustan* and, most precious, the *Shahnomeh* of Ferdosi lay under glass. The illustrations were marvellous. There were scenes of battles and of banquets laid with sweets and quince. Dark-haired beauties accepted gifts of fruit from bearded lovers. There were portraits of poets reciting for kings and the famous wrestling match between Rostam and Sohrab from *Shahnomeh*. The two mythic warriors were portrayed gripping each other's belts. They snarled at each other on the battlefield from behind their long black beards as their horses stood watch.

> Again their backs they wrestling bend,
> Again their limbs they seem to rend:
> They seize each other's girdle-band,
> And strain and grasp with foot and hand,
> Doubt hanging still on either side,
> From morn to sombre eventide.

Being in the same room with the heavy noble tomes, and the warriors etched on their pages, was as good a start to my revived travels as I could imagine.

I walked back to the centre of town from the museum as the traffic careened past. I had missed Iranians but I had not missed Tehran. I laughed as I found myself trapped behind a family out taking a leisurely walk together. Each time I tried to pass them they obliviously stepped into my path, blocking my way. When I tried to pass on the left, they drifted left. When I veered right, they did the same. I was hemmed in until they decided to go into a shop. I remembered this from my previous visit to Iran. The ability to block a sidewalk was a unique Persian trait; even a single strolling pedestrian could monopolize an entire walkway. The behaviour was not mischievous or intentional. It had something to do with the Persian sense of *douceur de vivre*, I thought. There were few things urban Iranians enjoyed more than these slow, meandering strolls. I found it charming, even when I was stuck behind them.

While in Canada, I read that a new law had passed in Iran banning qalyuns from public places. Happily, though, the law was not being enforced in Tehran. I found a dingy tea house beneath Ferdosi Square and smoked among workmen on their lunch breaks. It was a joy to fill my lungs with the sweet smoke once again, but the room was otherwise gloomy. The men, most wearing coveralls splattered in white paint, hunched over their kebabs and didn't speak.

Another man walked into the tea house. He had a white shirt and a pair of jeans slung over one arm, and held a watch in his hand. He was a hawker, and these items were his only merchandise. The man made a circuit of the tea house and held out the clothing and the watch to each customer. No one was interested. They each closed their eyes and tossed back their head, the Iranian gesture for "no" which seemed dismissive and rude but wasn't meant to be. The man, seeing he had no customers, opted for a break. He laid his wares on a chair and the proprietor brought him a glass of tea.

The gloom in the tea house struck me with a sort of déjà vu. I was so happy to return to Iran I'd almost forgotten the taste of disappointment that hung everywhere in this country. The sense of Persian melancholy I noticed a year before crystallized in the forms of brooding men and the hawker without a customer. Sadness was as Persian as swirling poetry and spinning pahlevans. I was back among a people who bemoaned what happened to their country, its hijacking by severe men in robes, and longed for what once was. For too many Iranians, their nation had the taste of a qalyun once the sweetness has charred away and all that is left is cinders.

I took a shared taxi to the Museum of Cinema in northern Tehran. The theatre at the museum was screening Michael Moore's *Fahrenheit 9/11*. I had seen the film in Canada but I wanted to watch it with an Iranian audience. I'd met a few Iranians who denounced George Bush, but far more who proclaimed their affection for the American president. I wondered what their reaction would be to a film that portrayed Bush as a scoundrel.

The cinema was housed in a converted nineteenth-century mansion surrounded by eucalyptus trees. The interior suited the building's noble pedigree. Plaster stalactites hung from the ceiling and transformed the room into a luxurious cavern. Intricate mouldings framed the projection booth. The floor was carpeted and clean, and the seats plush. I sat near the back and watched as the theatre filled with smartly dressed Tehranis. Many men wore suits with neckties, a Western fashion rarely seen outside a wedding hall in Iran. Their ties were a display of sophistication and signalled that this was not a crowd of average blue-collar Iranians.

The lights faded and the film began. The film was subtitled rather than dubbed, which was a relief, but many of the audience had to lean forward and flex their necks to read the titles on the bottom of the screen. Beneath the elaborate carved ceiling flashed images of bomb blasts, bandaged children and charred American bodies. The audience's reaction to the film was just like that of audiences in Canada. They gasped and clicked their tongues at the gore, and shook their heads as President Bush read to children on September 11.

They were still, though, when Moore reminded viewers that Iraq had never threatened America or killed a single American. After all, less than twenty-five years before, Saddam Hussein *did* attack Iran. I knew that every person in the cinema was thinking about their own country's long war with Iraq.

Soon after the Islamic Revolution, Saddam marched his troops across Iraq's border with Iran in an attempt to take over the strategic Shatt al-Arab waterway at the head of the Persian Gulf. He made dubious claims that Iran's Khuzestan Province was historically part of Iraq. His target, though, was not the barren desert province but the vast oil reserves that lay beneath it. Saddam knew that Iran's military had been a shambles since the Shah's army disbanded after the Revolution. Iraq also had military support from the United States, which was spooked by the Islamic Revolution and Khomeini's fiery rhetoric. The invasion should have been a picnic.

Saddam and his allies, though, miscalculated Persian nationalism. Just as the heroes of Ferdosi's *Shahnomeh* resisted Arab invaders on the battlefields of myth, and just as Ferdosi himself defended the Persian language from Arabic infiltration in the pages of verse, Iranians would not cower before yet another Arab invasion. Iran engaged Saddam's army with a fever that echoed the poetry of Ferdosi:

> A cloud of dust rose up, and there was such a din of war cries that the sharpest ears were deafened. Like fire glimpsed through a purple curtain, diamond lances glittered in the darkened air, spears struck against helmets, and men's heads were trampled by horses' hooves.

The world, though, is real. Unlike those versified battles, the Iran–Iraq War was not waged with swords and spears by honourable pahlevans of myth. It was a nightmare of trenches and gas plotted by the worst of men. Iraq killed one hundred thousand Iranians with nerve and mustard gas obtained from Western powers, making Iran the nation most affected by weapons of mass destruction after Japan. The ruling mullahs, outgunned and with little knowledge of war, sent waves of volunteer soldiers over the front lines, many unarmed, to attack Iraqi trenches. Allegedly, thousands of children, some as young as nine years old, were ordered to sweep over frontline minefields. They were sent in groups of twenty and were roped together to prevent the most frightened among them from deserting. Some reports say only young girls were used for these horrifying missions.

Iranians refer to the conflict as the "Iraq-imposed War" and those who fell on the field of battle are revered as martyrs who died in the protection of their homeland. Still, if Saddam started the war, Khomeini prolonged it. In the spring of 1982, the Iranian army managed to push the Iraqis back to their border. Saddam offered a ceasefire but by then Khomeini had his own territorial ambitions. He transformed his soldiers from defenders into invaders and ordered them into Iraq. He wanted to topple Saddam and liberate the Shiite holy cities of Najaf and Kerbala from his secular regime. Like Saddam's, Khomeini's invasion failed and cost another six years of war and hundreds of thousands more deaths. The conflict ended in a stalemate in 1988. Depending on who does the grisly accounting, between one and two million people died.

The Iranians in the theatre may have agreed that George Bush was a scoundrel, and they applauded at the end of the film, but surely no Iranian wept when the Americans wrenched Saddam Hussein from his pedestal.

The Ibn-e Babouyeh Cemetery is named for a distant relative of Imam Hossein whose elaborate tomb sits within the grounds. Babouyeh, though, is not the most famous man buried there. When I told my taxi driver to take me to the cemetery he asked if I was going to see Takhti.

Gholamreza Takhti was born in 1930 into a poor Tehrani family. He was a talented zurkhane wrestler until he discovered Olympic freestyle wrestling, while serving in the Shah's army. In the fifties and early sixties Takhti was one of the most dominant wrestlers in the world. He earned dozens of international medals and was an Olympic and world champion. He was dubbed "Jahan Pahlevan," the Pahlevan of the World. In Iran he was a god.

Takhti could have been a hero penned by Ferdosi. Like the mythical Rostam, Takhti was a noble warrior who battled for Iran's honour. He brought the ideals of the pahlevan from the zurkhane to wrestling mats around the world. Takhti was gracious and fair. In the final of the 1962 World Wrestling Championships, Takhti faced the Soviet Union's Alexander Medved, one of the most celebrated wrestlers in the history of the sport. Medved had suffered a leg injury before the match that made him ripe for a loss. Takhti refused to take advantage of Medved's weakness and never attacked the injured leg. His chivalry cost him the bout and the world title, but further endeared him to the Iranians.

Takhti's life, like Ferdosi's, collided with politics. Takhti retired from wrestling in 1963, but he was still revered by millions of Iranians. He was a devout Muslim and an outspoken critic of the Shah's anti-Islamic policies, and the authorities sought to discredit him. They forced him out of retirement and sent him to compete in the 1964 Olympics and the 1966 World Championships. The authorities knew that Takhti's skills had faded and hoped a weak showing would dull the lustre of his fame. The plan failed. Even though he won no medals in those last two tournaments—Medved won both of them—Takhti remains a hero to the Iranians.

The Pahlevan of the World died in a Tehran hotel room in 1968. When the government coroners declared his death a suicide Iranians rioted in the streets. Nobody in Iran believed Takhti took his own life. They believed that the Shah, unable to diminish Takhti's popularity, had murdered him.

My driver led me to the tomb. We stepped over graves littered with snack wrappers, plastic cups and broken bottles of rosewater used to sweeten the gravestones. Takhti's mausoleum was within a gated shed. He lay under a green marble slab beneath a peeling plaster ceiling and a bare lightbulb. Framed portraits of the champion hung on the walls and wrestling photos were pinned to a corkboard. The place looked dusty and unkempt. I expected a grander resting place for one of Iran's greatest heroes.

Then again, Takhti has no shortage of unofficial shrines; the Iranians have hardly forsaken their champion. There are posters of Takhti for sale in nearly every bazaar: images of the wrestler on the medal podium, praying in the mosque, kissing his mother and holding babies. There is a Takhti Stadium in many Iranian cities, and streets and squares around the country bear his name. The Takhti Cup, an annual tournament in Tehran, attracts some of the best wrestlers in the world.

A few months before my return to Iran, another Persian warrior became a hero to the Islamic Republic. At the Olympic Games in Athens, an Iranian judoka caused a diplomatic row when he allegedly refused to compete against an Israeli athlete. Arash Miresmaeili was the featherweight world champion and the flagbearer for the Iranian team at the opening ceremonies. A newspaper in Iran quoted Miresmaeili saying he would not fight the Israeli opponent he drew in the first round. Iran has a long-standing policy of barring its athletes from competing with Israelis, out of sympathy for the Palestinian cause. Miresmaeili denied that he had refused to fight, but was then disqualified from the tournament anyway, when he weighed in more than five kilograms overweight.

Miresmaeili's weight gain was suspicious; no elite athlete would ever show up to the scales that heavy, especially at an Olympic tournament he was expected to win. The Iranians claimed an unstated medical condition kept Miresmaeili from making weight and, unable to prove otherwise, Olympic officials cleared the judoka of wrongdoing. Most suspected that Miresmaeili's failure to make weight was intentional and that the athlete had little choice but to forfeit himself from the tournament at the urging of his government. President Khatami all but confirmed the boycott when he said Miresmaeili's actions were a proud moment in Iranian sport history, and that the judoka would receive the cash prize Iran offered to all its medallists.

I wondered, though, how Miresmaeili felt. Surely a warrior's loyalties lie with physical struggles rather than political ones. He had been robbed of his dream, and I felt sorry for him.

My driver whispered a few prayers at Takhti's tomb, then drove me back into Tehran. When I told him that I was interested in Persian poets as well as wrestlers he asked me what poets I knew.

"I know about Hafez, Ferdosi, Attar . . ."

At the mention of Attar my driver smiled. "Attar is my favourite." Then he lowered his voice and recited Attar's poetry to me until we reached my hotel:

> Do not delude yourself that from a burned heart
> I will discourse with palate and tongue.
> The body is impure, I shall cast it away
> and utter these pure words with soul alone.

I called Jamshid, the Persian beach hippie I had met the previous summer in Babolsar. Since then, he had moved to the capital and e-mailed me that he wanted to get together when I returned to Iran.

"Salaam, Jamshid. It is Marcello. From Canada."

"Marcello? Hello. You are back. How are you?"

"I am fine." I could hear the noise of a party going on in the background. "Where are you?"

"I am at my cousin's wedding. Where are you?"

"I am in Tehran. At a hotel."

"A hotel?" He paused. "Tell me where is the hotel. I will come and get you."

"Jamshid, you don't have to leave a wedding to come see me."

"Yes. I am coming."

I knew better than to argue with him. Within an hour he met me in the hotel lobby. My overprotective hotel manager raised an eyebrow at Jamshid as we greeted each other. Jamshid asked if I wanted to go for a walk, so I joined him in the quiet Tehran streets.

"Marcello, why you did not call when you came to Tehran?"

"I did call you. I called you tonight."

"Why not when you first came? You could stay in my house. You do not have to stay in a hotel."

"Thanks, Jamshid, but I don't mind the hotel. I was only staying for a couple of days anyway."

"I wish you called."

I shrugged at him. "Sorry."

"When will you leave Tehran?"

"Tomorrow morning. I am going to Mazanderan."

Jamshid was quiet for a few moments. It was obvious he was upset. We walked past the late-night street sweepers, men in yellow overalls charged with the Sisyphean task of clearing the streets of trash every night.

Jamshid broke the silence. "Marcello, will you stay at my house tonight?"

"Tonight? I have a hotel room."

"It is okay. You can come. We can get your bag."

"But why? I paid for the room. And it is already eleven o'clock."

"It is not late. Why won't you come?"

"I'll stay with you next time. My flight back to Canada leaves from Tehran so I have to come back here. I will stay with you then, I promise."

"I want you to stay with me tonight. Tomorrow I will drive you to the terminal for Mazanderan. It is close to my house."

"Jamshid . . ."

"Please. I want you to come."

I looked at Jamshid. He was pleading with me. Passing on his invitation felt like an act of cruelty.

"All right. I will come to your house."

He brightened. "Okay. Thank you. We will go get your bag."

We walked back along Lalehzar Street to the hotel. Coloured lights flashed from the windows of the lighting fixture shops, and the neighbourhood cinema was advertising a Farsi-dubbed version of *Kill Bill* called *Beel ra Bekosht.* I didn't know what to make of Jamshid's insistent welcome, but I knew I didn't like it. In Canada his actions would seem like a clumsy attempt at a seduction, and in most of the other places I travelled they would prelude a robbery. I was sure his intentions were neither sexual nor sinister but he made me feel uncomfortable nonetheless. His kindness bordered on coercion.

Jamshid waited in the lobby as I packed up my rucksack. The hotel manager gave me my passport and a disapproving look. We drove in Jamshid's pickup truck to his house in western Tehran. When I stepped out of the truck Jamshid reached over to ensure I locked the door properly. Then he secured an anti-theft bar around the gas pedal. He popped open the hood, exited the truck and checked to make sure he locked the driver's side door. Afterwards, he walked to the front of the truck, reached into the engine and pulled out an ignition cable. He tucked the cable into his pocket and checked both doors a final time.

"Afraid of thieves, Jamshid?"

"Yes," he smiled. "Tehran is bad."

Jamshid lived in the basement of his family's house. He had moved there only recently, and the place was a mess of half-empty boxes. There were piles of books and clothes, and a layer of cassette tapes on the floor. His computer sat on a desk in the corner. The back panel was missing and the electronic innards were exposed.

"I am sorry. It is very busy."

"Busy?"

"Sorry. I mean 'messy.' I am sorry my English. Sit down. I will play you music."

Jamshid was a classically trained musician. He played pretty melodies for me on his dotar and sitar. Then he showed me how to hold his tambur, a shallow drum with a skirt of metal rings similar to a tambourine. I was tired and tapped the skin a few times without much rhythm or enthusiasm. Jamshid got very excited. "Very good! We will play together." He started strumming his dotar but I shook my head and put down the tambur. Jamshid's insistence that I spend the night with him made my mood heavy.

"The tambur is from Kordestan," Jamshid said. "Have you gone there?"

"Not yet. I want to go on this trip."

"Me, also. When you get to Kordestan call me. I will come meet you and we will travel together."

"Thanks, Jamshid, but I prefer to travel alone."

His face fell. "But why? It is much better to travel with me. I can talk Farsi for you."

"Please understand. I like to travel alone. I learn more when I am by myself."

"But I want to travel with you."

"Sorry, Jamshid."

He paused and looked away. I had hurt his feelings again. He took a moment to recover then turned back to me. "Do you like rock and roll?" He lifted a disc from the pile on the floor, wiped it on his shirt and slid it into his computer. Soon the screen showed concert footage of a loud and terrifying metal band. "This is Man O' War. Do you know them?" I shook my head. He handed me a book of lyrics translated into Farsi. The songs had names like "Sign of the Hammer" and "The Demon's Whip." They were filled with medieval violence and references to Norse gods. It was terrible. "Do you like?" Jamshid asked.

"I don't listen to this sort of music much," I said.

Jamshid spent the rest of the night switching from disc to disc trying to find something I might like. It was all death metal. I had never heard of any of the bands, and after an hour of the guitar-driven gore I felt nostalgic for Chris de Burgh.

I looked over at Jamshid's dotar. "How can someone who plays classical Persian music listen to this?"

"I do not know. My teacher says I am sick. Sick in my head."

It was two o'clock before Jamshid turned off the metal and we went to bed. In the morning he fed me tea and hard-boiled eggs for breakfast and drove me to the bus terminal. As he was driving he reached across and rolled down my window for me, as if I shouldn't have to do it myself.

We were nearly at the station when Jamshid said, "Marcello, I want you to stay in Tehran for another night."

"Jamshid, I need to go to Mazanderan."

"You don't need. You can go tomorrow."

"I want to go today."

"But I want you to stay."

"Why?"

"I want to be with you."

I couldn't understand. Jamshid and I were hardly friends. His English was only slightly better than my Farsi, so our conversations were difficult and tiring. I couldn't imagine why he would want to spend time with me at all, much less why he seemed so desperate to do so. This was different from the Persian hospitality I enjoyed the previous year. Jamshid meant well, I am sure, but this was suffocating and oppressive. Worst of all, it forced me to be curt with someone who was only trying to be kind.

At the terminal Jamshid stepped ahead of me and purchased my ticket for me. I tried to protest but it was no use. He handed me my ticket and said, "Have a good trip. You call me when you come to Tehran."

"Yes. I will call. Thank you again for everything."

"I will be waiting," he said. Never did an offer of welcome feel so menacing.

12

MEN OF SOIL AND MYTH

The Persians owe a debt to the demons from the Valley of Light. Early in *Shahnomeh*, the monster Ghu marches a demon army into war against Persia. King Tahumers meets them on the field with a force of brave Persian soldiers. Together, they raise the stink of battle and the bodies of men collide with the demons' horned flesh. Tahumers finds Ghu amid the blood and flames, raises his mace and, with a single strike, dashes Ghu's brains across the ground.

Their leader slain, the demon army falls. Tahumers demands the prisoners die, but the demons beg for clemency. They vow that if they are spared, they will teach the Persians something marvellous. Tahumers agrees. The demons bring the king a box of books, pens and ink, and teach him the art of the written word.

Through the muscles of men, a warrior's mercy and the gift of demons, the poets of Persia were born.

The Nur River carves the Valley of Light from the mountains of Mazanderan. I followed the river to the village of Yush. En route, my driver said the river boasts the second-best-tasting fish in the world. "Only in the Mississippi, in *Amrika*, is there more tasty fish." We passed through the mountains and the freshness of the valley, where men sold squash and honeydew from heaps along the roadside.

The poet Nima Yushij was born in Yush in 1896. Like King Tahumers, young Nima learned to write from a demon. His teacher was the hot-tempered village mullah. The old man used to chase the truant and mischievous Nima through the streets and, upon catching him, tie him to a tree and thrash him with a cane. Were it not for Nima's mother, who used to recite for him the ghazals of Hafez, Nima might have had the poetry beaten out of him and ended up a farmer like his father.

I followed the steep dirt road up from the highway to Nima's childhood home and imagined a young Nima tearing around the corner with his cane-armed tormentor in pursuit. There were no cars in the streets. The gentle gurgle of water in the narrow streetside canals replaced the rattle of traffic. Nima's house was being restored into a museum. The heavy wooden doors were open and the rooms were filled with workmen splattered with white paint and plaster. A little man appeared to collect an admission fee, then vanished out the door.

Nima is buried in the courtyard beneath a simple wooden pavilion. The grave is a new addition to the house; the poet's remains were moved here from Tehran in 1994, thirty-five years after his death. I wove my way around the scaffolding to a room containing a collection of Nima's pens, inkwells and notebooks. Black-and-white photos showed the poet hunting, fishing and riding his horse in the valley. There was something whimsical about Nima's fat moustache and the storm of grey hair that ringed his otherwise bald head, but in the photos his face was always severe.

Nima's poetry, too, was serious. He wrote during the early days of the Pahlavi dynasty. The poet saw the reign of Reza Shah as a time of gloom and his verses were filled with pessimism and alarm:

It is night
A night of deep darkness.
On a branch of the old fig tree
A frog croaks without cease,
Predicting a storm, a deluge,
and I am drowned in fear.

Nima's poetry, though, is renowned more for its innovation than its themes. The poet transferred his youthful rebellion to the page. He was the first of the Persian scribes to abandon the centuries-old forms and write in free verse. For this, he is the father of modern Persian poetry.

There was no place to stay in Yush. The mosaferkhune planned for pilgrims to Nima's grave was not yet built. The workmen at the museum directed me to a private house across the lane. "They might have room for you." I thought of another of Nima's verses as I knocked on the door.

Standing before the village,
a single man,
knapsack on his back, hand on the knocker, murmurs
"Worry over this lot
ruins sleep in my tearful eyes."

A woman named Mahtab welcomed me inside. Her headscarf barely contained her henna-orange hair. I followed her into her courtyard and watched her daughters scatter to find cover for their heads. In a corner, a man tossed fistfuls of seed from a tin can to a flock of pigeons. He was Mahtab's husband, Amir. I sat with him until Mahtab delivered a tray of tea and biscuits.

Mahtab glanced at my feet. "I like your socks," she said. "They are thick and would be good for my husband. His feet are always cold and he gets sick."

I looked at Amir. He shrugged and nodded.

"I have an extra pair, if you want them," I said.

"That would be very nice."

"They are very dirty." Her daughters, who were eavesdropping, giggled.

"I can wash them," Mahtab said.

After tea I spent the afternoon walking through the village and the river valley. Ordered rows of trees, thin as pencils and tall, lined the Nur River. The reddish mountains loomed over everything. Nima's father once coaxed life from these riverside fields, and Nima himself used to drive his father's sheep through the valley, but the pastoral life did not suit Nima. He spoke of its monotony and the ignorance of the shepherds who populated the mountains. Nima preferred Tehran, and sought out "the cracks in the cities of light." Still, the beauty of the mountains was not lost on him. Nima refers to the landscape in many of his poems, and called the Nur Valley Iran's Champs-Élysées.

At night, I joined the family for dinner in one of their salons. The night outside was cold, and an electric heater warmed the room. Mahtab fed me squares of halva and dates flecked with coconut before a dinner of chicken and aubergine. A Turkish soap opera on the television claimed my hosts' attention, and against one wall, a huge pot of khoresht bubbled over a gas burner for the next day's guests. Mahtab periodically lifted the lid to stir the stew and the room filled with lamb- and lime-scented steam. The aroma infused the entire house and later, as I lay under heavy blankets, I dreamt of lamb stew.

I learned the previous year that every region of Iran has its own stereotype. Most, like the assertion that Qazvini men are pederasts, are rather nasty. Rasht is typecast as a sleepy backwater city, where the men are obedient imbeciles and their wives notorious sluts. I put little stock in these notions, and saw no evidence of them. Instead I found a city whose nocturnal streets were a happy chaos. Only Esfahan, and perhaps Tehran, were more interesting after dark.

Once the sun set, crowds of Iranians filled the narrow sidewalks in the town centre. The kebabi restaurants shut their doors and streetside grills offered skewers of lamb meat and kidney. Men crowded carts to buy tiny glasses of tea, or dishes of vinegar-tart fava beans. The open-air bazaar was jammed. Peddlers hawked cheap shirts and underwear from piles on the ground. Booksellers laid used volumes in even rows along the walkway. Men stood in front of fresh apricots and oranges and sang songs about their garlic. There were shopfronts loaded with a half-dozen varieties of pistachios, and trays of fish reddened with tart sumac. Women rummaged through piles of bras, men swarmed the cigarette sellers and children begged for plastic toys with flashing red lights. Everywhere was the smell of fish and tobacco, the noise of shouting vendors and blaring car horns.

I met Armin at one of the tea carts. He was about twenty years old and was thrilled to meet a Western traveller. He spoke to me in English. "I am tourist also!" he shouted. "Last year I go Thailand. You go Thailand?"

"No, not yet."

"Thailand very good. One month only fucking!"

"Pardon me?"

"Women Asia. Women Russia. Very much fucking!"

"That's great. Congratulations."

"Yes! One month only fucking! After one month, police take me. I go prison nine months."

I couldn't help but laugh. "You were in a Thai prison?"

"Yes, yes. Nine months. I have passport is fake."

"How was prison?"

"Very bad. Thailand prison very dirty."

"Yeah, I'll bet."

"But Thailand very good, good, good! Very much fucking!"

I declined Armin's invitation to drink araq with him and his friends. Instead I ate a dish of saffron ice cream in a cake shop. The woman behind the counter asked me where I was from, then whether I was married. I sat at the back of the shop and watched Rashti girls share cookies and conversation.

I returned to my hotel room buzzed from the tea and sugar and abruptly lost a contact lens. I spent two hours on my hands and knees searching for it but found only dust. I must have dropped it down the sink. Three days in Iran and already I was relegated to my glasses. So much for my Persian disguise.

I travelled west from Rasht, through the plastic orange palm trees that decorated the roundabouts in Somehsara, and into the more authentic pastures of Gilan Province. I was heading to Masal to seek out *gileh mardi* wrestling. My taxi was a battered Mercedes-Benz sedan. The fenders flaked with rust, the windshield was cracked and exhaust fumes leaked into the peeling interior. The car's luxury had decayed away years before. Still, the Benz retained a sense of morose nobility, like the venerable men in crumpled suits I sat beside in the tea houses.

My driver, though, was less dignified. "You are my new friend from Canada!" he shouted in English. "Canada very nice! Masal very nice! Gilan very nice! English very nice language!" He handed me a piece of paper from the glovebox. "Please! Write you name! Hurry up!"

I wrote my name. The driver grabbed the paper from me and examined it closely, trying to sound out the letters while the taxi swerved over the highway. The passengers in the back scolded him to watch the road. He read my name aloud about twelve times, then sang the alphabet song, ending with ". . . now I know my ABC's. Next time won't you sing with me."

Once I arrived in Masal I followed my driver's directions to a varzeshga. Masal seemed a typical Iranian small town. Pretty, but in a nondescript way, with tall trees shading the streets from the late-morning sun and workmen clanking on engines in the ubiquitous mechanic shops. I would see so many towns like this they would blend together, and I'd discern them only through the people I met there.

I met Iraj at the centre and asked him about gileh mardi. "Gileh mardi is the wrestling of the Talesh people," he said. "In our language, *gileh mardi* means 'man of the soil' because we usually wrestle on the ground. You must come back tomorrow night. There will be a practice at the varzeshga. I will meet you here, but now I must go home to take my lunch. Please, I would like you to come with me."

"No, thank you," I said, placing my hand over my heart the way Iranians do.

"It is no trouble. You are my guest."

"You are kind, but no."

"Please, you are welcome."

"Okay. Thank you." I smiled. I had missed ta'arof during my year away.

Iraj's house was like nearly all the homes I'd seen in Iran. Red carpets laid on the cement floor. There were cushions instead of furniture, and the whitewashed walls were nearly bare. A stuffed hawk shed its feathers next to a bouquet of silk flowers on top of the television. Iraj's tiny wife prepared a meal of grilled fish and rice while Iraj showed off his newborn son. Iraj's mother watched us from the corner, smiling at her grandchild and tucking back the strands of hair that fled her headscarf. Later, as Iraj and I shared tea and grapes, his mother napped in the adjacent room. I could see the soles of her feet, orange with fading henna, through the crack of the door.

The next day I arrived in Masal an hour before I was due to meet Iraj. I passed the time in a small tea house near the main square. The place was full of old Taleshi men with dusty blazers and deep wrinkles. Too dignified to fawn over a foreigner, they greeted me briefly, then returned to their conversations. I could not understand the language they spoke in, but I imagined them grumbling about the government, passing along gossip or relaying football scores.

Iraj was already at the sports centre when I arrived. He brought a friend with him, Hossein, who studied English at university. Hossein was so happy to have an English-speaking visitor he was vibrating. The words tumbled out of him. "Hello. Welcome to Masal. I am very happy to see you visit our city and show interest in our local, traditional wrestling. I am at your service. Please, you can call me any time. I would have met you yesterday, but, you see, I had to write an examination and, as you know, one must prepare if one is to do well. If one is to succeed. Yes? You will see that my English is not—how do you say?—without its flaws. I am learning day by day, but, you see, in Masal there are very few foreigners to practise with. Last year a German man came here. He was an anthropologist and spoke English. But his English, too, was not perfect. His name was Carlson, if I remember correctly . . ."

As we walked into the gymnasium about forty wrestlers jogged on the stinky wrestling mats that lay over half the floor. A karate team kicked and shrieked at the air on the other side of the gym. The wrestlers were about to begin a freestyle practice, but a coach selected two men to wrestle gileh mardi. He cleared the mats and the wrestlers stepped forward, brushed the mat with their fingers, then touched their lips and forehead like the bachoukheh wrestlers I'd seen in Mashhad. Then they turned towards the stands and jumped in place three times. Each wrestler tried to jump higher than his opponent. "They jump because they want to be closer to God," Iraj said. "The best wrestlers love Allah."

Next the two men walked towards each other and met at the centre of the mat. They hunched forward and each extended his left hand towards the other, palm down. The gesture was like a strange, tentative salute. I would learn that it signalled the beginning of a ritual unique to gileh mardi, a contest that preceded the actual wrestling and set the mood for the match. The wrestlers' right hands, meanwhile, hardened into fists at their sides and swung back and forth like pendulums. The first stage of the match would be a fight with right hands only. They circled each other on the mat, glaring into each other's eyes, until one man launched a punch at his rival's head. The strike was not a jab but a straight-armed swinging punch meant to strike with the side of his fist, the soft zone where the index finger curls inside the thumb. The defender threw up his hands to block the blow and caught his rival's punch just as it was about to connect with his temple.

The punch startled me. There were no such attacks in the wrestling styles I knew. Iraj was excited. "You see why gileh mardi is special? They hit like this." He smacked the side of his fist into his palm. "It is not like boxing. Not hard with knuckles. It is like farming. The Taleshi farmers swing their arms like this when they harvest rice. Men always wrestle gileh mardi after the harvest so they are in good practice."

Both wrestlers returned to their crouch, never breaking their stare, left hands still extended, right hands swinging next to them with the menace of loaded guns. They exchanged rice-harvest roundhouses, but the slow punches were easy enough to defend against and neither man landed a clean blow. To inflict pain, though, was not their purpose. The punches were not meant to do harm. They were meant to tire out an opponent and, most of all, inspire his fear of getting hit. This was a ritual of intimidation.

As a freestyle wrestler, I was taught to watch my opponent's hips during a match. All manoeuvres start from here and a seasoned wrestler can predict an attack by reading even a slight shift of balance. But during gileh mardi's opening salvoes, the wrestlers focused on each other's eyes. The progress of their psychological battle was written in their gaze. As the men continued to fight, I watched as one man's eyes hardened, daring the other to throw the next punch. His glare taunted his opponent, and announced that he, by bravery and force of will, was winning. His rival's eyes widened, red-rimmed and fearful, with a glare that confessed he had had enough. He was tired of throwing punches and didn't want to risk getting hit. He grabbed his opponent's left hand with his own to signal the end of the fisticuffs and the beginning of the actual wrestling. It was an act of surrender.

The two men started to wrestle. They attempted leg takedowns and shoulder throws. The wrestling itself was unremarkable and no different from the loucho bouts I'd seen in Babolsar the year before. Eventually, the quicker of the two men, the man with the harder eyes, scored a single-leg takedown that brought his opponent's knee to the ground. This was enough to win the match. The men shook hands, kissed each other on the cheeks and left the mat.

The coach approached me as the freestyle practice was beginning. He looked at my ears. "You are a wrestler," he said. "Would you like to try gileh mardi?"

"No, thank you," I said and I was happy he did not insist. I didn't want to exchange punches with anyone. I wasn't afraid of getting hurt. In my days as a wrestler, I endured fractured fingers, broken ribs and popped ankles. It was the idea of being struck on the head that terrified me. I may be a wrestler, but I am no man of the soil. I don't have the guts for that kind of violence.

13

Golestan

I watched a spice merchant at the Monday bazaar in Bandar-e Turkoman. Sacks surrounded him and each was unrolled to free its captive aroma: dried rose petals, barberries, musky turmeric as brilliant as the sun. The man had a shocking white beard and Asian-angled Turkmani eyes. There was a brass scale at his knee and a heavy stone mill stained with spice.

A traveller remembers what he wants. That is his privilege. I won't remember the stalls selling plastic housewares or the pestering beeps of Chinese-made alarm clocks. The banal does not linger. I will recall the women with floral headscarves, the girls in narrow dresses, and the spice man who silently weighed his garlic, bulb by bulb, as I fixed his face in memory.

The previous day, I had travelled east into Golestan Province. I made my way to Bandar-e Turkoman to see the bazaar and to visit Ashouredeh Island, a small disc of land a few kilometres out in the Caspian Sea. Ashouredeh was known for its natural beauty and traditional villages, but when I stepped off the speedboat I found the place populated only with trash and flies. I bought sour cherry leather and pistachios at a small shop ("Nobody lives on Ashouredeh," the shopkeeper told me, wondering why I'd come) and took lunch at the island's only restaurant. The sturgeon kebab nearly made the trip worthwhile.

I returned to the provincial capital, Gorgan. It was dusk, the bread-buying hours. In Iran, bakery lines and the smell of fresh sangak bread straddle the Persian sunset. The queues in front of bakery windows herald the night's approach as much as the fading light. Men and women stand in segregated lines, pile hot slabs of bread in their arms and hurry home to prepare dinner. The bakers prepare sangak on a bed of smooth black pebbles that form dimples on the loaves. The pebbles lie discarded on the ground beneath the bakery windows and are trod upon by the sundown clientele, but Iranians know to watch for the rare stowaway stone that stays lodged in the bread.

I found a room in a friendly mosaferkhune near the bazaar. Ali, the manager, had lived and studied in England. We spoke about wars with Iraq—Iran's, America's—about the uneasy marriage of religion and politics, and about beer.

"Please tell me, do you drink alcohol in Canada?"

"Sometimes."

"Do you like lager?"

"Yes, very much. I would like one right now."

"Yes, me too. But it is illegal in Iran. It is against Islam."

"I know."

"The government wants us to be good Muslims, you know. To follow all the rules of the religion. What do you think about our government?"

"I don't think the government can make you a good Muslim. Only God knows what is in your head."

"I think you are right. Tell me, how many lagers do you drink? How many pints?"

"After three I am in trouble."

"Really? When I was in England I used to drink six, seven or eight."

To feed another bad habit I went in search of a qalyun to smoke, but I couldn't find a tea house in Gorgan that offered water pipes. Nightly cups of saffron ice cream became my surrogate vice. Each night, after two ice creams and, often, a pound of pomegranates, I retired to my thin mattress at the mosaferkhune. There I listened to the BBC News on my short-wave radio and clapped at mosquitoes before going to sleep. I killed the slow, blood-swollen pests against the wall, leaving gruesome smears of insect parts and my own blood like hunting trophies.

In the eleventh century, a prince, poet and scholar named Shams al-Ma'ali Qabus erected a giant phallic tribute to himself. The Mil-e Kavus is the tallest brick tower in the world and stands fifty-five metres over the town of Gonbad-e Kavus like an earth-toned rocket. The construction of the tower turned out to be well timed; an assassin murdered Qabus only a few years after the structure was complete. Qabus's remains were placed in a glass coffin that hung inside the top of the tower, where the morning sun bathed his body through a small opening on the east side of the tower. The coffin disappeared long ago. Nobody knows where it went. The tower was empty when I visited; only a few birds and some marvellous acoustics remained.

Gonbad-e Kavus sits on the southern edge of the Turkman Sahra, Iran's most northerly desert and the home of a Turkmani wrestling style known as *alish*. I asked about alish wrestling at a cultural centre near the university. The men at the centre filled me with tea and macaroons, then instructed a driver to bring me to a varzeshga where I was ushered to the desk of a local wrestling official. He told me that alish wrestling bouts were usually held as part of Turkmani wedding celebrations. "Wait a minute," he said. He picked up his phone and spoke for a few minutes in a Turkmani dialect.

Then he hung up and smiled at me. "There is a wedding tomorrow. It is far away in the desert in a village called Hizler. You are invited."

My guide picked me up from my hotel the next morning. Nadir was a pudgy Inuit-looking man who walked with such a severe limp he seemed perpetually falling over. Before heading to Hizler we stopped for drinks and cigarettes. I had slept late that morning and hadn't had time for breakfast. I could feel the orange soda burning in my stomach as we sped out of town.

The Turkman Sahra widened into a coffee-hued expanse before us. Sandy hills sprawled over the landscape like lazing lions. Camels grazed at the roadside, moving in the half-dopey, half-elegant gait that camels have. Turkmani men sped past on motorcycles with their wives sitting behind them. Their long, narrow dresses meant they had to ride sideways on the saddle. The women sat still, held their hands in their laps and watched the scenery roll past as if at a cinema. I strained to see their faces through the greasy passenger window.

A sand track led off the highway to the village of Hizler. There was no sign; somehow Nadir knew where to turn. The village was a sparse collection of low brick houses. Camels were tied to skeletal trees in the spaces between the buildings and donkeys wandered freely but aimlessly. The wedding lent colour and clamour to the austere setting. Women moved in large noisy groups and attended to bridal errands while children buzzed around their legs. Fat, nervous sheep shuffled on their tethers. Guests spilled out of arriving cars. I loved that wrestling led me to such places.

Nadir brought me to a house where the village elders had gathered. About twenty men sat cross-legged before a plastic tablecloth finishing their tea. They slid over to make room for me and a servant delivered a small pot of tea in front of my knees. The men wore dusty blazers and buttoned-up shirts with no ties. Some had trim white beards and white turbans. Others wore fedoras and looked like gangsters from old movies. When I sat, a few of the men raised their hand to their breast in greeting. Others offered me nearly imperceptible nods. My arrival, though, drew no smiles from these venerable old men.

Until they reach a certain age, Iranian men are wonderfully gregarious. Young men greet each other with happy noise, and even direction-giving comes with a flailing, wild-armed dance. Drivers lean far out of their windows to holler at friends on the sidewalks. They joke and laugh, and exchange mock slaps at the taxi parks. Their lavish gestures would put my Italian relatives to shame.

But age seems to replace rowdiness with restraint. Elderly Iranian men are quiet and stately. They have economy in their movements. Every click of prayer beads. Every stroke of a beard. Every lump of sugar lifted from its bowl. Each motion is slow and deliberate. Theirs is an unhurried nobility. I felt no lack of welcome from the unsmiling men. I knew that their slight gestures held genuine salutations.

After we finished our tea an albino man named Abdul volunteered to be my guide and led me out of the house. We passed a group of giggling girls in pretty dresses, and a row of cauldrons half buried in hot coals and bubbling with lamb khoresht for the wedding feast. Abdul and I followed the crowds to a clearing where a white circle was painted in chalk on the soft ground.

Spectators already started to gather around the perimeter of the circle. The wrestlers hid behind a bus and changed into football-style jerseys and rolled-up trousers. An announcer shouted introductions into a loudspeaker on a small stage. Abdul introduced me to the officials, who considered me an honoured guest and gave me a place to sit on the stage. Abdul told the announcer my name was "Mister Marcello" and I was introduced via the loudspeaker as "Lister Macheh az Canada."

Soon, nearly a hundred spectators gathered to watch the matches. Most were men. The village women seemed preoccupied with wedding duties, though a few watched from a distance, sitting in the shade against the wall of a nearby house.

The announcer started to speak in low measured tones into the microphone. I turned to Abdul. "Is this poetry?" I asked. He nodded. "From Ferdosi?"

"No. It is Makhtumgoli." He put his hand on his heart. "A Turkmani poet. I love him too much."

> Only one with compassion in his heart is truly brave.
> The brave man's heart must be open, and he must be wise.
> In the open field be as shy as the crow;
> Appropriate virtue is what is needed:
> The brave man must go into battle like a lion,
> And behave as cunningly as the fox with the enemy.

The first two wrestlers stepped into the circle accompanied by a referee. One of the men raised his arms and the referee held a small white brick against the small of his back. The other man wrapped a long strip of cloth, called a shawl belt, around his opponent's waist, making sure to pass it over the brick. Then he rammed his head into his rival's chest and pulled on the two loose ends of the belt to tighten it. He wrenched on the shawl over and over, jerking the air out of his rival's lungs and nearly yanking him off his feet. Both men knew that the tighter the belt, the better the hold and the greater the pressure on the lungs. The match had not started but the battle had begun. Even before the whistle blows the wrestler is engaged.

When he decided the belt was tight enough, the second wrestler knotted it in front of his opponent's waist. The referee then took the brick away, giving the belt some slack and some relief to the man's compressed body. The wrestler inhaled; he was already short of breath.

Then it was his turn to tie on his adversary's belt. He butted his head into the other man's belly, and tried to tie the air out of him.

When both wrestlers were belted they took their position in the centre of the circle. Keeping their legs straight, they bent their bodies forward and each rested the top of his head against his opponent's shoulders. They turned their wrists into the shawl belts and gripped them tight. I recognized this position from the sixteenth-century *Shahnomeh* manuscripts at the Reza Abbasi Museum. Rostam and Sohrab held on to each other's belts as they fought. The wrestling of myth was made flesh in the Turkmani dust.

The referee ensured that both men were securely entangled before tapping them on their backs to begin the match. The announcer leaned over and touched my shoulder. "*Doh rayziz on,*" he said.

"I'm sorry," I said, "I don't speak Turkmani."

"Is English! *Doh rayziz on!*"

I thought for a moment. "'The race is on'?"

"Yes, yes! *Doh rayziz on!*"

The men did not move. They stood bound to each other, breathing hard, their fists tight and white. But they were wrestling, slowly exerting pressure with the belts and daring the other to strike first. The crowd was patient and wise enough to appreciate the nuance in the men's battle. I was used to wrestling as a crash of muscle. This was the opposite. These warriors did not collide; they were already fused. In nearly all the wrestling I'd seen in Iran, men were bound to each other. For them, wrestling meant emerging, dividing the single mass of flesh into two men: the victor and the vanquished.

Suddenly, one wrestler lunged forward, kicking up a puff of dirt, and heaved his rival off the ground by his belt. The crowd could sense a throw was coming and started to cheer. The lifted man struggled to keep his feet beneath him. His attacker was strong. His breath pulsed out of him in short bursts and his face went red with strain. I could see the belt dig into his wrists. He turned his rival's back towards the ground and they both crashed into the dirt. The man lay on his defeated foe until the referee helped them untangle. Both men stood and swept the dust from their shirts and faces as the crowd roared.

When the winner had received his prize, a bundle of cash wrapped in a blue handkerchief, he walked over to an old man in a white beard and a checkered turban who sat on the perimeter. The wrestler bowed and handed the old man the money.

There were a dozen bouts that morning. Two of the wrestlers were celebrities, members of the national alish team, and they received the loudest cheers when they stepped into the ring. Both dispatched their opponent with impressive ease. Every match concluded with a cloud of dust and two wrestlers lying in a heap of flesh, and each time the victor donated his winnings to a village elder. Nobody kept the money. "It shows respect for the old men," Abdul explained.

During the competition men patrolled the perimeter of the circle offering refreshment from a plastic cup and a bucket of water. Someone brought Abdul and me a bottle of chilled dugh made from sour camel's milk. Abdul was thrilled but I grimaced when I tasted it. "You don't like?" he asked.

"I don't like dugh," I said.

"But it is from a camel. It is the best." He was bewildered. Apparently, camel dugh was the champagne of salted sour milk.

Once the official bouts were finished, the wrestlers boarded a minibus parked nearby, and headed to another wedding in another village, where they would compete again later that afternoon. Now, two pairs of village children were invited to wrestle in the circle. The first two boys were about eight years old. They struggled in the centre of the ring until one fell into the dirt. The loser wept and rushed away before shaking his opponent's hand, and his unmanly tantrum earned rebukes from his father. Then a tiny pair of two-year-old twins were encouraged to wrestle. Following their father's instructions the boys held on to each other's waistband and stepped into the ring. The crowd laughed and hollered advice, but neither boy had any idea what was going on. They walked around the circle in their befuddled embrace until one tripped over his own feet and onto the ground. Everyone cheered. Someone handed the winner a banknote. The boy stared at it for a second then put it in his mouth.

All morning the bridegroom, who looked about seventeen, watched the bouts from a small table at the edge of the circle. His tidy suit and blue tie seemed out of place amid the dusty men who tussled in his honour. At first it was incongruous to me that the joining of a husband and wife was being celebrated with the combat of strongmen. But perhaps the wrestlers were meant to be an example to the groom as he entered manhood. The wrestlers were strong and robust. They respected their rivals and were charitable with their winnings. Each victor was modest. Each loser was gracious. These noble warriors embodied a masculine ideal, and there are worse role models for a young, nervous groom.

Makhtumgoli, the poet, wept when the camel slipped. The Persian bandits who stole his possessions and loaded them onto the camel were deft thieves, but their beast was clumsy.

It stumbled as it crossed over the Etrak River. The poet stood witness as his manuscripts spilled into the fast waters. He wrote:

> Making my dear life lost to all that's good,
> An evil fate wrought awesome sacrilege,
> Hurling the books I'd written to the flood,
> To leave me bookless with my grief and rage.

It was dusk when I crossed the same river to Makhtumgoli's tomb in the village of Ak Tokay, and the sunset spilled orange over the landscape. Two hundred years had passed since the jealous river swallowed Makhtumgoli's books, but his poetry remained the revered and undying voice of the Turkomen people. Makhtumgoli's poetry outlived the river that once claimed it; these days, the Etrak is nearly dry.

I hired a driver, Suliman, in Gonbad-e Kavus to take me to Makhtumgoli's tomb. Suliman drove slowly for an Iranian. His prudence was annoying. I'd become too used to flying along Iranian highways at perilous speeds. After half an hour Suliman pulled the car off the highway near an isolated roadside shop. He opened the hood and fiddled with the engine. I hadn't noticed that the car was labouring, but Suliman turned to me and said it would not make it all the way to Ak Tokay.

We returned to the car and drove into a nearby village. I thought Suliman was looking for a mechanic shop. Instead we stopped in front of a telephone office. I waited in the car while Suliman made a call. He returned a few minutes later. "What is going on?" I asked.

"The car is bad."

"Yes, but who did you call?"

"My brother-in-law. He has a new French car. A Peugeot. Iranian cars are very bad. He is coming in half an hour."

We drove back to the roadhouse to wait for the brother-in-law. The air was cool inside the mud-walled shop. Three teenage boys sold cigarettes and snacks to highway travellers. I sat at one of the metal tables, ate pistachios and watched Tom and Jerry cartoons on the tiny black-and-white television.

A half hour passed. Then an hour. I asked Suliman when the car was coming. He told me right away. Two hours went by before Suliman decided to call his brother-in-law again. He suggested I wait in the shop while he drove back into the village to make the call. "I will be right back," he said.

While he was gone three carloads of wedding guests arrived at the shop. They came in Paykans and pickup trucks decorated with plastic flowers. I could hear their approach from up the highway. Drivers blared their horns and men leaned out of the windows to point camcorders backwards at the happy caravan. When they stopped everyone tumbled out of the cars and filled the shop with ruckus. The children were the most excited. They fluttered from back seats like noisy angels and were eager for colas. Men bought single cigarettes, women tore open bags of potato chips and Iranian Cheetos, little boys in new shirts blew bubbles in their sodas with straws while their sisters laughed. They spoke Turkmani, a language with a gentle warble that made everyone sound happily intoxicated.

Their rest stop was brief. The flash flood of joy washed over the shop then flowed back into the cars. Engines revved and faded. Only the flotsam of candy wrappers and half-finished pop bottles remained. The quiet of the surrounding desert filled the empty space.

I hoped that the smiles of the wedding guests would lighten my mood, but I was getting impatient. Suliman had been gone for nearly an hour, and his Peugeot brother-in-law had not arrived. The boys at the roadhouse were kind. "You must be hungry," one said. He gave me a plate of khoresht and rice, leftovers from his lunch. I was starving and grateful.

Finally Suliman returned. "Where did you go?" I asked.

"To call my brother-in-law. I told you."

"You have been gone over an hour."

"Yes. He is coming."

"You said that three hours ago."

"He is coming now."

"Suliman, it is getting late. It will be dark soon."

"It is not late. Ak Tokay is only one hour away."

"But we have no car."

"He is coming."

Thirty minutes later a shiny blue Peugeot pulled up to the roadhouse. The driver, Amir, blinked at the sun through thick glasses. "Are you ready to go?" he asked. Suliman left his taxi parked at the roadhouse and we set off to Ak Tokay with no sense of urgency.

The highway snaked into the badlands of the Turkman Sahra. We passed steep, square-cut cliffs. Hills curved across the landscape like women's bodies. We could see Makhtumgoli's monument as we crossed the Etrak River. Its four tall pillars and white dome stood strong and immense against the earth-toned landscape. The structure was unadorned. There were no intricate mosaics or turquoise domes. Instead, the monument drew its drama from its dimensions and the starkness of its locale.

When we arrived at the tomb I knelt before it and placed my fingers on the gravestone. Makhtumgoli and his father, another poet, lie side by side under plain marble slabs. The two men were as close in life as in death. Makhtumgoli referred to his father as his "Qaaba," the stone at the centre of Mecca's shrine.

The Turkomen call Makhtumgoli "the Bestower of Happiness" but the poet's life overflowed with heartbreak. He was born in 1733 and trained to be a silversmith and leather-worker. In his youth, Makhtumgoli fell in love with a clever dark-haired beauty named Mengli and vowed that he would marry her, but when he returned from his studies he found that her father, a local pahlevan, had forced her to marry someone else. Makhtumgoli eventually married another woman, but the union was devoid of love: he remained devoted to Mengli. Makhtumgoli found brief joy in the birth of his two sons, but both died when they were still children.

Makhtumgoli's misery echoed the plight of the Turkomen people. In the poet's time, tribal strife made the Turkomen vulnerable to invasion and plunder. Sadness stained Makhtumgoli's poetry. He wrote of his sons' death, the wretchedness of old age and the pain that comes from love.

> Swept on, I gained the shores of love, shipwrecked—
>   so null
> Real and unreal were hurricanes within my skull.
> I fell exhausted, lost in wonderment.
> When love unsheathed its dagger, yes, I caught its blade!
> Love stripped me naked, left me stranded without shade.

It was dark by the time we left the village. A few kilometres from Ak Tokay, Amir braked suddenly. There was a camel in the middle of the highway. As Amir shouted and blared his horn the animal plodded off the road at its own unhurried pace. "These camels are very dangerous," Amir said, but I couldn't help smiling. When Makhtumgoli died, his devotees carried his body to the Turkman Sahra on the back of a white camel. In the glare of Amir's headlights, our camel was gleaming white.

14

On Azeri Slopes

"You speak Farsi very well," said my taxi driver as we pulled into Tabriz.

"I am learning. It is a beautiful language."

"Farsi is sweet," he said. "You speak it very well."

"You flatter me."

"No. It is true. I thought you were Iranian."

He dropped me at the hotel. "How much?" I asked.

"Nothing. You are my guest."

"Thank you. How much?"

"Nothing!"

"Many thanks. How much?"

"One thousand!"

I raised my eyebrow at him.

"Okay. Five hundred."

I handed him the bill, checked into my hotel and went in search of a tea house. The sidewalk on Ferdosi Street was being repaired and I had to step around the broken pavement onto the road. So much of Iran was under construction. Every day I dodged construction pits and stepped beneath scaffolding. All this work might have indicated economic health, but nothing I saw ever seemed complete. Concrete skeletons of unfinished buildings were everywhere and many looked as if they had been hastily abandoned by their work crews. Wheelbarrows lay tipped over on their sides. Cement mixers sat and yawned.

I walked past a shop selling only lemons and lemon juice, and paused to breathe in the powerful scent of citrus. Afterwards I found a humble tea house near a traffic circle. I chose a table and chair rather than sit on one of the takhts; I was still uncomfortable sitting cross-legged, even after all my months in Iran. Around me men with wet coughs conversed with lumps of sugar in their teeth. One man sat alone on the takht just across from me. He wore a crumpled suit, a blue shirt buttoned to the top and a white skullcap. His black leather shoes sat on the floor in front of his takht. I watched as he sipped his tea and pinched his cigarette between his thumb and index finger. The proprietor swept the crumbs off the adjacent takht with a short wicker broom. When he was finished he brought me a glass of tea. He looked at my ears and asked, "*Koshti giri?*" I nodded. He gripped my bicep and raised his eyebrows, pretending to be impressed.

Back home, wrestling was a sport few people understood and even fewer cared about. I endured countless jokes about homoeroticism—"You like rolling on the ground with half-naked guys?"—and had to explain how my sport was unrelated to the body-slamming spectacles that pollute the North American sports networks. In Iran, though, I felt proud of my years on the mat. My cauliflower ears meant I was part of a noble fraternity. I was honoured by honourable men.

I left the tea house and walked to the Masjed-e Kabud, the Blue Mosque of Tabriz. There were no poets or pahlevans there. No bearded men to honour. Still, the place had an air of graceful resilience about it. Built in the fifteenth century, the mosque was destroyed by an earthquake in 1779 and lay in ruins for two hundred years. Rebuilding began in 1979, and the restoration is ongoing. I passed through the great cracked portal into the sanctuary where men mixed plaster and pushed wheelbarrows. The walls leaned against crutches of scaffolding. Patches of broken mosaic made blue tattoos on the bare brick flesh. The mosque seemed an old warrior proud of his scars.

The Maqbarat-ol Shoara, or Poets' Tomb, stands atop a hill beside a park north of the Quri River. The modern monument is a series of pale stone arches, and a stairwell curves into an underground chamber where the remains of fifty poets, artists and scholars are interred. Many of them had been dead for centuries, but were moved there when the mausoleum was built in 1988 after the death of the renowned Tabrizi poet Mohammad Hossein Shahriyar.

It was not hard to see that Shahriyar is the most revered member of this college of the dead. While pressed-bronze portraits depict the other men in the tomb—each in turban and beard and indistinguishable from the others—Shahriyar stares down from a large painted canvas. The eyes beneath his angled brows are fierce and intelligent, his forehead ridged by a frown.

Shahriyar was born in a tiny Azeri village called Khoshkaveh in 1906. His father sent him to medical school but Shahriyar quit before completing his degree. Some say he grew bored with medicine, but a more poetic account has the scribe abandoning his studies to follow the woman he loved to Khorasan. He was a renowned poet by the time he returned, the first Iranian poet to produce significant work in the Azeri language. Shahriyar is called the saviour of Azeri in much the same way as Ferdosi is said to have saved Farsi. The poet's death was an occasion of great sorrow.

I browsed the small bookstall in the chamber. A bookseller sat trapped behind a huge table laid with volumes of poetry. We talked about Shahriyar, as recitations of his poetry haunted the chamber from small black speakers. I asked the man how Shahriyar died. "He was an old man," he said. "Eighty-two years. Also, he was addicted to opium. You can visit his home, if you like. It is a museum now. In the town centre."

I went back across the river and found Shahriyar's tiny apartment. There was nothing to distinguish the place from the other houses on the street, and the inside was unremarkable. Framed photos of Shahriyar hung on the walls. The poet's books and pens lay in glass cases and his sitar rested in a corner. Two couches and a television, each labelled smartly in Farsi, sat in the roped-off living room. That this ordinary apartment was now a museum proved the importance of the man who had lived here.

I shared tea with the two men who ran the museum. They told me that Shahriyar was not an opium addict, but he was fond of marijuana. "The marijuana kept him warm on cold winter nights," one of the men said.

"That is why we smoke it in Canada," I offered. The man laughed and handed me a thin volume of Shahriyar's poetry as a gift. It was an English translation of the poet's masterwork, *Hail Heydar Baba.* The verses describe the rural landscape where Shahriyar was born and are filled with pastoral beauty: rising partridges, sweetish plums, and the noble toil of farmers and their wives.

> Heydar Baba, when the thunder resounds across the skies,
> When floods roar down the mountainsides,
> And the girls line up to watch it rushing by,
> Send my greetings to the tribesmen and the village folk
> And remember me and my name once more.

I left Shahriyar's house and made for the tourism office near the bazaar to make inquiries about extending my visa.

The man at the desk greeted me with: "Hello. Welcome. Can I help you? My name is Nasser Khan. I speak eight languages. I have worked here for fifteen years. I am on page 205 of *Lonely Planet.* You have *Lonely Planet?*"

"Yes, I do."

"Give it to me. I will show you my name. Page 205."

"I don't have it with me."

"No? Why not? You should carry it with you always."

"Actually, I don't think it is very good."

Mr. Khan was taken aback. I'd trampled on his holy book. "No. It is very good. Very good. Maybe sometimes the prices are wrong."

I asked him about the procedures for extending my visa in Tabriz. Mr. Khan gave me the same information that I already read in my *Lonely Planet*, information that had proved wrong the previous year. Then I asked him about transportation to a village called Ostabin near the border with Azerbaijan. "Why do you want to go there?" he asked.

"I read somewhere that it is a pretty village."

"Nobody goes there. You should go to Masuleh. Have you been to Masuleh? Everybody goes. It is in *Lonely Planet.*" He narrated the guidebook from memory. "To get to Masuleh you must first go to Rasht. Then find a car headed to Fuman. From there you will find a car to Masuleh. There are two hotels. One place has a sign that says 'Cheap Hotel' . . ."

"Thanks for your help, Mr. Khan," I said, interrupting him. He gave me his card in case I needed anything else. Then I plunged into the bazaar.

The Tabriz bazaar is one of the largest covered bazaars in the world and I quickly became lost amid the corridors and clamour. Tight passageways divided rows of shops selling everything from cooking pots to qalyun parts. Porters rammed their pushcarts through the crowds of shoppers and squinted in the sunlight that flashed through occasional breaks in the ceiling. Only the carpet bazaar was tranquil and orderly, as if the rugs themselves absorbed the noise. I found a carpet-seller to change my money; they were the only merchants in the bazaar who dealt in foreign currency. We drank tea and bartered over the exchange rate for a quarter hour until we had a deal.

I wanted to find a quiet spot where I could read my new Shahriyar. I stepped into a kebabi and asked the owner if he knew where I could find a tea house.

"You want tea? I can make tea."

"Thank you, but a tea house would be better. I want to smoke qalyun."

"I will bring you qalyun. Sit."

The man pointed towards a table and sent a young boy out into the bazaar. The boy returned with a glass of tea and a smouldering water pipe. The qalyun was loaded with regular tobacco, not the sticky fruit-flavoured molasses I was used to. It was harsh and I choked. The man noticed my grimace and, ignoring my protests, sent his boy to fetch another pipe.

The man joined me at my table. His white shirt was translucent with grease and he spoke to me from beneath a fat moustache. He asked me about my job and I told him I was a writer. "Do you know about Persian poetry?"

"I am learning."

"Please, give me your pen." The man wrote a few lines on a napkin. "This is from Sa'adi," he said.

> You, the traveller, will be embraced by the world.
> The sand you kick up will be like kohl for your eyes.
> I've never seen anything clearer than water,
> But even water must move lest it grow stale.
> Go and see the world before the world goes from you.

The advice, transferred to me from an ancient poet through an unshaven kebab man, was better than any guidebook could ever give me.

A sign above the tomb of Sufi poet Sheik Mahmud Shabestari read, in English, "All respectable guests are welcome." I slipped off my sandals and entered the austere brick mausoleum. There was an old man in the corner. He cut a block of sugar into tea-sized hunks with a hinged blade attached to a cube of wood. "*Befarmyyid,*" he said as I entered. I knelt before Shabestari's alabaster gravestone as the sound of crunching sugar continued behind me, and it occurred to me how much time I spent kneeling at the graves of bearded, turbaned men.

I'd travelled to Shabestar that morning, skirting the bare red mountains that, according to my driver, would soon be white with snow. The town reclined against the mountain slopes. Pomegranate trees spilled over high mud walls flecked with black stones. Pairs of gender-specific knockers hung on heavy wooden doors: a narrow bar for men and an iron ring for women. Each made a different sound so inhabitants would know who was calling and who should answer. I walked to the tomb through the narrow bazaar. Men in fedoras and woollen Azeri caps looked up at me from their merchandise. I decided at that moment to wear a hat when I am an old man.

Shabestari was born into an Iran run by Mongols. When the armies of Genghis Khan first galloped into Persia in the early thirteenth century they butchered the Persians with bloody cruelty. The invaders slaughtered entire villages, raped women, defiled mosques and built pyramids of severed heads. Millions of Iranians were massacred or starved to death. Eventually, miraculously, the marauders were transformed. As if by some divine hand, Mongol leaders converted to Islam. They became devout Muslims and patrons of the arts. Under their rule different religious groups coexisted in relative peace. It was the Golden Age for Persian Sufis, and the great mystic Shabestari was one of their leading scribes.

The sugar man stood and urged me to sign the guestbook. Mine was the only English entry and this pleased me somehow. He sold me a dusty, leather-bound translation of Shabestari's *Golshan-e Raz*, or *The Secret Rose Garden*. The book is Shabestari's masterpiece, a series of poems about faith and morality. For Sufis, it is a guidebook to the mystic life. *The Secret Rose Garden* is filled with esoteric musings of the mystical: the ideals of wisdom, the perfection of the body and the concept of the perfect man.

> That man is perfect who through his perfection,
> Though he be master, serveth as a slave.
> When he at length shall reach his journey's end,
> The God of truth shall crown him as his heir.
> He through mortality eternity attains.
> Then once more from the goal pursues his course
> Back to the origin; his vest, the law;
> His robe, the pilgrim's path; in *certainty*
> His soul finds rest.

There was a disordered garden at the back of the shrine filled with a riot of marigolds. The caretaker followed me out into the garden. He pointed to a large tree. "Do you want *gordu*?"

I didn't recognize the word, and I couldn't see anything in the tree. "What is a gordu? Is it like an apple?"

"No, no. Come." He led me to the base of the tree and peered up into the branches. "There," he said, pointing. "You see? It is gordu."

I couldn't see anything aside from leaves. I shrugged at the man. "I will get it for you," he said. He fetched a long pole from a pile near the garden wall and reached into the tree to knock down a gordu. The pole, though, wasn't long enough so the man found a shaky wooden ladder and leaned it against the tree trunk. I tried to deter him but he was resolute. I held the ladder as he climbed to the top rung. Then he asked me to hand him the pole. The gordu, though, was still out of his reach.

"Thank you for trying, Agha," I said, but the man was not finished. He kicked off his shoes and climbed into the tree. He huffed and sweated as he climbed, and I worried he might fall. He made it halfway up the tree and asked for the pole again. I passed it up to him. He thrashed the upper branches until something fell to the ground.

I went to retrieve the prize but it bounced into a patch of tall grass. I knelt on the ground and combed through the grass with my hands. "Did you see it? Have you found it?" the man shouted, still in the tree. Finally my fingers fell on a single fresh walnut. I held it up to him. "Yes, yes! Gordu! Eat!" I laughed. This was a lot of effort for a solitary nut.

I pulled the green flesh from the nut, smashed open the shell with a rock and thought of Shabestari. According to *The Secret Rose Garden*, a nut is a metaphor for a life's journey. The husk is divine law, and the kernel certain truth. Between these lies the pilgrim's road.

Benjamin, my Jewish friend in Esfahan, had told me about the village of Shah Milarzan the previous year. It was his favourite place in Iran. "You must go," he said. "It is truly untouched." I followed the map he drew me in my notebook to Khotbeh Sara. There I found motorcycle taxis waiting to ferry passengers, one by one, up the mountainside to Shah Milarzan. Few cars attempted the steep and twisted road. My motorcycle journey was an hour of jerking and sputtering, and we paused midway to allow the overheated engine to cool. The surrounding hills were broccoli green and covered in jungle.

I met Oshin as soon as I slid off the motorcycle seat and dusted off my rucksack. It was as if he was expecting a visitor. He had a grey beard, thick eyebrows and the saddest-looking eyes I had ever seen. I told him I was a traveller and wanted to spend the night in the village. "Where would you like to stay?" he asked. His Azeri accent was difficult to understand.

"Can I stay at the mosque?"

"Come," he said. "You will stay with me."

Oshin led me to his house and we sat on the high, wide porch. His wife ceased all she was doing to prepare us tea. Word spread through the village that a foreigner had arrived. The bewildered eyes of a dozen children were on me before the tea was even ready. I smiled at a little girl with curly hair. She was afraid of me, though, and fled to the security of her mother's skirt.

"Why have you come to Shah Milarzan?" Oshin asked me once the tea was served.

"My friend told me about this place. He said the people were kind."

Oshin nodded. "You are welcome here. Tonight you will be my guest. But now I must tend to my shop. If you want to see the village, one of these boys will guide you." He gave instructions to the children and they all giggled in unison. I climbed off the porch into their care. A boy of ten, one of Oshin's sons, assigned himself as my guide. His name was Ali, and he wore tinted eyeglasses held together with white tape. Ali reached up and placed his hand on my shoulder as we walked. He wanted to assert to the other children that he was the leader. The rest trailed in a rowdy pack, growing serious only when I asked them to pose for a photo. I was sad that the only time their smiles dissolved was when they faced my camera.

We visited the village imamzadeh, peered into animal pens made of branches and bark, and waved bees away from our faces as we passed beekeepers' boxes. Cows wandered the alleys between the pale blue farmhouses. Ducks sipped from puddles left by washerwomen. The whole village smelled alternately of animal dung, wet earth and freshly cut leaves.

Ali led me to the mountain spring the locals used as a bath. An adjoining wooden tub held water that could be heated by hot stones taken from a nearby firepit. Aside from the mountain air and the rural charm, this was Shah Milarzan's chief attraction. On the pathway, three young children played with an enormous black bug. They placed the insect on a stick and ran through the village, screaming and laughing. Two members of my entourage shrieked and ran to catch the bug boys. For them, the novelty of my presence had already worn thin.

After the tour, I returned to Oshin's house. Oshin was in his shop, a tiny stall located underneath his porch. The shop was little more than a shed and was too small to stand up in, but the shelves were crammed with Iranian sundries—rice, cigarettes, washing powder—and a few soft tomatoes. I sat on an empty crate but Oshin suggested we climb back up onto the porch where there was more room. He kept an eye out for customers and roaming chickens, using a stick to shoo the birds away if they wandered near his shop.

"Are there any other villages beyond Shah Milarzan?" I asked him.

"Yes, there is another village on the top of that hill," he said, pointing into the distance.

"Is it far away?" I liked the idea of being at the end of the road.

"Not far, but you should not go there. There are wild dogs that will eat your flesh, and the place is full of thieves."

I smiled at this. I'd heard the same about Shah Milarzan from men in Khotbeh Sara. In fact, I heard the same warning wherever I travelled in Iran. According to the locals, the next village was always full of bandits and ambiguous dangers.

More tea arrived, then dinner, and soon the porch filled with Oshin's children. His eldest son, Mohammed, lived next door with his two wives, one of whom leaned on the railing of her porch and watched our gathering from across the pathway. Now and again she would shout a contribution to our conversation, but she never came over to join us. Each time I glanced over at her she held my gaze with her own. Her boldness made me blush.

A young girl came along the path and started a playful argument with Mohammed. They spoke in Azeri, and I could not understand what they were saying, but they appeared to be exchanging good-natured jibes. Mohammed's wife watched and smiled from the porch, but when she offered her own comment on the quarrel Mohammed frowned and everyone became silent. He left his father's porch, crossed the pathway to his home, climbed the steps and slapped his wife in the face. The smack sounded like a gunshot. She cried out, rubbed her cheek and returned to her sweeping.

I looked over at Oshin. He shook his head and clicked his tongue until Mohammed came back. I couldn't tell whether it was the slap he disapproved of, or his daughter-in-law's apparent insubordination. I didn't know how to react. I was angry and felt a strong desire to say something, but it was not my place to speak out. I opted for silence and felt like a coward.

The arrival of Reza, Oshin's favourite son, immediately lightened the mood. As soon as the eleven-year-old climbed onto the porch Oshin embraced him, kissed his cheeks and called him "Baba." Reza squirmed out of his father's embarrassing embrace and asked me if I could write something for him in English. "What would you like me to write?" I asked him.

"Just something," he said.

I tore a bit of paper from my journal and wrote my name, my age and where I was from. I handed it to him. "Will you write something for me in Farsi?" I asked.

Reza smiled and rushed off to find more paper. He returned with a page torn out of his mathematics workbook. Oshin shook his head and scolded Reza for always destroying his schoolbooks. Reza took my pen and wrote two lines on the paper. "This is poetry," he said.

> Answer my pleas,
> You who are the Friend of love.

"Is this your poetry?" I asked.

He shook his head. He didn't know who wrote it. "I memorized it a long time ago," he said.

I spent the rest of the night at the house chatting with Oshin and his children. It was a struggle to understand their Azeri accents, so our conversations were slow. I felt happy just to be their guest, sipping tea while wrapped in the blanket the mother had provided me with when once she saw me shiver.

The mother prepared a room for me with some blankets and a foam mattress. As I said good night to the family one of Oshin's daughters poked me in the shoulder. "Please, Agha, will you take my picture?" She had been eyeing my camera all day.

"Yes. I would like that, but we should wait until tomorrow when the sun is up."

She smiled. "Tomorrow? In the morning?"

"Yes. When the light is better."

"Because now it is dark."

"That's right."

"Good night."

I fell asleep staring out the window. The sky was so thick with stars it made me forget the darkness.

15

INTO THE WEST

The Kurds of western Iran empathize with travellers, because they, too, inhabit a country that is not their own. For thousands of years the Kurds have called parts of Iraq, Syria and Turkey their home, but nationhood has always eluded them. They are a people without a homeland. Among them, though, I felt at home.

I admired their fashion almost as much as their hospitality. Men wore double-breasted suit jackets, baggy pants with cummerbunds, white slippers called givehs and fringed turbans that looked as if they had fallen on the men's heads from a second-storey window. I shared the Friday-quiet streets of Mahabad with these men and snacked on boiled chickpeas wrapped in greasy flat bread from street stalls. I had no success finding anyone who knew about traditional Kurdish wrestling, though a man selling fat black grapes told me that *koshti kurdi* is practised mostly by the Kurds in Iraq.

I met Parvis at my mosaferkhune. He was drinking tea when I checked in and was delighted to hear that I spoke English. "I wanted to go to Canada!" he said. Parvis had a way of bellowing when he spoke, like every sentence was a glad announcement. "I was a sailor in the Shah's navy before the Revolution. I trained in U.S.A. and had girlfriend in Milwaukee. Really! She was very much with the dancing. She wanted us to go to Canada, but I didn't want to leave the navy. Please, where are you going?"

"I was going to go for a walk," I said.

"May I come with you? We can have conversations."

I spent the afternoon with Parvis talking about poetry and politics. He was a devotee of the Persian poet Molana Jalaludin, known better as Rumi in the West, whose tomb in Turkey is a place of pilgrimage. "When I was in the navy, every day I read Molana on the ship. Every night before I sleep. Really! Molana tells you how to live. Molana tells you how to grow your children. He tells how to love your wife. He tells how you want to be. Everything. Also Attar. You know Attar? He also tells about how to live. He is second for me, behind Molana. When you read Molana, you cannot see only the story," he said. "You must look always *behind* the story."

Parvis and I walked to a nearby park. He hooked his arm in mine as if we were old friends. Groups of teenaged boys smoked qalyuns in the shade of the tall trees. Old men sat cross-legged on flattened boxes and played dominoes. Parvis and I found a bench and he told me about the Revolution. "Before 1979, the officers say to the soldiers and the sailors, 'You must stay in the army or we will put you in jail.' But the soldiers and sailors were not afraid. We knew that Shah was finished. Really! So me and many other soldiers left the army. After the Revolution, and Shah was gone, I became a sailor for the new government. For Ayatollah Khomeini. Then the war with Iraq came. I went to China because China was selling rockets to Iran's army. I was in China for most of the war training on the rockets."

Parvis rubbed his hands against his thighs, then clasped them together. "I think that Khomeini was Jesus, Mohammed and Moses," he said.

"Really?"

He put his hand on his heart. "Really!"

"Most Iranians say they don't like Khomeini. They say life was better under the Shah."

Parvis clicked his tongue. "These men who tell you this are trying to look like smart man. They do not know the society. Before Khomeini, all Iran was like Afghanistan. All villages. Really! Only Tehran and Esfahan and Shiraz were cities. This place," he waved his arm around to indicate Mahabad, "was only one road. There was no park. The only parks were in Tehran, Shiraz, Esfahan. Really!

"People do not have it right in their memory. People say to me that Shah was better because bread was only three rials. But they forget that salary was very small. My father had eight children. He was in the army. They gave him one thousand rials each month. That is only one hundred rials for each mouth. Eight children and one father and one mother. I went to school five kilometres in the morning, five kilometres back home for eating lunch, then five kilometres back to school in the afternoon. And five kilometres for coming home. Four times a day I walked. The bus was only two rials, but our family walked. We could not pay. And we were high in the village.

"Now the army gives me four million rials. I am same rank as my father. Now villages have lights and roads. Every house has telephone. Really! At time of Shah we did not know what car was! But people say it was better because bread was only three rials."

For all his respect for Khomeini, and his bile for the Shah, Parvis did not praise the current government. He felt that the regime had betrayed Khomeini. Khomeini's ideals of an Islamic government were simple and logical, according to Parvis, but the regime had abandoned Islam's inherent common sense for harsh conservatism. It was strange, and wholly counterintuitive, to hear Khomeini described as a liberal thinker.

"What is in your head is the right way," Parvis said, tapping his temple. "Khomeini believed this. But today, in Iran we do not follow what is in our head. There is a very famous man, an Islamic thinker. His name I forget. He went to the West and lived with the people. When he came back he said, 'In America I saw Islam but no Muslims. Here I see Muslims but no Islam.' Really!

"In the West they walk along the right way. In the Islamic world, and very much in Iran, we look at the way, we say the way is beautiful, we make prayers to the way, but we do not walk on the way. We stay in one place."

Parvis paused and smiled, clearly pleased by the wit of his last statement. "I talk too much. Maybe I make you tired."

"Not at all."

"I tell you all that I think," he said as we left the park. "But maybe I do not know. Maybe I make mistake."

After I said goodbye to Parvis I had a dinner of chicken liver soup and qormeh sabzi. The boy at the mosaferkhune invited me to watch a pirated copy of *Evil Dead 3* on his laptop computer. I opted for sleep, with Parvis's words in my head. Surely the great mystic poets would share Parvis's passions. Attar's birds had to shed their egos to find God. Shabestari insisted men disregard notions of status and structure, and travel through life unburdened. Molana taught his readers that severity led away from wisdom. For them, the way forward, for a nation as much as a single man, is organic. "What is in your head is the right way."

I didn't know whether Khomeini shared these views. I never thought him a mystic, but my Western television education only ever portrayed him as a scowling villain. Most of the Iranians I met hated him and longed for life as it was under the Shah, but few had actually lived under the Shah's notorious and corrupt regime. In Iran, it was somehow fashionable to forget the excesses of the Shah until only nostalgia remained. Then again, when haven't poets found their greatest joys in the past?

The next morning I found a tea house in the bazaar and ate a Kurdish breakfast of boiled potatoes and eggs smashed together with a pat of butter. I bought honey-flavoured tobacco from a qalyun merchant, and watched a street vendor serve ladlefuls of dugh flecked with dried rose petals.

Mahabad was a pretty town, but even here the traffic was vexing. Iran's national aroma is diesel fumes. The instances when my nose snared something other than exhaust were rare and lucky moments. I always slowed my pace when I passed the lemon seller in Tabriz, the coffee roaster on Tehran's Enqelab Avenue, Mashhad's saffron bazaar, or the top of stairwells leading down to fruit-smoky tea houses.

At night I returned to the park where I had sat with Parvis the day before. I ordered a qalyun from a small shop on the grounds. The shopkeeper joined me on the terrace. When he heard that I was writing about Iran he told me to be sure to write that life is hard for the Iranian Kurds.

"We are second class," he said. "I do not feel Iranian. I am first a Kurd. We are one people. In Iran, Iraq, Turkey, Syria. We will have our own country: the Democratic Republic of Kurdistan."

"When will that happen?" I asked.

"In one year."

"Do you really think so?"

"Enshallah," he said. God willing. *Enshallah* is one of the most pervasive expressions in the Islamic world. Its three breathy syllables are loaded with hope, wishful thinking and the resignation that so much is out of mortal hands. My shopkeeper's "enshallah" was heavy with doubt. We both knew that his wish was unrealistic, that the year would pass without a free Kurdistan, and this saddened me a little.

That night the Iranian national football team played the team from Germany at Azadi Stadium in Tehran. It was a charity match; the proceeds would go towards the victims of the Bam earthquake. Every man in Mahabad found a spot in front of a television. I doubt there were many men in Iran who were not watching. I joined the crowd of men at the restaurant adjoining my mosaferkhune to watch the game.

Nights in Iran were often dull. I found myself showering in the evening just so I had something to do. The football game was a welcome nighttime diversion. Still, it seemed incomplete watching a football match without lager at the ready. Tea and team sports are poor mates. Even the ads on the side of the field were for beer, albeit a non-alcoholic German brew called Bitburger. The game offered the Iranians little to cheer about. The home team lost, two to nil. Nobody was surprised. "Germany good play," one man told me when I expressed some sympathy for the loss.

As I waited for my bus to Sanandaj the next morning, three young beggar girls came into the terminal. They wore colourful dresses and headscarves, and demanded money from each passenger. They didn't beg or make sad eyes with stories about dead fathers or sick mothers. They just stuck out their hands and commanded donations. Unlike the eyeless old men I'd seen begging elsewhere—one hand held out for coins, the other rubbing an empty eye socket—these girls treated their poverty as a game. After touring the terminal they took turns at the water fountain. They giggled and splashed until a man behind the ticket counter told them to go away. Then they scattered into the sunlight.

A notice at the front desk at my hotel warned guests that

> The home that has been delivered is yours up 2pm. Otherwise that's prolongation and whole of the expense will be received.

I considered this to be a good omen; there is something cheerful about really poor English. My porter, Mohammed, was a slim boy of about seventeen. He had a thin, teenage moustache and spoke with a slight lisp. Mohammed studied English and was eager to speak with me. When he opened the door to my spartan room he asked, "Mr. Di Cintio, is it beautiful?"

"Beautiful? Yes, very beautiful."

"Are you sure? The television is broken."

"That's fine. I cannot understand Farsi very well anyway."

"Some television is Kurdish. Do you speak Kurdish?"

"I'm afraid not."

"Okay. Goodbye."

I asked the hotel manager if he knew anything about koshti kurdi. He shrugged and told me to visit the zurkhane a little way down the main road. I took a detour through the bazaar en route. Stalls sold packets of henna and piles of sumac. Tailors sewed together those impossibly baggy Kurdish trousers. At the abattoir, the intimate parts of sheep—lungs, stomachs and testicles—lay on trays and collected flies. Another section of the bazaar was devoted to tiny Playstation booths. The game booths were large enough to house three televisions and six small stools. Glassy-eyed boys crammed inside, elbow to elbow, and played digital soccer matches against each other. Their calloused thumbs were a blur. As I passed by a one-chair barber shop, a man inside asked me in a whisper if I would like to buy some alcohol.

Outside the bazaar, the streets were busy and colourful. The Kurdish women wore layers of bright fabric, often festooned with sequins. Some wrapped two headscarves in different colours around their head and chin and reminded me of Bedouin nomads. Many reddened their hair with henna. Others boasted thicker moustaches than young Mohammed at the hotel. There were givehs everywhere, and the loose turbans and cummerbunds that seemed to hold the old men together.

I bought boiled red beets and fava beans from glass cases on the sidewalk. On a street corner a man sold old photographs behind squares of glass framed with masking tape. I bought one of a dervish girl with snakes in her mouth. On another corner, a lunatic waved a photo of Khomeini and hollered at the crowds on the sidewalk. Teenage boys taunted him until he shook with rage.

The men at the zurkhane were hesitant to let me in at first; they didn't want a foreigner defiling the sanctity of the zurkhane with camera flashes. But when I explained my interest in traditional koshti, they warmed to me. It was early in the afternoon and the day's exercises were still hours away. The room was nearly empty. One man was quietly revolving a pair of mils over his shoulders, but he put them down when I entered and joined me on a bench at the side of the gohd. He was still sweating and short of breath.

The man had never heard of koshti kurdi but was happy to talk to me about the zurkhane, especially about the power poetry had over men. He told me that of all the poetry the morshed might recite during the ritual, he was especially stirred by verses of the mystic. He closed his eyes and swayed his arms back and forth to mimic the trance-like effect the poetry had on him. "I always ask the morshed to sing Hafez, Sa'adi and Khayyám," he said. This was different from the pahlevans I met in Qazvin who were inspired by Ferdosi's brawny heroes. "In other sports—football, volleyball, basketball—a man is too old to compete after he becomes thirty years old," the man told me, "but the pahlevans in the zurkhane continue to train even as old men. It is because of the poetry. This poetry, this mysticism, gives us our strength."

I found a minibus headed towards Palangan. The bus was filled with jovial old men with missing teeth who joked and laughed with each other the entire journey. When one man sang poetry softly to himself, the others quieted down to listen to his song. He finished just as we approached the turnoff to Palangan. One of the men, bearded and wearing a white cap like a tier of a wedding cake, pointed to a dirt road that descended into a river valley. "There you will find Palangan."

I'd seen a poster of Palangan at my hotel in Sanandaj. It looked like another pretty cliff-clinging mountain village like Saragh-Seyed, and I was anxious to visit it. The road ended at a fish hatchery but I could not see the village. A fish farmer pointed to a covered aqueduct that ran above the river and along the steep mountainside. I climbed onto the aqueduct and followed it around the bend.

I found a man with an accordion. He sat on a blanket next to an old woman who must have been his mother. They were drinking tea and eating sunflower seeds out of a black plastic bag. I said hello, and when the old woman realized I was a foreigner she opened her eyes wide. "Please sit down with us," she said.

I made the customary refusals then sat down. The accordion man offered me the bag of seeds while his mother poured tea. "I like talking to young people," she said. "All my children have grown and moved away. How old are you?"

"I am thirty-one."

She gasped and put her hands to her face. "But you have so much white hair!" We all laughed. "Are you married?" I showed her Moonira's photograph and she sighed. "She is so beautiful."

Her son, Fariboz, told me that the accordion was not his. It belonged to his brother. "My brother is down at the river fishing with his friends. Will you join us for lunch?"

"Thank you, but I came to see Palangan."

"So did we. We can go see it now. And afterwards we will eat together."

"Don't you want to fish with your brothers?"

"I do not like to fish. I prefer music and literature."

"Me, too," I said.

Fariboz and I walked towards the village. The aqueduct was about twenty metres above the river. From this height we could see his brother and the other fishermen. They waved up at us as we passed. Two Kurdish girls in sequined dresses led cows along the riverbank. Three more girls passed us along the aqueduct. One wore a dress of green taffeta and carried a metre-long scythe over her shoulder.

Palangan clung to the steep mountainsides that flanked the valley; the river and a narrow bridge divided the village into halves. The homes were built of bricks that were the same sepia as the surrounding rock, and the village might have been invisible were it not for the blue window frames and the colourful dresses the women wore. I could not see their faces from the pathway—they were too high—but their dresses shimmered against the uniform brown. They moved like wandering jewels, stood on the edges of rooftops and shouted greetings to each other from across the valley. It was one of the most beautiful sights I have ever seen and I felt profoundly happy.

I walked with Fariboz back to the picnic blanket. He envied my life in the West. "Here in Iran it is forbidden even to think. During Ramazan, food is haram. But in Iran, every day is Ramazan for thinking."

The fishermen returned from the riverbank with baskets of small whitefish. There was Fariboz's brother, his friend, his wife and his four-year-old daughter, Mahtol. The men collected firewood and built a fire while the two women sharpened green sticks into skewers and cleaned the fish. They threaded the fish onto the skewers along with cubes of lamb, cherry tomatoes and peppers. As the men roasted the skewers on the fire Fariboz's brother squeezed Italian, Russian and Israeli folk songs out of his accordion. All the while a cigarette hung from his lips, its ash growing long during each tune.

I joined my hosts in front of a tablecloth when the food was ready. We waved away flies and plucked stowaway embers from the roasted fish. The others pressed me to eat more and dropped chunks of roasted lamb in front of me despite my objections and full stomach. When we were finished we tossed the fish bones and charred skewers into the valley. There were apples and melon seeds for dessert. And cups of tea.

Afterwards we all walked back into Palangan. We watched two girls haul firewood from the river up the steep incline to the village. The old woman shook her head and said, "Life here is very hard." Little Mahtol suddenly looked up at me and said, "One, two, three, four, five, six, seven, eight," but grew shy when I asked her where she had learned English.

Dusk came and with it the cliffs glowed orange. There were no cars leaving Palangan so my hosts offered me a ride. "You have no room for me," I said. "I'll stay here and find a ride back to Sanandaj tomorrow."

"No. It is no trouble. We can all fit." Seven of us pressed into their Paykan. I sat in the front with one of the men and Mahtol who quickly fell asleep against my shoulder. The family was going only as far as Karyaran, the first town of any size along the highway to Sanandaj. When we arrived the old woman said, "It is late. Stay with us tonight. You can find a car to Sanandaj in the morning."

"Thank you, Khanun, but you have already given me so much," I said.

I knew nothing about this family, I hardly knew their names and they would surely forget mine, but our brief encounter bound us together the way only strangers can be bound. They would remember me, and tell their friends about a solitary Canadian who joined them for lunch near Palangan. I will never forget the Kurdish family who fed me fish and played accordion. The sweetest travel passes not just through geography, but through the everyday lives of strangers. Experiences like these graft themselves on a traveller's cells. I knew I would never see the family again, and this saddened me.

The old woman filled my pockets with apples and seeds. "I hope you can visit with us again someday."

"Enshallah," I said.

The gardens and fourth-century stone reliefs at Taq-e Bostan attract mobs of Iranians from Kermanshah. It was Friday when I visited and the place was busy. Families posed for photographs next to the carvings, then enjoyed picnics in the garden or refreshments from the open-air tea houses and kebabis.

The carvings honoured the ancient Zoroastrian king Khosro II who was a famed warrior and hunter. Some of the reliefs commemorated Khosro's investiture as king and his victories on the battlefield. Others depicted royal hunting parties. Bearded noblemen on stallions and elephants chased stags and herds of wild boars across the stone wall. The bas-reliefs were another display of Persian brawn.

It was a happy irony, then, that here amid the stony manliness I met a woman traveller. Muriel was from Belgium and was travelling alone. We shared some lunch in one of the tea houses and reminisced about beer. "I am not a big drinker," she said, "but I've been dying for a beer since I arrived in Iran."

"Have you tried araq? The liquor they brew themselves from raisins?"

"I haven't. Is it any good?"

I laughed. "It's no Belgian beer. Iran could use a few of your Trappist monks."

I told Muriel about my interest in Persian poetry. "So you must know about Hafez and Sa'adi," she said. "I have to do an errand for an Iranian friend in Antwerp. She wants me to bring copies of Sa'adi and Hafez back for her. She says her house is incomplete without them."

"How are you finding Iran?" I asked. "Travelling alone as a woman, I mean."

"It's fine," she said. "I've had no problems. Not at all. Sometimes the Iranian women ask me if I am scared. They assume I must be afraid because I am a Westerner. I tell them that I am afraid of crossing the street in Tehran. This makes them laugh because they're also afraid.

"The women here are so wonderful." Muriel's face brightened. "I've been invited into private homes a few times. We always go into a room separate from the men and shut the door. Right away everyone throws off their chadors and headscarves. Then someone turns on a stereo and we all dance. Sometimes there were three generations of women dancing in the room. We dance and sing and laugh. The laughing is the best part. When they are around men, the women can be so serious, but when they get together they laugh and laugh. After we got tired of dancing, we always sat and watched wedding videos. I have spent hours watching Iranians get married. Wedding videos and Chris de Burgh. What's the Iranian fascination with Chris de Burgh?"

"I'm jealous," I said. "I haven't met any women here. The men are different. They are always cheerful until the discussion turns to politics, which it always does." I twirled my finger over my head in reference to the ruling mullahs.

Muriel nodded and we were both quiet. She had only been in Iran for a couple of weeks, but she knew the sadness, black as a chador, that hung over the Persians.

The waiter arrived to break the silence and clear our plates. I ordered a pipe. "You speak Farsi," Muriel said. She seemed impressed.

"A little. I studied back home."

"It is a beautiful language. I love it."

"The Iranians say, 'Farsi is sweet.' It is difficult to learn, though. At least for me. I don't have a knack for languages."

"Farsi is the reason why I came to Iran. I watch Iranian films all the time in Belgium. I don't speak Farsi so I have to read the subtitles to understand, but I love to listen to the language. I love the sound of it. It is very musical. I decided to travel to Iran just to hear the language every day."

"That is the best reason for travelling I have ever heard," I said.

When we were finished Muriel and I walked past the Taq-e Bostan towards the taxi stand. Iranian families lined up to do laps around the nearby pond in a speedboat. The pond was no larger than a regulation swimming pool; it took about seven seconds for the boat to go around once. Muriel shook her head. "These poor people," she said. "What they have to do for fun."

In Islam Abad I went in search of *zhir-o bal* wrestling. I knew little about the style other than the words *zhir-o bal* mean "under-up" in Farsi. I followed a teenaged boy from a sandwich shop to a wrestling salon. A practice was about to start. While the team warmed up on the mats I asked the coaches about zhir-o bal. Only one man had heard of it.

"Zhir-o bal competitions happen in the summer," he said. "Not now. All these wrestlers here are Greco-Roman wrestlers. Are you a wrestler?"

"I used to be, but I wrestled freestyle."

"Would you like to wrestle today?"

I hadn't been on the mat since my last practice with Jeremy before I left Canada. I looked into the gymnasium. The athletes jogged and tumbled on the mats to prepare their bodies for training. The warm-up had just begun, but the air had already grown warm with the heightened pulse of two dozen men. There was a captivating scent of pending combat in the room. "I would like to wrestle," I said.

The coach called out to his athletes. Two of them broke out of the tumbling ranks and fetched extra shorts, a shirt and wrestling boots from their sports bags. I slid them on and joined the warm-up. The coach also assigned one of his athletes to be my partner. "You can wrestle freestyle with him. Later I will show you zhir-o bal."

I followed the team in their somersaults and cartwheels until my breath was fast and my forehead began to sweat. A senior member of the team led the stretching, then everyone paired off to find a spot of mat. I was happy to find that my partner and I were evenly matched. We grappled for about ten minutes, alternating attacks and takedowns. It was just practice, but I relished the locking of our limbs and the happy strain of our contest. And it was a relief that here, unlike in Kuhrang the year before, I was not the centre of attention. The other wrestlers in the room were focused on their own wrestling. They were disciplined athletes. My presence did not distract them.

Soon the coach called me over to the side of the mat. He had been showing one of his athletes how to wrestle zhir-o bal so he could demonstrate for me. The two men stood chest to chest. They gripped their left hands together as if in a handshake. Then they leaned forward into each other. Their hands remained clasped underneath their chests. "The left hand is *zhir*," the coach said. Under. Next, each man hooked his right arm up under his opponent's left arm. "This is *bal*." Up. The wrestlers must stay in this position for the entire bout. The first man to bring his opponent down to the ground, either by a trip or a toss, is the winner.

The two men demonstrated the style. They pulled at each other for a few seconds until the coach managed to catch his wrestler off guard, trip him with his left leg and bring him to the mat. "Now you try," he said, lifting himself off the ground.

The coach helped me get into the under-up lock with the other wrestler, then tapped us on the shoulder to start the bout. We pushed our bodies together and wrenched on each other's left hand. My opponent took a step between my legs and lifted me off the ground, but he wasn't able to bring me to the ground and I squirmed back to my feet. I stepped to the side and nudged my man backwards. He recovered and pushed into me. I stepped forward and hoisted him off his feet. He flung his legs back but I twisted my torso and threw him onto his back.

"Very good," the coach said, helping us up. "That was a good throw. What do you think of zhir-o bal?"

"I think I like it very much," I said. I was just happy to get back on the mat. After long days on crammed buses, the feeling of blood moving through my veins was exhilarating.

My mosaferkhune in Khorramabad was horrifying. The rooms smelled vaguely of orange blossom water, which was pleasant enough, but they caught all the racket and smog from the highway below. The toilets were filthy and my bed was crawling with ants. The worst feature, though, was the shower. The shared sinks emptied directly into the solitary shower stall. As I stood under the frigid water I noticed tea leaves swirling around my feet. Apparently someone was washing a teapot. Then I heard a man snort up a packet of mucus, spit it into the sink and rinse it my way. I vowed to pay a little more for my accommodations from then on.

I went to a sports centre to inquire about *lori* wrestling. When I arrived about a dozen young wrestlers, all with battered faces and bruised ears, waited outside for the doors to open for practice. None of the wrestlers had heard of lori wrestling, but an old man, the grandfather of one of the boys, stood up. "We do not call it lori wrestling here," he said. "It is called *zur-o-safoneh.* But no one wrestles like that any more. Not since the Revolution."

"Why not?"

He shrugged. "After the Revolution, everything changed."

It was the same story I'd heard before. The Revolution did more than replace a monarchy with a theocracy. It did more than close the discos and drape women in hejab. The Revolution rendered centuries-old traditions obsolete. All eyes looked forward to a utopian Islamic future. I wondered how much of Persian culture had been lost in the past quarter century, shuffled away by the mullahs into the memories of a few old men.

The man told me that zur-o-safoneh was practised mainly in the villages. Wrestlers wore traditional lori dress and competed on the bare ground. Like the other traditional styles, poetry was recited before zur-o-safoneh bouts. "They read *Shahnomeh.* Always *Shahnomeh.* Listening to Ferdosi makes men strong." He quoted the poem from memory:

> And still they struggled hard—still sweat and blood
> Poured down at every strain. Rostam, at last,
> Gathering fresh power, vouchsafed by favouring Heaven
> And bringing all his mighty strength to bear,
> Raised up the gasping Demon in his arms,
> And with such fury dashed him to the ground,
> That life no longer moved his monstrous frame.

The man stepped close to me, wrapped his arms around my torso and locked his hands behind my back. "The wrestlers held each other like this," he said. Then he squeezed. He was nearly seventy years old but had the strength of a bear. My breath choked out of my lungs and the boys laughed. The man held the grip and spoke into my ear. "In zur-o-safoneh you must stay in this position. You cannot touch your opponent's legs. But you can throw." He cinched me even tighter and hoisted me off my feet and into the air. For a moment I thought he would dash me to the concrete like Rostam's demon, but the man stopped the throw short and placed me back on my feet.

I rubbed my ribs. "You are very strong," I said.

He looked to the sky. "Thank you, Ferdosi!"

I left the wrestlers and walked to the Falak-ol-Aflak, the clatter-named fortress that stands over Khorramabad. The castle was built in the twelfth century and now houses a small museum and tea house. It is most famous for its collection of Lorestan bronzes, ancient housewares dating back to 1000 BC that were unearthed in the nearby hills.

I briefly toured the museum and settled in the tea house for an apple qalyun and a pot of cinnamon tea. A man approached me as I was writing in my notebook.

"Excuse me. Are you a foreigner?" the man asked me in Farsi.

I looked around to see if anyone else was listening before nodding. My Farsi had improved enough that I had paid the Iranian price for my ticket. I didn't want to blow my cover.

"Where are you from?"

"Canada."

"Canada. English?"

"Yes, I speak English."

"You speak Farsi, too."

"A little."

"Very good. Please, may I take your picture?"

I smiled at his camera lens, flattered that I was a tourist attraction. Then the man handed me a sheet of paper. "Please, can you write something for me in English?"

"What would you like me to write?"

"Whatever you like."

I took the paper and wrote: *Hello. My name is Marcello Di Cintio. I am from Canada. I like Iran very much. Iranians are very kind.* I handed him the paper and translated it for him.

"Thank you very much," he said placing his hand on his heart. Then he went back to his table, wrote me a message in Farsi and handed it to me as he left the tea house. It was a poem.

> A garden,
> The mother of flowers of different colours.
> I wish you knew that one day a horserider will pass
> through this garden.
> His footfalls are frightful,
> And his name is Autumn.

At the bottom of the page, the man added, *My name is Ahmed. I am pleased to meet you, kind gentleman. I wish you health and safe travels. I am happy that I now have a friend in Canada.*

A few minutes later another man approached my table. He greeted me in English. "Excuse me, may I sit with you. I am working at this museum. You are a tourist, yes?" I nodded, ready to hand over the extra tomans for my admission fee, but he didn't ask about my ticket. "I am in charge of restoration," he said. "Would you like to see the laboratory?"

I followed him out of the tea house and into a room filled with microscopes and long lab benches. "We restore many of the artifacts here," he said. He walked over to a large floor safe in the corner of the room. "Now I will show you something very wonderful." He spun the combination lock until the door clunked open. Then he removed a locked box from the safe and opened it with a key on his belt. He lifted a decorated metal bowl from the box, blew off the dust and handed it to me. "This is Lorestan bronze," he said. "It is three thousand years old."

Ancient artifacts never interested me much; a half hour earlier I had given the bronzes on display in the museum little more than a momentary glance. But holding the bowl in my hands made my pulse jump. I had never held three millennia in my fingertips before. The man removed more objects from the box—another bowl, an axe head, the hilt of a dagger—each thousands of years old. A millennium before Christ a man might have split branches into kindling with the axe. A woman may have filled the bowl with grapes and quinces. These everyday objects had passed from those ancient hands to mine. Our fingers had held the same metal coolness. For a moment I knew what eternity felt like.

"Will you display these things at the museum?" I asked.

"No. We will send them away."

"To Tehran?" I'd seen similar bronzes at the National Museum.

"Not Tehran. To Paris. To the Louvre. The Iranian government is not interested in these things any more, because they are from before Islam." He twirled his finger over his head. These bronzes would suffer the same fate as zur-o-safoneh and the other forgotten traditional wrestling styles. They were regarded as artifacts from a bankrupt age and devalued by a regime that decided being Muslim was far more important than being Persian. I could not understand why it was impossible to be both.

"I love these bronzes. I love, love, love, love them," the man said. Then he kissed each piece and returned them to the safe.

16

Esfahan

I'd been longing for easy Esfahani days since I returned to Iran. Every day I travelled felt like one step closer to the tea houses, the Zayendeh River and the Nagsh-e Jahan.

My taxi dropped me at the Takhti junction, where a bust of the legendary wrestler stood with cauliflower ears carved from stone. The driver overcharged me—Esfahani taxi drivers were notorious swindlers—then I stepped through the glass doors at the Amir Kabir. Shapur, the hostel manager, recognized me. "You are back," he said. He collected my passport and wrote the details down in the register. Then he rattled off a list of warnings: "Please leave your money, air ticket, camera, credit card with us. We are not responsible if you lose something. Please come back to the hostel after ten o'clock. Beware of men on motorcycles who will steal your bag. Never give anything to any man who says he is policeman. He is fake. Real policemen will not stop tourists. Do not go into an Iranian house. Only take real taxis, not fake taxis. Real taxis are blue. If a man come into the hotel and says he is a guide do not go with him because he is not a real guide."

Dodging phony policemen, taxi drivers and guides made sense, but curfews and warnings against Iranian hospitality seemed paranoid. "Is Esfahan more dangerous than last year?" I asked.

"Not dangerous, but you should be careful. There are some bad people. We must tell every guest about the dangers. If someone from this hotel gets robbed, and we have not warned them, the police say we are responsible. We will have to pay back the money to the tourist."

There were posters in many Iranian hotels that featured a quote from Imam Ali. The Imam stated that if any traveller to an Islamic country is robbed during his travels it is the responsibility of the government to compensate him for his loss. The posters always made me smirk; I didn't believe for a moment that the Iranian government would reimburse me if someone picked my pocket. According to Shapur, though, I should not have been so cynical. He told me that thieves stole money and an airline ticket from a German tourist in Esfahan a few months before. The man reported the robbery to the police and they repaid him the money he lost and purchased another ticket for him.

"You are joking," I said.

"It is true. Now the police say every hotel must warn tourists about thieves. If we do not, and someone is robbed, then we must give the tourist his money back. We have to do the job of the police."

I laid my rucksack in my room and made my way towards the Nagsh-e Jahan. I needed to buy some Iranian currency from the money-changers on Sepah Street. Esfahan's illegal money-changers were less bold than the men in Tehran who waved brick-sized stacks of cash on street corners. In Esfahan they stood on the sidewalks whispering, "Doh-lar, euro, doh-lar," to everyone who passed and holding up small calculators to display the day's rates. I chose one of the men at random; I never knew if one money-changer was more honest than the next. We stepped into a nut shop, haggled over the commission and exchanged a few American notes for two piles of rials.

I bought a day-old *Tehran Times* and walked out into the square. Immediately a short man about my age approached. "I am from Nomad Carpet Shop," he said. "I am on page 284 of the *Lonely Planet.* Do you have *Lonely Planet*? You can come to my shop. Just to look. Drink tea. Free Internet. Clean bathrooms. Whatever you like. I can help you. Here is my card." I smiled and walked past; it felt good to be back on the square, despite the carpet-sellers and souvenir touts.

It was the early-afternoon "quiet time," according to Shapur at the hotel, and the square was nearly abandoned. I climbed up the stairway to the Qeysarieh tea house. The same old man sat at the same desk. "The Canadian has returned," he said.

I was overjoyed. A traveller strives for anonymity. To be able to wander unnoticed as the proverbial fly on the wall is a gift, and thanks to my Persian-enough features I was able to do this in Iran. To be remembered, though, after over a year was an even greater gift. It meant I was not just another tourist passing through. His greeting honoured me. To both stand out and fit in is the traveller's dream.

The tea house was crowded with tourists, mostly retired Germans who waved around camcorders and looked lost. Two Germans filmed me as I smoked qalyun. The few Iranians in the place grinned at them.

When I returned to the hotel that evening, there was an Iranian man walking through the courtyard. When he saw me pass on the balcony he called out hello and asked me for my nationality.

"I am Canadian," I said.

"My name is Farzad. I like you very much!"

"Thank you."

"What is your language?"

"English."

"I know twenty-two thousand English words."

"That is more than I know, I'm sure."

"I think you are very handsome."

"Thank you."

Later, I saw Farzad in the lobby. He was kissing Shapur's hand. "I kiss his hand because he gives me kindness. My mother is a psycho. She insulted me. She drove my brother and me apart. For ten years I was a reckless."

"A reckless?"

"Yes. A reckless. Like a hermit."

"You mean a recluse."

"Yes. But two Swiss prayed for me and now I have a friend named Jesus. What is your education?"

"I have a university degree."

"What did you study?"

"Biology."

"A tumour can be malignant or benign," he announced.

I walked through the gardens off Chahar Bagh Street and watched the couples on the grass. It was an exercise in voyeurism, to be sure, but I enjoyed the Esfahanis' demure flirtation. Half hidden behind low shrubs, young lovers leaned into each other and talked close. They read poetry and shared sweets. Sometimes a man lay on his back and placed his head so that it just touched his lover's leg. A hand might briefly touch a knee, though it would never rest there. There was nothing as brash as a kiss or an embrace. One day I saw a woman holding her companion's face in her hands and was shocked at her boldness.

There was something sweet about this sort of courtship. I never knew how such couples behaved in private—perhaps their passion was hot-blooded and wild—but their public intimacy was coloured by innocence. I envied the Persian dalliances. The lightest of touches. A glance held just a little long. There was more poetry in the smallest of gestures than in the lustiest kiss.

I left the couples and walked to the tomb of the poet Sa'eb Tabrizi. Another garden. Another still fountain. Another gravestone to kneel before. The scent of flowers flavoured the cool morning air. Sa'eb rests beneath a mirrored ceiling supported by pillars. Verses of his poetry are rendered in calligraphy mosaics on a facing wall. There was an arabesque depression carved into the tombstone that formed a shallow pool. Tiny flowers left by Sa'eb's visitors floated on the water. I plucked a pink blossom from the garden and dropped it.

Sa'eb Tabrizi was born at the beginning of the seventeenth century in a village near Esfahan. Like many of the Persian poets, Sa'eb was a great traveller. He made a pilgrimage to Mecca and wandered through Afghanistan and India. Shah Jahan, the Mongol emperor of India, appointed Sa'eb as a court poet. Six years later, Sa'eb's aged and lonely father went to find Sa'eb and bring him home to Esfahan. The reigning king was an enthusiastic patron and made Sa'eb his poet laureate, but he was not happy in Esfahan. Three centuries ago, Sa'eb's complaints foreshadowed those of future Iranians when he bemoaned the rising power of the mullahs. Like so many of today's Iranians, he longed to leave Iran.

Benjamin was one of them. I saw him at the Qeysarieh later that day. He told me that it was lucky I arrived in Esfahan when I did. He had arranged to emigrate to New Zealand and would leave in ten days.

"What will you do in New Zealand?"

"I am going to cooking school."

"You want to be a chef?"

Benjamin shrugged. "I will do anything. It is only a way to leave Iran. After three years I will get a New Zealand passport. That is all I want. I want to be free. I love Iran, but I need to leave."

Benjamin's disenchantment with Iran had crystallized the previous summer. He travelled with a group of friends to the Caspian Sea. There were three men and two women; no one was married or related. "We were sitting on the beach. We were doing nothing wrong. The women were wearing good hejab. But a policeman came to us and asked for our ID cards. When he found out that we were not married he arrested us. He put handcuffs on all of us and brought us to the police station. We got lashes."

"You were whipped?"

"Yes. On the back. Because we were together. That was our crime. A police officer held a Quran under his arm and whipped each of us sixty times."

I thought of the couples I spied on in the park. "But I see young men and women together all the time. Are they always married?"

"No, but they are always risking lashes. It happens all the time. It is life for us."

This made me furious. When I read that the regime closed reformist newspapers and punished protestors, I was not surprised. The fate of Zahra Kazemi, though tragic, was not really a surprise. Despotic governments show little tolerance for their critics.

Benjamin's lashing, though, was something different. He and his friends were not punished for breaking laws or committing immoral acts. They were whipped because, according to Iran's leaders, men and women cannot be in the same space without giving in to sin. Their intentions are assumed to be immoral. I wondered what the authorities meant to accomplish. What did they mean to lash away? I couldn't understand how young people could live this way.

Perhaps this is one of the reasons why Persians so venerate their poets. Surely this adoration long preceded the Revolution, but I wondered whether the importance of poetry has changed since 1979, at least for some Iranians. After all, only within those ancient verses are the ideals of Persian culture free from the mullahs' grip. Only in poetry can Persians exchange kisses with their lovers in rose-scented gardens. Only in the *Divan* of Hafez does ruby wine flow free. So much sweetness has been lost in Iran, and it is only found in the rhymes of ancient measured lines.

Benjamin continued. "I have travelled to New Zealand before. I like it, but I do not fit in there. I do not *want* to live in New Zealand. It is not my home. My home is Iran. But how can I live here? Everyone wants to leave. I love Iran, but I must go."

I would receive an e-mail from Benjamin a year later that read:

> Here I am in New Zealand, I am not having a good time at all. Got no friends and just can not stand New Zealand and New Zealanders any longer. Hopefully soon I shall go back to Iran.
>
> I always wanted to leave Iran and live somewhere else. New Zealand sounded so good. I spent the whole year this year doing a course in cookery. I am doing the last month of the course, the work experience. Did all this just to find out I don't want to live in New Zealand any more.
>
> I am so lost. I long so much for a minute back in Esfahan. The people here ask me where I come from. I tell them Iran. The next thing they say is, always, WELL YOU ARE VERY LUCKY THAT YOU ARE IN NEW ZEALAND. Always the same. I am doing my work experience in a big hotel. My boss asked me if I needed to get a job. I said yes, that would be good. He says, I BET YOU DO ANYTHING TO STAY IN NEW ZEALAND, NOT TO HAVE TO GO BACK TO THAT SHIT HOLE!!!! I don't know, Allah is the knower . . .

Benjamin's note reminded me that despite the government's crimes, Persians are proud to be from Iran. The country may have become, for many, a place to flee, but what we call home never relinquishes its claim. Our homeland can betray us, it can become unlivable, but it remains the place where we belong. Perhaps Iran's greatest tragedy is that it has become so hard to love.

The next day, Ramazan descended on Esfahan like a sudden hush. It was the first day of the Muslim fasting month. From dawn until dusk, the pious refrained from eating, drinking, smoking and sexual intercourse. Before I left Canada, an official at the Canadian embassy advised me against travelling in Iran during Ramazan. He told me that even though I, as a non-Muslim, was not expected to observe the fast, most restaurants would be closed during the day and it might be difficult to find food. Also, hunger sometimes led to short tempers.

When I mentioned to Khadije that I might be in Iran for the holy month she had only encouragement. "I am very envious," she sighed. "I wish I could go to Iran for Ramazan. In Iran, we can hear the prayers on the television and on the radio. I relax with those sounds. They are like musical sounds. In Canada, it does not feel like Ramazan." I was intrigued. I wanted to know what Ramazan felt like.

I spent the day with Kevin, an American I met at the hotel. Kevin had been travelling his entire life and seen more of the world than anyone I'd met, yet he was refreshingly modest. He was also wickedly funny. I was sold on his companionship the moment he said that he was struck less by Iranian monotheism than "monobrowism." Wandering through the city with him was a pleasure.

Kevin and I went to the immigration department to extend our visas. We didn't need medical exams; apparently the rules had changed again. Then we walked back into the centre of town. There were no restaurants open but I stopped at a dried fruit and nuts shop and bought a half-kilo bag of pistachios. I asked Kevin if he had tried Iranian pistachios. He hadn't. "They're wonderful," I said.

"They could kill me," he said. Kevin had a very serious nut allergy and carried an epinephrine shot with him at all times in case he had a reaction.

He told me about his flight to Iran from New Delhi. Kevin sat next to an Iranian man who spoke a little English. During the in-flight meal, the man noticed that Kevin did not eat the small walnut cake he was given for dessert. Kevin told him about his allergy and asked if he could write a description of his condition on a slip of paper in Farsi. That way he could show the paper to the staff at Iranian restaurants. The man agreed and scrawled out a note in Farsi.

For several days after his arrival in Iran, Kevin showed the Farsi note at every restaurant, kebabi and sandwich shop that he visited. The staff always read it, nodded politely and prepared his meal. Eventually, an Iranian friend translated what the paper actually said. It did not announce his allergy to nuts. Instead it read, *I am sick and can't eat cake.*

We took a city bus to the Manar Jomban, the famous "Shaking Minarets." It was nearly noon and the bus was filled with schoolchildren on their way home for a lunch break that, for the first time that year, would not include any lunch. Our presence on the bus distracted them from their hunger. The boys mobbed Kevin and me, and shouted out all the English they knew at random: "Excuse me! What is your country?" "Excuse me! What time is it?" "Excuse me! I love you!"

The Manar Jomban was an odd tourist site. It reminded me of the idiosyncratic roadside attractions I'd find back home, like the giant Ukrainian Easter egg in Vegreville or

Torrington's gopher museum. The Manar Jomban was the tomb of a fourteenth-century holy man named Amu Abdollah, but the place was most famous for its pair of minarets. If one minaret was shaken, the other also began to shake. The reasons for this movement were unclear and much disputed—some claimed it was the manifestation of Amu Abdollah's holiness, others suggested it was shoddy construction. Whatever the explanation, Manar Jomban was a very popular place, especially for Iranian tourists. Shapur at the hotel said—with exaggerated drama—that if we hadn't seen the Manar Jomban we had not seen Esfahan.

The caretaker of the tomb asked if Kevin or I would like to shake the minarets. Kevin opted out, but I followed the man as he unlocked a short wooden door at the base of the tomb. He directed me to a staircase that coiled up the inside of one minaret. When I reached the top of the tower the caretaker yelled up at me, "Push! Push!" I leaned back and forth against the walls in an attempt to shake the minaret. At first nothing happened; it felt like pushing against a brick wall. Eventually, though, I managed to overcome the minaret's inertia and it began to swing. Then the other minaret started to shake. It was barely perceptible, but a bell on the other minaret rang as proof that it was actually moving. Kevin clapped his hands.

The whole ordeal seemed rather silly and hardly worth the energy. I was breathless by the time I climbed back down. Kevin laughed and shook his head. "You looked ridiculous," he said.

"I could have shaken the thing better if I wasn't so hungry." It was a joke, but the truth was we were both famished. We had not eaten at all that day. I had my pistachios in my bag, but I could not eat on the street. Eating in public during Ramazan would be immensely rude, if not illegal.

By the time we returned to the Amir Kabir, there were only a couple of hours left before *iftar,* the dusk breaking of the day's fast. Kevin, though, did not want to wait. He knocked on the back door of a tea house near our hotel. The proprietor opened the door an inch. "We are not Muslims. Do you have any food?" Kevin asked.

"Come in," the man said. We snuck in by the back door as if it were a Prohibition-era speakeasy. "We have only soup." He scooped out two bowls of a thick green soup and served it to us with a piece of stale bread. We were thrilled. We sat on one of the takhts and spooned up our contraband.

We were half finished when a young man kicked off his sandals and climbed onto the takht directly across from us. He stood on the takht, turned in our direction, closed his eyes and began his *namaz*. As he bowed, kneeled and prostrated towards us I realized we were sitting between this man and Mecca. He was sending his prayers westward over two soup-slurping infidels on the first day of Ramazan. Kevin and I felt profoundly guilty. We waited until he finished his devotions then apologized for our insensitivity. "You are not Muslims," he said. "It is okay."

Farzad the lunatic was in the lobby when we entered the hotel. "Hello, my Canadian friend," he said, then turned his attentions to Kevin. "I speak twenty-two thousand English words. Where are you from?"

"I am American," Kevin said.

"George Bush is a liar, a thief and a homosexual." Farzad was quickly becoming my favourite Iranian.

17

WAITING FOR IFTAR

When I asked my hotel manager in Kashan, "How is Ramazan?" he stuck out his tongue at me. It was pasty and white.

"Today I have no water, no tea, no soda and no food," he said.

"Neither have I."

"Why not? You can go to the bazaar, bring some food to the hotel and eat it here. It is okay."

"I know, but I am fasting, too."

"Are you a Muslim?"

"No."

"Then why do you fast?"

"I am in Iran. It is Ramazan. I want to try it. Maybe for just a few days. When is iftar?"

"Soon. You will hear the mosque." Then he began to mimic the call to prayer: "Allah, Akbar! . . ."

I had been fasting for only a few days and it seemed I spent all my waking hours waiting for iftar. The first two days of my fast were the most difficult. I felt sluggish and had little enthusiasm for travel. But by the third day I started to get used to the foodless hours. I took advice from the locals and became strategic with my eating. I kept some dates and a bottle of water next to my bed, set an alarm to wake me just before dawn, and had a small breakfast before going back to sleep. I added a second dinner to my evenings and ate something light just before bed.

As I walked on the street, my body felt taut and fit, and there was a pleasant lightness in my head. As a non-believer, I was not fasting for spiritual reasons, and I wasn't exactly sure what Ramazan represented for pious Muslims. Still, as I watched the sun descend in the west and listened to the sundown call from the mosques, I felt a new kinship with the Iranians. I shared their hunger and knew the tightness in their bellies. I'd made a physical connection. A bond of flesh rather than faith.

I watched my hotel manager and his son prepare their dinner in the moments before sunset. They washed fruit, laid out some naan and dates, and sliced sausages into coins. Then they sat quietly in front of the food and waited for iftar. I left the hotel and went in search of my own dinner. The sidewalks were busy. Most of the stores were closing early as shopkeepers rushed home for iftar. The cake shops, though, were doing good business and the streets were crowded with Iranians carrying boxes of sweets tied with pink ribbons.

On a street corner near the bazaar, three men stood behind an enormous cauldron and handed out free soup. As I passed, one of the men looked at me and shouted, "*Biya!*" Come. I stepped forward and he thrust a plastic bowl in my hand. His friend filled it with hot soup and the third man gave me a plastic spoon.

"Merci," I said and stepped aside as crowds rushed forward to claim their own bowls. The soup man's generosity attracted dozens of people who rushed to get the free meal. A happy mob gathered, and the men ladled out the soup until the pot was completely empty.

Everyone in the entire bazaar now had a bowl of soup but nobody had started to eat; the day's fast had not yet ended. I sat on the curb with the others, my soup beside me, and waited for the call from the nearby mosque. I placed my notebook over my bowl to keep out the dust from the road. When the call echoed over the streets the entire bazaar dipped their spoons in unison. My soup had chilled a little, and there was a gummy skin forming on the top, but being a part of this tiny celebration made me feel a part of the community of believers.

Kashan is a pretty oasis town. I toured the traditional houses for which Kashan was famous, and got lost amid the intricate plaster mouldings, stained glass, courtyards and reflecting pools. I paid visits to the requisite mosques and tombs, and wandered the bazaar. Bottles of rosewater, distilled from the gardens in nearby Qamsar, crowded every market stall and shopfront and the passageways smelled of roses.

Kashan's mud walls and rose-scented corridors were once home to the modern mystic poet Sohrab Sepehri. I first heard of him when I was in Esfahan; he was Benjamin's favourite poet. Sohrab was also a translator of Japanese haiku and a celebrated painter. He was born while his mother was on a journey from Kashan to the holy city of Qom in 1928, and remained a passionate traveller. His journeys led to Japan, India and Pakistan. He studied lithography in Paris and exhibited paintings in Europe, Egypt and New York.

Sohrab Sepehri studied fine arts in Tehran and, upon graduation, worked in a number of government culture institutions. He found the work dull and eventually left the offices to support himself with his painting and poetry. His life was typically bohemian. He endured bouts of poverty, travelled constantly and never married. It took cancer to end his nomadism. Sohrab died of leukemia in 1980 when he was only fifty-two.

The next morning I took a minibus to the nearby village of Mashhad-e Ardehal. The village is most famous for the burial complex for a descendant of the fifth Shiite Imam, but I had come to visit the tomb of Sohrab. I found his gravestone in the corner of the imamzadeh and knelt before it. In life, Sohrab was often invited to Mashhad-e Ardehal but he never visited. Nobody understood why he refused. Some believed the poet had a sense of foreboding about the place, that he had a premonition that linked it to his death. Regardless of what the poet might have known or sensed, he lay there beneath a plain stone, nearly lost amid all the marble, tile and domes.

I left the imamzadeh and walked through the village. It was deserted. Ramazan made the calm midday hours all the more silent. The fast robbed the air of the sounds and smells of cooking pots. I walked through alleyways and past flat-topped houses built of mud and stone until I heard the call to prayer. Then life began to filter into the streets. I followed the call to a simple mosque and watched the slow procession of believers. Men with thick glasses walked with canes and bent backs. Breezes made black chadors billow. The faithful greeted each other on the steps of the mosque as piles of shoes grew before each open door, one for men and one for women. A man saw me sitting in the shadows, mistook me for a believer and invited me to come in. I shook my head. We had only the fast in common.

Qom is a forest of turbans and chadors. Stern mullahs with impeccable beards rushed past me on the morning streets. Shrouded women moved in inky streams over the bridges that spanned the paved parking lot where a river once flowed. Some women allowed only their eyes to peer out through an opening in their chador. Others covered their entire face and saw the world through a fine black mesh. When they were still

I could not tell which way they were facing. Everything was black and serious. Even the local sweet, an oily pistachio brittle called *sohun*, was heavy.

After Mashhad, Qom is Iran's holiest city and the site of the Hazrat-e Masumeh, the gold-domed tomb of Imam Reza's sister Fatimeh. The shrine transformed this small desert town into a place of pilgrimage, and Qom developed into the religious heart of the nation and an international centre for Shiite scholarship. Many of Iran's most unyielding clerics studied in Qom, and it was from here that Ayatollah Khomeini gathered his most fervent supporters.

I was lucky to find a hotel room. The war in Iraq, for all its horrors, was good for business in Qom. Journeys to the Shiite Iraqi holy cities of Najaf and Kerbala were deemed too perilous. Instead, pilgrims opted for the safety of Iran's holy shrines. Pilgrims came from everywhere: Turkmenistan. Afghanistan. Iraq. Africa. I followed the crowds into the *hazrat* and tried to avoid the eyes of the officials who wore oversized blazers and patrolled the sacred environs armed with striped nylon dusters. Officially, non-Muslims were not permitted within the Hazrat-e Masumeh. I made a promise to Khadije, though, that if I went to Qom I would give her greetings to Fatimeh.

Two domes soared over the tomb complex. An intricate star pattern of painted tile covered one of them. The other was coated with gold. The iwan at the women's entrance to the shrine dripped with mirrored stalactites. The sound of prayers and chanting competed with the jackhammers that pounded out a symphony of unending expansion. Like the shrine in Mashhad, the Hazrat-e Masumeh was an ongoing construction project.

Fatimeh, who is known as "the Infallible One" by believers, died in Qom in AD 816 on her way to meet her brother in Mashhad. Imam Reza said that anyone who makes a pilgrimage to his sister's tomb will be guaranteed a place in heaven, and thousands of pilgrims come every year. They prostrate themselves before the shrine and place kisses on the heavy wooden doors. At the same time, families have picnics and children play tag. I watched two boys wash cucumbers in the ablution fountains where men wash before prayers.

I slipped off my sandals and carried them into the heart of the shrine, where Fatimeh lies. Inside, a golden grille surrounds the tomb, and the ceiling is covered in a million tiny mirrors that reflect the green light like emeralds. I mimicked the other pilgrims, placing my hand over my heart as I approached the tomb, then pressing my face against the grille. Behind it, Fatimeh's casket was shrouded with green cloth and surrounded by donated banknotes the faithful pushed through the grille. I closed my eyes and whispered a message from Khadije. Then, with my hand again on my heart, I stepped backwards out of the shrine, never turning my back on Fatimeh until I crossed the threshold.

Fatimeh was not the only woman I'd come to see. I knew that somewhere within the complex was the tomb of Parvin E'tesami, the most famous of Iran's female poets. Khadije was one of Parvin's devotees and spoke of her with nearly the same reverent tones she saved for Fatimeh. "I love Parvin very much," she said. "Like me, she is from Tabriz. And like me, she is a woman." Khadije had drawn me a map of the Hazrat-e Masumeh in my Farsi notes and marked the location of the poet's tomb with an X, but even with the map I could not find it. Risking expulsion from the shrine, I asked one of the dustermen for directions. The man wanted to know my name and where I was from, but wasn't interested in the details of my faith. He escorted me to an obscure corner of a courtyard and unlocked a door. Inside a small room were two gravestones, one for Parvin, the other for her beloved father, E'tesam-al Mulk. On her gravestone were the verses:

Beneath this soil which verdure refuse,
Lies Parvin, literary star and muse;
Who, while suffering the bitterness of Times,
Composed charming, sugar-laden rhymes.

Parvin E'tesami was born in 1907. Her toys were books of poems instead of dolls. Parvin attended poetry readings with her father at the age of six and began writing her own poetry by the time she was eight. Parvin's father, wanting to familiarize his daughter with Western culture and learning, enrolled Parvin in the American College for Girls in Tehran. She taught there briefly after her graduation, but soon returned to her family to work as a poet. Her father was the founder of a literary magazine called *Bahar.* He published Parvin's writings and introduced the young poet to such luminaries as her fellow Tabrizi scribe, Shahriyar.

Parvin was modest but uncompromising in her principles. Some of her couplets scolded the Iranian women of the day, who yearned for riches rather than wisdom:

Not by wearing earrings, necklaces, and coral bracelets
Can a woman count herself a great lady.

What are colourful gold brocades and glittering ornaments good for
If the face lacks the beauty of excellence?

The hands and neck of a good woman, O Parvin,
Deserve the jewels of learning, not of colour.

Parvin also resented the corrupt regime of Reza Shah and refused to tutor his wife, the Queen. She also declined a medal bestowed upon her by the Ministry of Education. Her energy earned her many admirers, especially among the women in Iran whose plight Parvin described.

Early endings and "the bitterness of Times" betrayed Parvin's early promise. A marriage in 1936 ended in divorce after only ten weeks. Her father's death in 1938 broke Parvin's heart and abruptly severed her link with the literary community. Without her father acting as her agent, Parvin had no access to the male-dominated literary circles of the time. Then, four years later, typhoid truncated Parvin's own life. She died of the fever before her fortieth birthday.

I paid my respects to Parvin then left the Hazrat-e Masumeh through the heavy wooden doors. It was nearing sundown and men were laying two long plastic tablecloths on the ground in a plaza just outside the gate to the shrine. They set the cloth with plastic plates then added three dates, a bit of cheese and some naan to each setting. People began to crowd around, men at one cloth and women at the other, in the hope of getting a spot in front of one of the plates.

I approached a man at a nearby sweet shop. "Where does this food come from?" I asked.

"It is a gift from the city government. For Ramazan."

"Who gets to eat it?"

"Anyone can. You can go if you like."

"I am not Muslim."

"That is not important. Go ahead."

I did not join the men at the tablecloth, but I watched as they sat cross-legged and elbow to elbow until the call from the mosque soared over the city. Everyone began to eat and a television camera recorded the festivities. The man at the sweet shop pulled his own dinner from beneath the counter. "Please come here," he said. He tore a piece of naan, wrapped it around some cheese and a walnut and handed it to me. "Go ahead. Eat. You are welcome."

18

AN OASIS OF DATES

It wasn't easy to reach Garmeh, a tiny village in the Kavir Desert. I started in Na'in on the desert's southern edge. The manager at the mosaferkhune could not offer me any advice on how to get to Garmeh. He had never heard of the place. He only wanted to ensure that I was out of the mosaferkhune by eight in the morning.

"Why do I have to leave so early?" I asked.

"Because I am going."

"Where are you going?"

"To sleep! It is Ramazan. I am tired."

According to my map, Khor was the only town of any size near Garmeh. I inquired about buses to Khor at the terminal. They told me that no regular buses went from Na'in. I would have to wait at the junction at the edge of town and try to flag down a passing vehicle. I managed to hitch a ride as far as a police checkpoint at the Tabas–Damghan crossroads, where truckers had their loads and papers inspected. The officers at the checkpoint were unhelpful and I waited for two hours before finding a ride in a pickup truck. I volunteered to sit in the bed of the truck, but the driver insisted I squeeze into the cab. I sat next to his young son who was covered in cookie crumbs that smelled of coconut. The driver dropped me in Farrokhi where I found a taxi to Khor. Then a final taxi into the desert to Garmeh.

My driver guessed my destination. "You are going to Maziar's place," he said. I'd read that Maziar, an artist and musician, had renovated a traditional desert mansion into a hotel. I was longing for some desert quiet and was intrigued by the pictures I'd seen of the place. My driver stopped in front of a large mud-brick house next to a mosque. An old man opened the door and greeted me in English. "I am Seyed. Maziar's father," he said. I followed him through a mud-plaster corridor into a central courtyard and salon.

A young woman sat on the floor in front of a bowl of black dates. She had full red lips and large beautiful eyes. The woman wore no headscarf; her dark curly hair tumbled freely over her shoulders. It was the first time I'd seen a woman's hair in weeks. "This is Maziar's wife, Ariane," the man said. "She speaks French. Her mother is a Frenchwoman."

Ariane curved her lips into a smile and said hello. I caught myself holding my breath. I'd never seen such a beautiful woman. She looked just like the women I'd seen in the illustrated manuscripts of Hafez. Here was the "sugar-lipped charmer" who freed poetry from the pens of men.

"Would you like some tea?" Seyed said.

With effort, I coaxed my eyes from Ariane. "If you are fasting I will not take any tea. I can wait for iftar."

"I am not fasting," he said. "I am not well. I have to take pills for my heart so I cannot fast. Please, have some tea with me." He went into an ancient kitchen to prepare the tea while I sat in the salon and chatted with Ariane. I spoke to her in Farsi and filled the holes in my vocabulary with French. She pushed the bowl of dates towards me. "These are from our orchards," she said. I plucked a date from the bowl. It melted like molasses on my tongue. I abruptly ended my Ramazan fast. This woman could have talked me into anything.

"Do you have any other guests?" I asked.

"There are seventeen French people here. Twelve adults and five children. They live in Tehran. They are out with Maziar right now but they are coming soon. We will have dinner after they come."

"Five children? How long are they staying?"

"For two more days. They are very noisy."

Just as Seyed delivered the tea I heard the front door slam open and the clamour of young voices. The children poured into the courtyard followed in turn by a dozen exhausted adults. The last to enter was Maziar. I held my breath again. Maziar was a giant. He was well over six feet tall and had long black hair and a huge beard striped with grey. The mass of hair made his head the size of a bear's. He shook my hand. His voice had all the rumble of distant thunder but none of the malice. If Ariane was a maiden penned by Hafez, Maziar was Rostam.

The French filled the hotel with commotion. A mother tried to pry her daughter away from her Gameboy and into the shower. Two other children chased a small goat into and out of the guest house. One woman immediately began chain-smoking cigarettes. They were all friendly with me, but I was disappointed. I wanted Garmeh to be an oasis of silence. The French had invaded my desert retreat.

My mood turned to forgiveness after dinner, though, when one of the men pulled a bottle of pastis from a rucksack. "Would you like some?" he asked. I nodded; I hadn't had a drink since Heathrow airport. Two fingers of pastis were made milky with water, and as the chilled licorice slipped over my tongue I felt more forgiving.

The French all worked for multinationals in Tehran. I asked them about the alcohol. They told me that once a year a truck crossed the border from Turkey filled with beer and spirits. The annual delivery involved a few requisite bribes, but it all happened without incident. Also, many Europeans working in Tehran made their own wine. "Surely the authorities know what is happening when European expats buy grapes by the truckload," one man said, "but nobody gives us any trouble as long as we don't sell it to the locals."

"How do you like living in Iran?"

"It is fine. We have a good community and any time there is trouble all the expatriates bond together. We all knew about Zahra Kazemi and what happened to her. And, of course, there was the German."

When foreigners in Iran spoke of "the German," they always referred to Hamburg businessman Helmut Hofer. In 1998, an Iranian court convicted Hofer of having sex with an unmarried Iranian woman and sentenced him to death. The sentence was eventually quashed, but Hofer spent two years in prison and paid nearly thirty thousand dollars in various fines. The ordeal of the German was enough to deflate the temptations of the most randy of Iran's visitors.

I woke late the next morning and nearly missed breakfast. The French were going on a day trip with Maziar into the desert near Mesr. One of the mothers asked if I'd like to join them. "No, thank you. I think I'll stay in Garmeh today. I want to walk around the village a little."

"All by yourself? Are you sure? You can come with us. We have plenty of room."

"No, thank you."

She looked at me for a moment. "Are you sure?" She was afraid I would be lonely. It was a mother's concern and it made me feel warm.

"Yes. Thank you. You are very kind. I will see you at dinner."

The seventeen French assembled into their respective vehicles and drove off into the desert. And suddenly the world was silent. I walked out into Garmeh's dusty and narrow streets. At the edge of the village I passed a woman pulling weeds from her garden and stepped into the forest of date palms. The dates were in varying stages of ripeness: some red, some yellow, some fat and black. All hung from golden stems that were bright against the green. Ripe dates fell from the trees onto the pathway. The honeyed mash lodged in the treads of my sandals, and the stickiness collected pebbles as I walked.

I returned to the guest house just after noon. Seyed sat in front of the camel pen outside. He pointed to the building next to the hotel, a huge crumbling citadel made of mud. "You see this fort? It is maybe four hundred years old," he said. "The fort used to shelter people from bandits. When the bandits came, all the families went inside the fort. The door was very heavy. It was six hundred kilos. There were two rooms for each family inside."

"How long did people stay there?"

"Until the bandits went away. Sometimes for fifteen or twenty days. People came out in the day to tend to their fields and animals. But at night it was too dangerous so they came into the fort. I remember it, but very little. I was only seven years old."

He stood. "Come inside. We will have lunch. Today you will eat camel burger." I sat in the salon with Seyed. Soghra, Maziar's mother, joined us. She wore layers of coloured cloth and laughed often. We ate camel burgers, then hot tea, fresh dates and pomegranates. The pomegranates were especially wonderful. Soghra said it was because the water in Garmeh was a little salty. It added flavour to the fruit.

I lifted another pomegranate from the bowl. "Are there any poets from this part of Iran?" I asked.

"There are two poets buried in Khor," he said, then paused. "But I write poetry also."

"Really?"

"One time, some years ago, I talked to an old man about the traditions of the village. He told me about the old fort, and how the date farmers used to share the water that comes from the desert springs. These sorts of things. Village things. I wrote the stories down in my book and I made them into poems. I have maybe five hundred of them, but I have not put them together."

"I would like to see them."

"They are all in Farsi," he said, suddenly bashful. "And I have not put them together."

The morning greeted me with stomach pains. Perhaps it was the second round of pastis the previous night. I opted out of breakfast and Soghra brought me a glass of tea flavoured with saffron sugar. "This is *chay nabod*. It will settle your stomach," she said. The French packed their bags, settled their account with Maziar and exchanged affectionate farewells with their hosts. Then the convoy of vehicles snaked out of Garmeh to the main highway.

As I waved goodbye it occurred to me that although I spent two nights in their company, none of the French ever learned my name. I never properly introduced myself. It wasn't a conscious omission, but it pleased me somehow. I liked that I was able to float in and out of people's lives, leave a light impression and disappear. I cannot do this at home where even casual relationships require disclosure. On the road, I could connect without giving anything up, and there is something romantic about being the nameless stranger.

As sunset approached I followed Seyed and Soghra through the village to a friend's home. Though none of us were observing Ramazan, we had been invited for iftar. While the women busied themselves in the kitchen, Seyed and I sat on the floor of the salon where a long tablecloth lay. We were among the first to arrive but soon thirty guests crowded around the cloth waiting for dusk. Women shuttled back and forth from the kitchen to lay out naan, plates of cheese, green herbs and three colours of dates. When the day's fast was over—we received official word from the television set—everyone began to eat. We nibbled on the cheese and dates, then bowls of *ghalamkar*, a thick soup made of barley, lentils, beans and fresh herbs. Fried fish and mounds of rice followed the soup.

I regretted that I'd stopped fasting two days before. I felt as if I was missing something. The food was delicious but, for me, the meal was mere sustenance. For the others, it was a sacrament. Every date, every bit of cheese and spoon of rice had an extra sweetness. Each mouthful was an expression of faith. I felt honoured to be invited to such an event, and was treated with sincerity, but my joy was of a lesser kind. I turned to Seyed and said, "Tonight I wish I was Muslim."

He understood and smiled at me. "Even if you were a Muslim, you would not make fast. You are a traveller. The Quran says that the traveller must not fast."

"I know that, but today I have not travelled."

"It does not matter. You came here only three days ago. Until you stay for ten days then you are still a traveller."

"I've never heard of that rule."

"It is true. You are a traveller when you go twenty-four kilometres from your home. And you are a traveller until you stay in the same place for ten days."

"Is that what it says in the Quran?"

"No. The Quran only says a traveller must not fast. In Iran, we say twenty-four kilometres and ten days. Maybe in other places it is different. Maybe in Arabistan it is twenty-two kilometres and nine days. I don't know."

I spent the next day hiking with Maziar and Ariane. We trekked out of Garmeh, through the date plantations and into the bare mountains that surrounded the oasis. We found shade in an outcrop of rock and ate the fruit we carried in our rucksacks. Maziar pointed into the desert. "Nasir Khosraw came this way," he rumbled, referring to a famous eleventh-century poet and explorer. "He went from Na'in to Garmeh. He wrote that he 'came through the desert into a forest of palms.' We are walking in his footsteps." The three of us returned to Garmeh through the same forest of palms, and stopped to pluck fresh dates from the scaly-trunked trees as we passed.

Two young friends of Maziar were waiting at the house when we returned, and an old man from the village who came to visit Seyed. He wore thick glasses and spoke as if he were being strangled. Soghra and Ariane served dinner in the salon. We passed around naan and a dish of delicious *kashk bademjan*, fried eggplant with dried whey and mint. Maziar's friends spoke good English and talked to me about Persian poetry. "My wife and I agree that we could live in a house that is only two metres wide and two metres tall if we had a copy of Molana."

"I met a sailor in Mahabad that said the same thing," I said.

"Sometimes I go running with my friends for exercise. There are maybe six or seven of us. One of my friends always brings some poetry. He reads us the poetry before we run."

"What kind of poetry?"

"Sometimes Molana and Hafez. Sometimes new poets. All kinds."

I tried to imagine what the men I wrestled with at home would think if I read poetry to them in the gym between sets of bench presses. "That would never happen in Canada," I said.

The man frowned and shook his head. He couldn't understand why not. Neither could I.

I excused myself soon after dinner was finished. I would travel to Yazd the next day and the bus left at sunrise. I wanted to get some sleep. As I said goodbye to everyone, I realized that I never once felt like a client in their company. I always felt that I belonged. In the morning, Seyed woke to see me out into the chilled dawn. He prepared a breakfast for me to take along: some naan, a piece of cheese and two hard-boiled eggs. He also gave me a basket of sticky dates. "This is a gift," he said. Then he made me promise I would return someday.

I thought again how people back home considered Iranians dangerous, and that I must be brave, or foolish, to want to travel here. I would never convince them of the Iranians' warmth and welcome. It bewildered me that people were so comfortable being afraid.

19

BAM LIVES

The earthquake lasted twelve seconds. Walls shuddered and cracked with the earth's fever. Mud bricks dissolved into sand. The day after Christmas, while the rest of the world woke with holiday afterglow, the people of Bam drowned in dust. Twelve seconds of violence killed thirty thousand.

News reports counted bodies, global donations and babies born in the field hospitals. As in all disasters, there were miracle stories: A ninety-seven-year-old woman spent eight days under the rubble, then asked for a glass of tea. She wrote a poem while she recovered in the hospital. Another man survived for thirteen days. Rescuers were surprised and overjoyed, but the man fell into a coma and died a few days later.

Back home, I tucked fifty dollars into a box at a Red Cross fundraiser, for all the good it might do. I looked over my photos of Bam and thought of the people: the children among the date palms, the boys in the qanaat and the mullets on motorcycles. These were faces I had only glimpsed, people whose names I never knew. This was not my tragedy, but something inside of me crumbled.

As I rode a bus from Kerman, the man on the seat next to me asked me where I was going.

"To Bam," I said.

"There was an earthquake there last year. A very big one."

"I know."

"There is nothing left. Many people died. Why are you going there?"

"I am a journalist," I said. I felt ashamed at my lie, but I didn't know what else to say. I spent the previous night in Kerman trying to figure out why I was going back to Bam. I didn't know if I was a mourner or just a voyeur; I didn't want to admit to myself that I was a disaster tourist.

Nor did I know what to expect. I was surprised that there were still regular buses headed to Bam from Kerman. There was a makeshift bus terminal on the edge of town and the place was busy with taxis, minibuses and fruit sellers. I thought Bam would be a ghost town—a quarter of the population died in the earthquake—but it was as busy as when I visited the previous year.

A taxi driver offered me a ride into town, but I opted to walk. Makeshift shops and market stalls built from shipping containers lined the main road. Some had windows cut out of them. Air conditioners hung on the outside of others. A barber set up a shop in a tent provided by Oxfam. He cut hair in front of a single mirror as two customers waited on a seat torn from a car. There were shops selling televisions and jewellery. Grocers sold pomegranates and dates from stalls assembled from scraps of wood, old fruit boxes and palm fronds. The entire street was busy with commerce. The city was far from dead.

I walked off the main road towards Akbar's place. A wall on the street corner once held a sign directing travellers to the guest house. The wall was gone, only an outline of bricks remained, and I was happy I remembered where to turn. From the side streets the scope of the disaster was obvious. Tents grew from the remains of fallen houses. There were piles of bricks and fallen electric poles. Power lines draped over branches into prefabricated shelters. Everything seemed temporary except for the date palm trees that stood tall and defiant over the rubble.

I knew that Akbar was alive—I had seen him on television after the earthquake—but the guest house was destroyed and two travellers died when the dormitory walls came down. Whether Akbar's son, Mohammed, survived was less clear. I read that he died in the earthquake, and that Akbar heard his son's screams from below the rubble but could not reach him. Other reports said Mohammed survived. What was certain was that Akbar helped dig his guests from his collapsed guest house. "They are my family too," he was heard to say.

I reached Akbar's place. There was little left of it. Only the front gate was standing. A neat pile of bricks stood in what was once the dormitory, but a prefabricated shed was freshly painted with "Welcome to Akbar's Tourist Guest House." Somehow, even amid the devastation, the place was cheerful.

Akbar stepped out into the sun as I approached. He smiled at me through his glasses against the background of ruin. His grin seemed out of place. He didn't remember me, but when he greeted me he held both my hands. "You were here before the earthquake?" he said. "Thank you for coming back."

"I wasn't sure if you were still accepting guests," I said.

"Of course I am. What else would I do?"

"You look good," I said. It had been eight months since the earthquake. I don't know why I expected him to look battered.

"Thank you. I am keeping well, all things considered."

I didn't know what else to say to him. "Akbar, I am so sorry. How are you doing?"

He took a deep breath. "It has been hard, of course. We lost everything, as you can see. But I am rebuilding. Do not worry about that. Now I only have tents, but my prefab sheds for guests are arriving today. And I am going to make them very nice. Very fancy."

I laid my rucksack in one of the tents. Both were emblazoned with the faded logo of the Iranian Red Crescent. Akbar and I sat at a table in the courtyard. His wife brought me some water and a bowl of dates.

"I saw you on television," I said to Akbar.

"Yes. It was incredible. Everybody interviewed me. CNN, BBC, everybody. After the disaster I did five interviews a day."

"You are a celebrity."

"I suppose so."

I took a sip of water. "How is your family?"

"We are fine. It has been hard, like I said, but I am an optimist. Everything will be good again."

Akbar was one of the few who did not lose any members of his immediate family in the disaster. He told me that Mohammed did not perish below the rubble. It was Mohammed's childhood friend who died that night. "But he was like a son to me," Akbar said. "I knew him his entire life."

"And two travellers died here?"

"Yes. It was very sad, but people have been wonderful."

Five days after the earthquake a German traveller arrived at the remains of Akbar's guest house. She had stayed there before, and bought a ticket to Iran as soon as she heard of the disaster. "I was standing with my wife. We said, 'What are we going to do now?' Then Anna came. She was the first to come back. She left a two-year-old child in Germany to come and help. I couldn't believe it," Akbar said. "Then two Dutch couples came. They had also stayed with me before. They were here ten days and helped us dig out. They cleared debris, moved bricks. It was not a holiday for them at all. They worked very hard.

"Since the day that Anna arrived, I have had at least one visitor every night. Many people have come back. Everyone has shown us so much generosity. It is these people that keep me strong."

Afterwards, I left the guest house to walk around town. Young boys on motorcycles passed me on the street, shouted greetings to me in faulty English, then laughed like madmen. At least that hadn't changed. Buildings fell and thousands died, but the people of Bam still found foreigners absolutely hilarious.

The sweet shop where I used to get my fix of saffron ice cream was gone, though the guitar-shaped fountain was still there. I walked down the main street towards the bazaar. A tea-house sign hung from a slanted pole, but when I turned the corner I saw that the tea house itself, and the entire bazaar, was gone. Only a bulldozed field of littered earth remained. Some of the buildings that remained intact leaned to one side. The Jomeh Mosque survived, but nearly every dwelling was destroyed. The Arg, which had survived for centuries, looked like a sandcastle after the first wash of surf.

There was little evidence of rebuilding anywhere in the city. New structures were improvised and temporary like the shops on the main road. Piles of salvaged bricks and construction materials were ready to be reused, but according to Akbar there was no money for rebuilding. Locals complained that the government broke its promises to rebuild the city, and government officials claimed that the international community reneged on their donations. Even though the city was alive and busy, everything had an air of impermanence and frayed patience.

There had been killer earthquakes in Iran before. In 1962, the earth shuddered beneath the town of Bou'in-Zahra, near

Qazvin, and killed twelve thousand people. The Shah's government at the time was slow to respond to the disaster. A group of Tehran University students were frustrated and decided to help the victims at Bou'in-Zahra themselves. They collected supplies and mobilized medical students and interns to help the injured. The students found a leader in the wrestler Gholamreza Takhti. The famed pahlevan led the caravan of students to Bou'in-Zahra.

Their procession, though, would never arrive. The Shah was not about to let a crowd of students draw attention to his government's inept relief efforts, so he sent in the National Guard. Armed soldiers blocked Takhti and the students as they neared Qazvin. They ordered them back to Tehran and promised to fire on whoever disobeyed. The students dispersed, and not long afterwards Takhti was found dead in a hotel room.

After the Bam earthquake, Takhti's son Babak told a reporter that if his father were still alive he would have been in Bam helping the victims, just as he had in 1962. In a way, the pahlevan did just that. An Iranian painter, Behzad Sishegaran, organized an exhibit called "With Takhti in Bam" to raise money for the relief effort. The exhibition acknowledged Takhti's contribution to the victims of the 1962 quake in Bou'in-Zahra. Various artists gathered at the Reza Abbasi Museum in Tehran and donated art to be auctioned. Sishegaran sold his portraits of Takhti, but the most sought-after item was a poem, handwritten on the spot by the Iranian poet Simin Behbahani:

> Rise Takhti, it is dawn
> Morning's on the horizon
> Again the world is turning
> Again the earth is quaking

Absorbed in fantasy,
I found a path to your grave,
On your sleeping chamber,
My hand knocked sadly.

Rise and usher, Takhti,
This people to industry,
Rays of gloom have appeared,
It is time for a journey.

With tears and sympathy,
Arrange a Caravan afoot
Carpets, kilims, and tents
Anything of worth, collect. . .

Someone paid 14 million rials for the poem, proving that Takhti's legendary chivalry still touches Iranians forty years after his death, and stirs them to action.

By the time I returned to the guest house, Akbar's prefab shelters had arrived. Three men were busy hammering together the sheets of corrugated tin. "You see," Akbar said to me. "I am not sitting back. These will be ready soon."

Then he asked me, "What do you think? Do you think there will be tourists here again? Do you think that people will come to Bam?"

"I think so, enshallah."

"I think so, too," he said. "I am very confident. Travellers have always been good to me."

Just then, two backpackers walked into the guest house: a Turkish woman and a Spanish man. They had crossed the border from Pakistan that morning. Akbar was excited to have more guests. He offered them one of the tents. "You see how romantic this is?" he joked. "It is the most romantic room in all of Iran."

"How much?" the Turk asked.

"Six thousand tomans. Three thousand tomans each."

"That is too much. We will give you four thousand."

Akbar grinned. "I am not going to bargain with you. I do not like to bargain. You can bargain elsewhere. The price is six thousand. This is my price."

"No. Four thousand."

"The price is six thousand," Akbar said. He shrugged his shoulders. "If you do not want to pay six thousand, then you can stay here for free. I do not care. Be my guest and pay nothing. But do not bargain with me. The price is the price."

"Six thousand is too much."

"Please understand. My price is six thousand." Akbar's grin was tight.

"This is only a tent," she said.

Akbar paused. His strained smile straightened and vanished. "We have been living in a tent for eight months. My whole family. The whole city. Do you know what has happened here?"

"Yes, I am very sorry, but I will only pay four thousand. Six thousand is too much for a tent," the Turk said.

"There isn't even a shower," said the Spaniard.

"A shower?" Akbar was on the edge of tears or rage, I couldn't tell which.

"Four," the Turk held up her fingers.

"But we have lost everything." Akbar seemed to shrink. For the first time all day he seemed like an earthquake victim.

"Okay, we will pay you five thousand for the both of us," the Turk said.

Akbar was shaking. "Fine. Five thousand," he said and walked into his shed. The Spaniard sat next to me at the table. He gave me a victorious grin, as if I should be impressed with him, but then he read my expression.

"It is only a tent," he said. I buried my head in my notebook.

Akbar and his wife stayed in their shed until the Turk and the Spaniard went out in search of dinner. He was still angry when he emerged. "I am very insulted," he said. "You know, this is the first time I have ever lowered my price. Even before the earthquake I would not bargain."

Akbar's wife pointed across the way and said something to Akbar. A man was coming out of his tent with a pretty young woman. They distracted Akbar from his anger. "You see that man? He lost his whole family in the earthquake. His wife, his children, his mother-in-law. Then, after a few months, he is married to this young girl. She is only seventeen years old!"

"Good for him," I said.

"Yes. He is the envy of the neighbourhood." He laughed.

I sat on the table and pulled a pomegranate from my bag. "Did you buy that in town?" Akbar asked.

"Yes, would you like some?"

"No, thank you. How was your walk?"

"Good. It made me sad, but I was surprised that the city is so active. I was expecting to find a city of ghosts."

"Bam lives," he said.

"Did many people leave after the earthquake?"

"Who could leave? Everybody was dead." It was a morbid joke. "In truth, some people went to be with their families in Kerman or Tehran, but most people came back. This is still home for these people."

"Did you consider leaving?"

"Not for one second. I will never leave this place. If there is one man left standing in Bam it will be me. I love my city too much."

20

UNDER THE BRIDGE

Sa'adi was a traveller long before he was a poet, and he was the sort of observant and modest traveller that I longed to be. The trappings of royal courts bored him. He never sought company among the nobility and its wealthy men in silks. Instead he wandered the souks of Morocco, the desert towns of Arabia and Cairo's cramped alleyways. Sa'adi was happiest in the humble tea houses of ordinary men. His friends were bazaaris, dervishes and thieves. Their lives fascinated him, and their stories informed his poetry.

Sa'adi was born in Shiraz, sometime at the end of the eleventh century. He studied in Baghdad before he began to wander. Sa'adi's journeys took him to the western reaches of the Islamic world in Morocco and as far east as Kashqai. Crusaders captured him in northern Africa and forced him into slave labour in Tripoli, but a Muslim trader offered him salvation on the condition that he marry his daughter. Sa'adi wrote that in agreeing to the marriage he exchanged one sort of slavery for another.

Sa'adi travelled for thirty years before returning to Shiraz. He was already an old man when he began to ink his travels into verse. He lived for nearly a century, and now rests beneath a turquoise dome in a garden filled with cypress trees and citrus.

I visited Sa'adi's tomb on a bright morning. I had arrived in Shiraz from Bam the previous night and was happy to be back in this city of poets. I climbed the steps to Sa'adi's gravestone and placed my fingers on the marble slab. The stone was etched with verses.

From the tomb of Sa'adi, Son of Shiraz,
The perfume of love escapes.
Thou shall smell it still one thousand years after his death.

I bought a translation of Sa'adi's *Golestan* at the garden and found a shaded bench where I could read. *Golestan* was filled with common wisdom. Sa'adi wrote about dervishes, tax collectors and kings both wicked and benevolent. He also wrote about wrestlers. He tells the story of a great wrestler who mastered 360 holds. The wrestler took on a young protegé and taught him all but one of the techniques. Under the tutelage of his master, the youth became a great wrestler himself. He boasted that no man was his equal. The Shah grew weary of the boy's arrogance and arranged a competition between the youth and his master. Spectators gathered from around the kingdom. At the outset of the match, the youth "made an onslaught like a lusty elephant with an impulse which might have uprooted a mountain of brass." The old master, though, employed his 360th hold, lifted the boy off his feet and hurled him to the ground. The youth was indignant, but the wise master offered the sage advice: "Never give your friend so much power that, if he becomes hostile, he can do you harm." Sa'adi wrote:

Either fidelity itself does not exist in this world
Or nobody practises it in our time.
No one had learnt archery from me
Without at last making a target of me.

Four young women sat on the bench across the path from mine. My book's English cover betrayed me as a foreigner and I could hear them whispering English phrases. The most daring of the four called out hello. I looked up from Sa'adi, grinned and said, "Salaam." They all giggled. Then another said, "Welcome."

"*Khayli mamnun*," I said.

"You speak Farsi?"

"A little bit."

"Where are you from?"

"Canada."

They huddled together and began talking among themselves. I returned to Sa'adi, but could hear their discussion. They were arguing which of them should come over and talk to me. They made their decision and a woman wearing an orange manteau over a pair of blue jeans stood up and crossed the path. I could smell her perfume before she reached me. The woman held a bag of candy in her hand. "Excuse me," she said in English. "Would you like some sweets?"

I lifted a foil-wrapped toffee from the bag. "Thank you."

She pointed to a pink candy. "Try one of these. They are delicious."

"Thank you," I said as I took the candy.

"What is your name?" she asked.

"Marcello. What is yours?"

"I am Sara," she said. "Bye, bye."

She returned to her friends and they held another conference. "Excuse me," Sara called out. "Do you have a wife?"

"Yes," I said. They conferred again, then Sara asked, "Excuse me?"

"Yes."

"Where is your wife?"

"In Canada."

Another huddle. "Excuse me?"

"Yes."

"Are you Muslim?"

"No, but my wife is."

This continued for a while. Eventually Sara walked over to me again. She was growing tired of calling to me from across the pathway. "Do you have Yahoo?" she asked.

"You mean an e-mail address?"

"Yes."

"I do. Would you like it?"

"Yes, please."

Sara sat down next to me and I wrote my e-mail address on a piece of paper for her. The others, inspired by Sara's boldness, joined us. They were all university students in Shiraz, studying either computers or mathematics. I took a photograph of them with their camera. Then I asked if I could take their photo for myself. Three of the women agreed and posed in front of my lens with serious expressions. The fourth didn't want her photo taken; she didn't think it was proper to offer her image to a foreign man.

After visiting Sa'adi the women planned to visit another garden in central Shiraz. They asked if I wanted to join them. Then it was my turn to consider what was proper. I thought of Benjamin's lashing, and politely declined. Sara wrote her e-mail address on a piece of paper along with the message "Good luck . . . !?" Then they left the garden.

It was a joy to share conversation with Iranian women. Our discussion never strayed from the banal and I received no real insights into their lives, but at least I made some sort of contact. In a way, this was as far as I could go without endangering anyone. I was happy that after over four months in Iran it finally happened.

I walked back into central Shiraz from Sa'adi's tomb. I was hungry and stopped in a sandwich shop. Even though it was Ramazan and most restaurants were closed during the day, a few places stayed open to serve people not observing the fast. These were most often simple sandwich shops. The owners covered their windows with newspaper so hungry passersby could not see those eating inside. The restaurant was full when I entered. Young men hunched over their sandwiches and left greasy fingerprints on coarse grey napkins. The paper on the windows lent the shop an odd light and a sense of shame. I ate a gummy hamburger with the other Ramazan cheaters and felt like a criminal.

In the evening I enjoyed another forbidden pleasure. After a meal beneath the vaulted ceilings of the Hamam-e Vakil I asked my waiter for a water pipe.

"No qalyun," he said. "Qalyun is illegal in Shiraz."

"Everywhere?" I was mortified.

"Yes, everywhere."

"That's terrible."

"Not terrible. It is good. Qalyun is very bad for you. Shiraz is a healthy city."

On my way back to the hotel I walked along the pedestrian mall that stretched from the bazaar to Martyrs' Square. Teenaged boys played football under the street lamps. Near the Zand Castle a man in a brown sweater-vest ran an outdoor tea stand. He had a burner to brew tea, some plastic cups, a pot for boiling eggs and, happily, some qalyuns to smoke. I asked him about the qalyun ban as he lifted a few hot embers from a tray and readied a pipe for me. "I have a special permit," he said with a sly smile.

I cared little about legalities; I would be leaving Iran soon and was happy to get my qalyun fix. I felt like a junkie as I smoked in the near darkness and huddled against the night's chill. "I'll see you tomorrow night," I said when I ran out of smoke.

I took the long way back to the hotel and stopped at the Mausoleum of the King of the Lamp, the imamzadeh where

Imam Reza's brother rests beneath a fabulous egg-shaped dome. I passed through the giant wooden doors of the main gate to the courtyard. Like all of Iran's holy places, the complex was a marriage between the social and the sombre. There was no intimidation or silence here. Children rode bicycles around the central fountains while young men discussed football scores on their cellphones.

I left my sandals at the shoe repository and passed beneath the carved wooden ceiling into the inner sanctum. It was like stepping into a diamond. Tiny mirrors formed mosaics on the walls and ceiling. Some were made with green-, silver- and gold-coloured glass. Even here children played, but the boys who ran barefoot on the carpets earned whispered admonishments from their fathers. Most men were praying. Some clung to tiny Qurans and read scripture. Others read newspapers. I stared into the million mirrors and watched my face shatter into fragments of light.

A man called out to me in English outside the shrine. "Hello! My name is Aram. How are you? Where are you from? Please sit down." I joined the man on a bench.

Aram was in his late thirties. He was studying to be an English teacher at a nearby language academy. He showed me his notes and textbook. The chance to speak with me had him vibrating. "You are Canadian? I like Canadians. I also like Americans. Americans are very strong!" he said and flexed his arms. "They are not afraid of anybody. I am also not afraid of anybody! I am strong like an American. I am strong and very good-looking. When I see teenagers on the street I am not afraid of them. They think that they are strong but I will fight them and steal their girlfriends because I am so strong and handsome. Do you think I am handsome?"

Aram was balding and a little flabby. His pursed lips made him look like a Persian Mr. Bean. "Gorgeous," I said.

"I know! Gorgeous!" He closed his eyes and giggled. "I am also very fast," he continued. "I can run very fast! When I was sixteen I played football. I could run one hundred metres in ten seconds. The big football boss said that I was like a horse child. He said I was a horse child because I run like a horse with my head up and my neck up." He stretched out his neck by way of demonstration. "Like a horse going to his mother. I can still run very fast. Have you seen the national Iranian football team?"

"Yes. I saw them play Germany."

"Yes. I am faster than all of them." He laughed again. "How is my English?"

"It is very good."

"Really?"

"Yes."

"What level is my English?"

"What do you mean?"

"Am I low or intermediate or high intermediate . . . ?"

"You are high intermediate," I said, with false authority.

"Thank you. Please. Test my English. Ask me very difficult questions."

I told him I didn't know how to test his English. Instead, I helped explain a list of English expressions his teacher had given him to learn. They included:

Whoops
Yuck
Geeky
Geeked out
Knockout
Blow him off.
Blow him off the face of the earth.
I'm gonna knock your block off.
Punch his lights out.

Afterwards, when I stood to leave, Aram said, "I want to thank you for helping me. I would like to buy you an ice cream, but I have no money. Tomorrow my mother will send me some money, but tonight I have nothing. I am ashamed. I feel shame. She sent me money last week, but I spent it already. I think I spend money too fast."

"Just like you run."

"Yes, yes! That is exactly correct!"

I spent my last Persian days in Esfahan. I changed my air ticket so that I could fly out of Esfahan without having to return to Tehran. I wanted to end my journey in a place that I loved, not in Tehran's brown smudge. I e-mailed Jamshid and told him that I would not be coming through Tehran after all. I thanked him for his hospitality and told him to be sure to keep in touch, but I never heard from him. I must have hurt his feelings again.

I arrived back in Esfahan on the last Friday of Ramazan and walked from the Si-o-Seh Bridge to my hotel. A film called *Girls' Dormitory* was playing at one of the cinemas on Chahar Bagh Street. Three young Iranian girls in hejab stared demurely out from the movie poster. I smiled. Surely this film was more wholesome than a Hollywood film with the same name would be.

I passed Sepah Street just as a wave of people flowed out from the square. It was the largest mob I'd seen in Iran. I asked someone what was going on. "It is Al-Quds Day," the man said. "Every year, on the last Friday of Ramazan, we make demonstrations against Israel."

"Just in Esfahan?"

"No. Everywhere. All the world. In Iran, Palestine, Lebanon. Even Germany and Britain."

"Is it over?"

"Yes. All finished. You must wait until next year."

I wove through the mass of protestors and made it to the hostel. I met two Australians there, Emma and Christian, who had attended the demonstration that afternoon. They watched figures of George Bush and Ariel Sharon burn in effigy. People chanted "Death to America" and "Death to Israel," and torched flags. "It was amazing. We took some fabulous photos," Christian said.

"Was it all right for you to be there?"

"Are you kidding? People loved us. One man led us up a stairwell so we could have a better view. Some wanted to take photos with us. It was incredible. Like a big festival."

I was disappointed that I had missed the demonstration. This was my only opportunity, and my last chance, to see Iranians live up to their flag-burning Western stereotype and I was too late by an hour. The images reported by Emma and Christian were intriguing. The vitriol against Israel didn't surprise me. This was an expression, however crude, of their support for the Palestinian cause. It was the demonstrations against America that I could not understand. I knew that the shouted hatred of the U.S. did not represent the feelings of most Iranians. I lost track of the times I heard men declare love for America and George Bush. I wanted to know who these protestors were. I wondered what urged them to take to the streets and set the flags ablaze. Most of all, I was saddened that the world would watch it all on their televisions and believe that this sort of hate fuelled all Iranians.

I made my way to the square. The Qeysarieh was closed for the entire month of Ramazan so I descended into the Azadegan, a subterranean tea house beneath an overflowing army-surplus stall. The chaykhune was long and low-ceilinged. With its collection of archaic weapons and stuffed animal heads, it seemed the set of a Gothic horror film. Not an inch of space on the walls or ceiling was bare. Iranian soccer heroes and pahlevans stared out of dozens of cracked frames. There were old photos of Esfahan, zurkhane mils, old battleaxes and coloured lamps. My favourite was a photo of a local strongman wrestling a lion.

The Azadegan was not an especially welcoming place for women. They were relegated to an area in the back of the room separated by a curtain, and were not permitted to even walk through the men's section. They had to enter and leave through a separate door. It was like an Iranian bus.

The place was no more friendly for foreigners, and unlike most places in Iran, I felt as if I was being tolerated rather than welcomed. The frowning proprietor always overcharged me, but I was too charmed by the Persian clutter and stubble-charred faces of the clientele to stay away for long.

The tea house was busy when I arrived. The waiter who shuttled teapots and pipes was harried and sweating. There were no empty tables, but I spotted Benjamin's friend Makan near the barrier to the women's section. He was reading a French translation of Omar Khayyám's poetry. He looked up from the book when I said hello, and made room on the bench for me.

"Did you go to the protest today?" I asked.

Makan scoffed and tossed his head back. "Stupid fanatics. They just want to be on television," he said.

I pointed at his book. "You like Omar Khayyám?"

"Yes, of course. Khayyám is very excellent. He was a free-thinker at a time when Europe was still full of barbarians. Do you understand French?"

"A little bit."

"Listen." He read aloud his favourite poem. "It is so beautiful," he said. "Tomorrow I am guiding some French tourists through the city. I want to give them a gift of Khayyám. I want to write out some of the poems in French for them, but my writing is very bad."

"I could do it for you," I offered.

"Is your writing very nice?"

"It's pretty good. And I have some good paper at the hotel."

"That would be excellent."

He marked the poems that he wanted me to copy. They were all about love and wine. "Thank you very much," he said. "Please write at the top '*Un souvenir de Makan.*' I think they will like it."

I promised to leave the book and the paper at the hotel desk in the morning. Makan thanked me again, crushed his cigarette in a copper ashtray and left the Azadegan. I finished my tea and walked back to the hotel with my happy errand.

I wasn't sure if I wanted my last days in Iran to be social or solitary, but I could not resist the companionship of Emma and Christian. I was warmed by their enthusiasm for Iran. They were travelling through the Middle East and had been in Iran for less than a day before declaring Iran their favourite destination. I accompanied them on a shopping trip into the bazaar to purchase qalyuns. In exchange for my self-proclaimed qalyun expertise, I implored Emma's help in selecting a gift for Moonira.

"I am going to propose to Moonira when I get home," I said to Emma as we perused turquoise-coloured enamelware. The ease with which the declaration slipped from my lips startled me; I'd never told anyone this before. Emma, a woman I'd met only hours before, was the first to know. There is something about travel that breeds disclosure. Somehow, the world of strangers can be a more fitting storehouse of secrets than the ears of friends.

"Congratulations," Emma said. "We'd better find something nice then."

Later that afternoon, Emma, Christian and I stepped out of the covered bazaar into a crowd of about fifty young

Afghan men. In the centre, a street performer demonstrated feats of strength for the gathered audience. When the crowd noticed our arrival, they immediately turned their attention from the strongman to us, especially to Emma for whom they shifted to make room at the front of the circle. The strongman was crestfallen and annoyed at the interruption, but managed to regain the eyes of the crowd by hoisting a small boy seated on a pole high over his head. Then, for his finale, he stuffed a live snake down the front of his shirt.

The mob applauded and dispersed. A gang of about a dozen boys escorted Emma, Christian and me through the bazaar until we reached the main road. The sight of three foreigners had them laughing so hard they draped their arms over each other as they walked to keep from falling over.

I left Iran on the final day of Ramazan. It was a holiday, and one of the most anticipated days of the Islamic calendar, yet by the time darkness fell I felt only sadness. My flight would leave at midnight, and I had only a few hours before I would take a taxi to the Esfahan airport.

I packed my rucksack for the last time and left it behind the hotel's front desk. Then I joined Emma, Christian and a few other travellers at a restaurant near the Sheik Lotfallah Mosque early that evening. It was my farewell dinner and I shared it with people whom, though they were friendly and interesting, I knew I would never see again. Afterwards, we assembled at the chaykhune next to the hotel.

At the tea house my mind drifted away from their conversation like the smoke from my lungs. All I could hear was the bubbling of my last pipe, and all I could think about was leaving. I excused myself from their company. I wanted to be among Iranians. I strolled down Chahar Bagh Street to the crowded riverside.

I walked by the picnics and the paddleboats to the Khaju Bridge. I stepped past the stone lions and descended the stairs to the bridge's lower tier. Men had gathered to sing beneath the softly lit arches. I walked along the bridge in measured steps and listened to their spontaneous music. Some of the singing was lively. It inspired happy shouts, clapping hands and forbidden public dance. Most of the songs, though, were plaintive and slow and better matched my own melancholy.

I thought of my time among the men of Persia. In the worst of ways, all men are the same. Men everywhere are capable of the same braggadocio, the same cruelties and the same foolishness. Yet in Iran, men hold within themselves a poetic civility. Noble verses are inscribed on their hearts like tattoos on muscle, and ancient verses direct them towards kindness.

The Persians have a word for this: *fotovat*. It is the combination of unabashed masculinity with chivalry and kindness. The word is old-fashioned and is rarely used any more, but lingers in the memories of men like the perfect world of poetry and the skills of old wrestlers. I learned much from the Persians, and could strive for fotovat, but I would never have what they had. Through war and sorrow, revolution and oppression, crown and turban, through all that Iranians have lost and may yet lose, they will never lose this. Civility is their birthright, the gift of their culture, and the inheritance of poets and pahlevans.

I wandered into a small chamber at the end of the bridge. A man stood alone in the centre and sang verses into the night. He stared at the damp stones at his feet or up into the domed roof, never once looking at the audience of men who gathered to listen to him. His poem was beautiful and sad. The bricks of the chamber swelled with his voice. When he finished he clasped his hands behind his back and, without looking up or acknowledging his applause, walked away.

I wanted to follow him. I wanted to ask this man why he sang, but my time in Iran taught me that the man would only shrug. The question had no answer; poetry is what Iranians do. I might as well ask the man why he breathed. My body trembled as I walked back along the river. I was grateful for the dark that hid the sadness filling my eyes. And in that darkness I knew that this anonymous poet was the sort of man I wanted to be.

I thought of him as I waited in front of the statue of Takhti for my taxi, and as Emma, breaking an Iranian taboo, placed a demure kiss on my cheek to say goodbye. I thought of his lonely song in the sky above Iran. As I reflected during my final journey home, back to where men don't do such things, this man became Iran to me. All the beauty I'd seen, all the marble tombs of poets I knelt before and the stone valour of the pahlevans. All the sorrow of good men, the pomegranate blossoms and the eyes of Persian girls. All were distilled into that singular moment beneath the bridge, in the voice of a solitary man who sings poetry into the glowing night. Then walks away.

Acknowledgments

I owe a great debt to Richard Harrison, John Vigna, Maryam Nabavi and, especially, Michael Schellenberg at Knopf Canada whose efforts made this a much better book. Thanks to Diane Martin, publisher, for first taking an interest in this project, to Random House's Trish Kells, and to the staff at Pages bookstore in Calgary for facilitating the introduction to the good people at Knopf Canada.

To that end, I must also thank Louise Dennys, Frances Bedford, Ron Eckel, Marion Garner, Kelly Hill, Deirdre Molina and Adrienne Phillips.

Special thanks to my patient Farsi teacher, Khadije Abadi, who taught me far more about Iran than just the language—*Khayli mamnun.* For help with some of my translations, and for making the best fesenjan in Calgary, thanks to the Khezri family at Atlas Restaurant. Thank you to the University of Calgary Wrestling Team, especially Jeremy Podlog, for helping me reorient myself on the wrestling mat. For their ongoing support of my writing and my travelling, thank you to CBC Radio in Calgary, the Calgary Public Library, Raj Pal, Adrian Kelly, Wayson Choy, Alberta and Dwayne Ennest, Bruce Kirkby, Ron Reive, Gabrielle Cran, Annie Vigna, my friends and family and everybody who has ever come to a reading or tolerated me babbling about my travels.

I am indebted to the work and research of the following writers: Iraj Bashiri, Sandra Mackey, Farzad Nekoogar, Dr. Behrouz Homayoun Far and Martin Turner.

I would like to thank the countless Persians who made my visits to Iran such a joy, especially, but not exclusively, Mr. Nabavi, Ali Akbar, A.R. Assadi, Maziar and Ariane Aldavood, Seyed Hadi, Soghra Beygom, Bijan Mirvani, Soroush Chalak, Amin Asadina, Rohim in Shahr-e Kord, A. Hossein Zadeh, Afshin Noserat, Dr. Raisi Dehkordi, Ramazan and his family in Shah Milarzan, Hamid in Tehran, and my good friend "Benjamin" whom I wish every happiness. Thanks, too, to fellow travellers Olivier Gambari, Emma and Christian Power, Kevin Meredith-Jones, Rory MacLean and all those who made the sometimes dull Iranian nights a little more interesting.

An early draft of the book was awarded the Dave Greber Freelance Writing Award. I would like to thank the Dave Greber Foundation for this generous and well-conceived prize. Thanks, too, to the Alberta Foundation for the Arts for their financial support.

Lastly, special thanks, and all my love, to Moonira Rampuri. I don't know which is harder to endure, my long absences when I am travelling, or my grumpy presence when I am writing. Thank you for forgiving both.

Permissions

The author gratefully acknowledges the permission to reproduce the following material. Every effort has been made to contact the copyright holders.

From *The Hand of Poetry: Five Mystic Poets of Persia*, "Looking for Your Own Face, written by Farid al-Din Attar, "My Response to Your Offer," written by Hafez, and "Shiraz," also written by Hafez, all translated by Coleman Barks. Copyright © 1993. Reprinted with permission from Omega Publications.

From www.hafizonlove.com, Qazal 374, by Hafez and translated by Shahriar Shahriari. Copyright © 1999. Reprinted with permission from Shahriar Shahriari.

An excerpt from *The Conference of the Birds*, written by Farid al-Din Attar and translated by Dick Davis. Copyright © 1984. Reprinted with permission from Penguin Classics.

From "50 Poems from Shah Nematollah Vali", poem 34. Reprinted from the website of Bonyad Erfan Gonabadi.

An excerpt from *Sunset of Empire: Stories from the Shahnameh of Ferdowsi*, Volume III, translated from Dick Davis and published by Mage Publishers. Copyright © 2004.

From *Music of a Distant Drum: Classical Arabic, Persian, Turkish and Hebrew Poems,* an excerpt of a poem written by Farid al-Din Attar and translated by Bernard Lewis. Copyright © 2001. Reprinted with permission from Princeton University Press.

From "Nima Yushij and New Persian Poetry", an excerpt from "Moonlight," written by Nima Yushij and translated by Iraj Bashiri. Copyright © 2000. Reprinted with permission from Iraj Bashiri.

From *Songs from the Steppes of Central Asia: The Collected Poems of Makhtumkuli: Eighteenth Century Poet-Hero of Turkmenistan*, excerpts of "The Pains of Love" and "Making my Dear Life Lost", written by Makhtumgoli and translated by Yousef Azemoun. Copyright © 1995. Reprinted with permission from The Society of Friends of Makhtumkuli.

An excerpt of "A Woman's Place" written by Parvin E'tesami and translated by Heshmat Moayyed. Reprinted with permission from Heshmat Moayed.

An excerpt of "Takhti" written by Simin Behbahani and translated by Korosh Khalili. Reprinted with permission from the poet and translator.

MARCELLO DI CINTIO is a former wrestler and author of *Harmattan: Wind Across West Africa*, which won the Henry Kriesel Award for Best First Book. It was also a finalist for the Wilfred Eggleston Prize for Best Nonfiction at the 2003 Alberta Book Awards. In 2003, he won the Maclean Hunter Endowment Prize for Creative Nonfiction. His travel writing has appeared in *Geist*, *enRoute*, *Prairie Fire* and *Prism International.* He lives in Calgary.